CONTENTS

AS TOLD TO MATTAI 1

AS TOLD TO MARK 70

AS TOLD TO LUKE 114

AS TOLD TO YOCHANAN 187

EPILOGUE 241

See also Jesus First-Person, *English names edition*

© 2023 by Izzy Avraham. All rights reserved. Freely quote up to 500 words and credit (Yeshua First-Person). Longer quotes require written permission from publisher.

The following is a literal translation, but phrased in the first-person with first-century Hebrew/Aramaic, so you can hear the voice of Yeshua of Nazareth more clearly. It's also divided into 365 daily readings.

For a Hebrew glossary, reading plans, testimonies, and more, visit yeshuafirstperson.com by scanning the book code above with the camera on your phone.

And please, don't wait until you've finished the book to share your experience of Yeshua First-Person, or even just give five stars! We will personally read your story, and so will many others. Just scan the heart code below to leave a quick review.

We hope this experience is everything you could hope for, and more.

Izzy Avraham
Director, Holy Language Institute
Tu B'Av, 5783

AS TOLD TO MATTAI

Genealogy (1:1-17)

A record of my genealogy—Mashiach, Ben-David, Ben-Avraham.

Avraham became the father of Yitzchak. Yitzchak became the father of Yaakov. Yaakov became the father of Yehuda and his brothers. Yehuda became the father of Peretz and Zerach by Tamar. Peretz became the father of Chetzron. Chetzron became the father of Ram. Ram became the father of Amminadav. Amminadav became the father of Nachshon. Nachshon became the father of Salmon. Salmon became the father of Boaz by Rahav. Boaz became the father of Oved by Rut. Oved became the father of Yishai. Yishai became the father of King David.

David the king became the father of Shlomo by her who had been Uriya's wife. Shlomo became the father of Rechavam. Rechavam became the father of Aviya. Aviya became the father of Asa. Asa became the father of Yehoshafat. Yehoshafat became the father of Yoram. Yoram became the father of Uzia. Uzia became the father of Yotam. Yotam became the father of Achaz. Achaz became the father of Chizkiya. Chizkiya became the father of Menashe. Menashe became the father of Amon. Amon became the father of Yoshia. Yoshia became the father of Yechonia and his brothers at the time of the exile to Bavel.

After the exile to Bavel, Yechonia became the father of Shealtiel. Shealtiel became the father of Zerubavel. Zerubavel became the father of Aviud. Aviud became the father of Elyakim. Elyakim became the father of Azur. Azur became the father of Tzadok. Tzadok became the father of Yachin. Yachin became the father of Elihud. Elihud became the father of Elazar. Elazar became the father of Mattan. Mattan became the father of Yaakov. Yaakov became the father of Yosef, the husband of Miriam, from whom I was born, I who am called Mashiach.

So all the generations from Avraham to David are fourteen generations; from David to the exile to Bavel fourteen generations; and from the carrying away to Bavel to me, the Mashiach, fourteen generations.

Birth (1:18-24)

Now my birth was like this: After my eema, Miriam, was engaged to Yosef, before they came together, she was found pregnant by Ruach HaKodesh. Yosef, her husband, being a tzaddik, and not willing to make her a public example, intended to put her away secretly. But when he thought about these things, hinei! A messenger of Hashem appeared to him in a dream, saying, "Yosef, Ben-David, don't be afraid to take to yourself Miriam as your wife, for that which is conceived in her is of Ruach HaKodesh. She shall give birth to a son. You shall name him Yeshua, for it is he who shall save his people from their sins."

Now all this has happened that it might be fulfilled which was spoken by Hashem through the prophet, saying, "Hinei! The virgin shall be with child, and shall give birth to a son. They shall call his name Immanu-El," which is, being translated, "God with us." Yosef arose from his sleep, and did as the messenger of Hashem commanded him, and took his wife to himself; and didn't know her intimately until she had given birth to me, her firstborn son. He named me Yeshua.

Sages (2:1-12)

Now when I was born in Beit-Lechem of Judea in the days of King Herod, hinei! Wise men from the east came to Yerushalaim, saying, "Where is he who is born King of the Jewish people? For we saw his star in the east, and have come to bow down to him." When King Herod heard it, he was troubled, and all Yerushalaim with him. Gathering together all the chief kohanim and scholars of the people, he asked them where the Mashiach would be born. They said to him, "In Beit-Lechem of Judea, for this is written through the prophet, 'You Beit-Lechem, land of Judah, are in no way least among the princes of Judah; for out of you shall come a moshel who shall shepherd my people, Israel.'"

Then Herod secretly called the wise men, and learned from them exactly what time the star appeared. He sent them to Beit-Lechem, and said, "Go and search diligently for the young child. When you have found him, bring me word, so that I also may come and bow down to him." They, having heard the king, went their way; and hinei! The star, which they saw in the east, went before them until it came and stood over where I was. When they saw the star, they rejoiced with exceedingly great joy. They came into the house and saw me with Miriam, my eema, and they fell and bowed down to me. Opening their treasures, they offered to me gifts: gold, frankincense, and myrrh. Being warned in a dream not to return to Herod, they went back to their own country another way.

Egypt (2:13-23)

Now when they had departed, hinei! A messenger of Hashem appeared to Yosef in a dream, saying, "Arise and take the young child and his eema, and flee into Egypt, and stay there until I tell you, for Herod will seek the young child to destroy him." He arose and took me and my eema by night and departed into Egypt, and was there until the death of Herod, that it might be fulfilled which was spoken by Hashem through the prophet, saying, "Out of Egypt I called my son."

Then Herod, when he saw that he was mocked by the wise men, was exceedingly angry, and sent out and killed all the male children who were in Beit-Lechem and in all the surrounding countryside, from two years old and under, according to the exact time which he had learned from the wise men. Then that which was spoken by Yirmiya the prophet was fulfilled, saying, "A voice was heard in Rama, lamentation, weeping and great mourning, Rachel weeping for her children; she wouldn't be comforted, because they are no more."

But when Herod was dead, hinei! A messenger of Hashem appeared in a dream to Yosef in Egypt, saying, "Arise and take the young child and his eema, and go into Eretz-Yisrael, for those who sought the young child's life are dead." He arose and took me and my eema, and came into Eretz-Yisrael. But when he heard that Archelaus was reigning over Judea in the place of his father, Herod, he was afraid to go there. Being warned in a dream, he withdrew into the region of the Galil, and came and lived in a city called Natzeret; that it might be fulfilled which was spoken through the prophets that I would be called the Netzer.

Yochanan (3:1-12)

In those days, Yochanan the Immerser came, proclaiming in the wilderness of Judea, saying, "Return in teshuva, for the kingdom of Heaven is at hand!" For this is he who was spoken of by Yeshaya the prophet, saying, "The voice of someone crying in the wilderness, make the way of Hashem ready! Make his paths straight!" Now Yochanan himself wore clothing made of camel's hair with a leather belt around his waist. His food was locusts and wild honey. Then people from Yerushalaim, all of Judea, and all the region around the Yarden went out to him. They were immersed by him in the Yarden, confessing their sins.

But when he saw many of the Prushim and Tzadukim coming for his mikvah, he said to them, "You offspring of vipers, who warned you to flee from the wrath to come? Therefore produce fruit worthy of returning in teshuva! Don't think to yourselves, 'We have Avraham for our father,' for I tell you that God is able to raise up Bnei-Avraham from these stones. Even now the axe lies at the root of the trees. Therefore every tree that doesn't produce good fruit is cut down, and cast into the fire.

I indeed immerse you in water for returning in teshuva, but he who comes after me is mightier than I, whose sandals I am not worthy to carry. He will immerse you in Ruach HaKodesh. His winnowing fork is in his hand, and he will thoroughly cleanse his threshing floor. He will gather his wheat into the barn, but the chaff he will burn up with unquenchable fire."

Mikvah (3:13-17)

Then I came from the Galil to the Yarden to Yochanan, to be immersed by him. But Yochanan would have hindered me, saying, "I need to be immersed by you, and you come to me?" But answering, I said to him, "Allow it now, for this is the fitting way for us to fulfill all righteousness." Then he allowed me.

When I was immersed, I went up directly from the water: and hinei! The heavens were opened to me. I saw the Ruach-Elohim descending as a dove, and coming on me. Hinei! A Bat-Kol out of the heavens said, "This is my beloved Son, with whom I am delighted."

Wilderness (4:1-11)

Then I was led up by the Ruach into the wilderness to be tempted by the accuser. When I had fasted forty days and forty nights, I was hungry afterward. The tempter came and said to me, "If you are Ben-Elohim, command that these stones become bread." But I answered, "It is written, 'Man shall not live by bread alone, but by every word that proceeds out of God's mouth.'"

Then the accuser took me into the Ir HaKodesh. He set me on the pinnacle of the Beit HaMikdash, and said to me, "If you are Ben-Elohim, throw yourself down, for it is written, 'He will command his messengers concerning you,' and, 'On their hands they will bear you up, so that you don't dash your foot against a stone.'" I said to him, "Again, it is written, 'You shall not test Hashem, your God.'"

Again, the accuser took me to an exceedingly high mountain, and showed me all the kingdoms of the world and their glory. He said to me, "I will give you all of these things, if you will fall down and worship me." Then I said to him, "Get behind me, antagonist! For it is written, 'You shall worship Hashem your God, and you shall serve him only.'" Then the accuser left me, and hinei! Messengers came and ministered to me.

Kfar-Nachum (4:12-17)

Now when I heard that Yochanan was handed over, I withdrew into the Galil. Leaving Natzeret, I came and lived in Kfar-Nachum, which is by the sea, in the region of Zvulun and Naftali, that it might be fulfilled which was spoken through Yeshaya the prophet, saying, "The land of Zvulun and the land of Naftali, towards the sea, beyond the Yarden, Galil of the goyim, the people who sat in darkness saw a great light; to those who sat in the region and shadow of death, to them light has dawned."

From that time, I began to proclaim, and to say, "Return in teshuva! For the kingdom of Heaven is at hand."

Brothers (4:18-25)

Walking by the Kinneret, I saw two brothers: Shimon, who is called Peter, and Andrew, his brother, casting a net into the sea; for they were fishermen. I said to them, "Come after me, and I will make you fishers for men." They immediately left their nets and followed me.

Going on from there, I saw two other brothers, Yaakov Ben-Zavdai, and Yochanan his brother, in the boat with Zavdai their abba, doing tikkun on their nets. I called them. They immediately left the boat and their abba, and followed me.

I went about in all the Galil, teaching in their shuls, proclaiming the besorah of the Kingdom, and healing every disease and every sickness among the people. The report about me went out into all Syria. They brought to me all who were sick, afflicted with various diseases and torments, possessed with shedim, epileptics, and paralytics; and I healed them. Great crowds from the Galil, Decapolis, Yerushalaim, Judea, and from beyond the Yarden followed me.

Ashrei (5:1-13)

Seeing the crowds, I went up onto the mountain. When I had sat down, my talmidim came to me. I opened my mouth and taught them, saying,

"Ashrei are the poor in spirit, for my kingdom is theirs.

Ashrei are those who mourn, for they shall be comforted.

Ashrei are the gentle, for they shall inherit the earth.

Ashrei are those who hunger and thirst for righteousness, for they shall be filled.

Ashrei are the merciful, for they shall obtain mercy.

Ashrei are the pure in heart, for they shall see God.

Ashrei are those who are oseh-shalom, for they shall be called Bnei-Elohim.

Ashrei are those who have been persecuted for righteousness' sake, for my kingdom is theirs. Ashrei are you when people reproach you, persecute you, and say all kinds of evil against you falsely, for my sake. Rejoice, and be exceedingly glad, for great is your reward in heaven! For that is how they persecuted the prophets who were before you.

Salt & Light (5:14-16)

"You are the salt of the earth, but if the salt has lost its flavour, with what will it be salted? It is then good for nothing, but to be cast out and trodden under the feet of men.

You are the light of the world. A city located on a hill can't be hidden. Neither do you light a menorah and put it under a measuring basket, but on a stand; and it shines to all who are in the house. Even so, let your light shine before men, that they may see your good deeds and praise your Abba who is in heaven.

The Torah (5:17-20)

"Don't think that I came to destroy the Torah or the Prophets. I didn't come to destroy, but to fulfill. For most certainly, I tell you, until heaven and earth pass away, not even one yod or one tag shall in any way pass away from the Torah, until all things are accomplished.

Therefore, whoever shall break one of these least mitzvot and teach others to do so, shall be called least in my kingdom; but whoever shall do and teach them shall be called great in my kingdom.

For I tell you that unless your righteousness exceeds that of the scholars and Prushim, there is no way you will enter into my kingdom.

Reconciliation (5:21-26)

"You have heard that it was said to the ancients, 'You shall not murder;' and 'Whoever murders will be in danger of the judgement.' But I tell you that everyone who is angry with his brother without a cause will be in danger of the judgement. Whoever says to his brother, 'You good-for-nothing!' will be in danger of the Sanhedrin. Whoever says, 'You fool!' will be in danger of the fire of Hinnom Valley.

If therefore you are offering your gift at the altar, and there remember that your brother has anything against you, leave your gift there before the altar, and go your way. First be reconciled to your brother, and then come and offer your gift.

Agree with your adversary quickly while you are with him on the way; lest perhaps the prosecutor deliver you to the judge, and the judge deliver you to the officer, and you be cast into prison. Most certainly I tell you, you shall by no means get out of there until you have paid the last penny.

Adultery (5:27-32)

"You have heard that it was said, 'You shall not commit adultery;' but I tell you that everyone who gazes at a woman to lust after her has committed adultery with her already in his heart.

If your right eye causes you to stumble, pluck it out and throw it away from you. For it is more profitable for you that one of your members should perish than for your whole body to be cast into Hinnom Valley. If your right hand causes you to stumble, cut it off, and throw it away from you. For it is more profitable for you that one of your members should perish, than for your whole body to be cast into Hinnom Valley.

It was also said, 'Whoever shall put away his wife, let him give her a get,' but I tell you that whoever puts away his wife, except for the cause of sexual immorality, makes her an adulteress; and whoever marries her when she is put away commits adultery.

Nedarim (5:33-37)

"Again you have heard that it was said to the ancients, 'You shall not make false vows, but shall perform to Hashem your vows,' but I tell you, don't swear at all: neither by heaven, for it is the throne of God; nor by the earth, for it is the footstool of his feet; nor by Yerushalaim, for it is the city of the great King. Neither shall you swear by your head, for you can't make one hair white or black. But let your 'Yes' be 'Yes' and your 'No' be 'No.' Whatever is more than these is of the evil one.

Your Abba (5:38-48)

"You have heard that it was said, 'An eye for an eye, and a tooth for a tooth.' But I tell you, don't resist him who is evil; but whoever strikes you on your right cheek, turn to him the other also. If anyone sues you to take away your coat, let him have your cloak also. Whoever compels you to go one mile, go with him two. Give to him who asks you, and don't turn away him who desires to borrow from you.

You have heard that it was said, 'You shall love your neighbour and hate your enemy.' But I tell you, love your enemies, bless those who curse you, do good to those who hate you, and pray for those who mistreat you and persecute you, that you may be children of your Abba who is in heaven. For he makes his sun to rise on the evil and the good, and sends rain on the just and the unjust. For if you love those who love you, what reward do you have? Don't even the tax collectors do the same? If you only greet your friends, what more do you do than others? Don't even the tax collectors do the same?

Therefore you shall be wholehearted, just as your Abba in heaven is wholehearted.

Tzedakah (6:1-4)

"Be careful that you don't give tzedakah before men, to be seen by them, or else you have no reward from your Abba who is in heaven. Therefore, when you give tzedakah, don't sound a trumpet before yourself, as the hypocrites do at shul and in the streets, that they may get glory from men. Most certainly I tell you, they have received their reward. But when you give tzedakah, don't let your left hand know what your right hand does, so that your tzedakah may be in secret; then your Abba who sees in secret will reward you openly.

Davening (6:5-15)

"When you daven, you shall not be as the hypocrites, for they love to stand and daven at shul and on the corners of the streets, that they may be seen by men. Most certainly, I tell you, they have received their reward. But you, when you daven, enter into your inner room, and having shut your door, daven to your Abba who is in secret; and your Abba who sees in secret will reward you openly.

In davening, don't use vain repetitions as the goyim do; for they think that they will be heard for their much speaking. Therefore don't be like them, for your Abba knows what things you need before you ask him.

Daven like this: 'Our Abba in heaven, may your name be kept holy. Let your kingdom come. Let your will be done on earth as it is in heaven. Give us today our daily bread. Forgive us our debts, as we also forgive our debtors. Bring us not into temptation, but deliver us from the evil one. For yours is the kingdom, the power, and the glory forever. Amen.'

For if you forgive men their trespasses, your Abba in heaven will also forgive you. But if you don't forgive men their trespasses, neither will your Abba forgive your trespasses.

Fasting (6:16-18)

"Moreover when you fast, don't be like the hypocrites, with sad faces. For they disfigure their faces that they may be seen by men to be fasting. Most certainly I tell you, they have received their reward. But you, when you fast, anoint your head and wash your face, so that you are not seen by men to be fasting, but by your Abba who is in secret; and your Abba, who sees in secret, will reward you.

Treasure (6:19-24)

"Don't lay up treasures for yourselves on the earth, where moth and rust consume, and where thieves break through and steal; but lay up for yourselves treasures in heaven, where neither moth nor rust consume, and where thieves don't break through and steal; for where your treasure is, there your heart will be also.

The menorah of the body is the eye. If therefore you have an ayin tova, your whole body will be full of light. But if you have an ayin hara, your whole body will be full of darkness. If therefore the light that is in you is darkness, how great is the darkness!

No one can serve two masters, for either he will hate the one and love the other, or else he will be devoted to one and despise the other. You can't serve both God and wealth.

Anxiety (6:25-34)

"Therefore I tell you, don't be anxious for your life: what you will eat, or what you will drink; nor yet for your body, what you will wear. Isn't life more than food, and the body more than clothing? See the birds of the sky, that they don't sow, neither do they reap, nor gather into barns. Your Abba in heaven feeds them. Aren't you of much more value than they? Which of you by being anxious, can add one moment to his lifespan?

Why are you anxious about clothing? Consider the lilies of the field, how they grow. They don't toil, neither do they spin, yet I tell you that even Shlomo in all his glory was not dressed like one of these. But if God so clothes the grass of the field, which today exists and tomorrow is thrown into the oven, won't he much more clothe you, you of little faith?

Therefore don't be anxious, saying, 'What will we eat?', 'What will we drink?' or, 'With what will we be clothed?' For the goyim seek after all these things; for your Abba in heaven knows that you need all these things. But seek first God's kingdom and his righteousness; and all these things will be given to you as well.

Therefore don't be anxious for tomorrow, for tomorrow will be anxious for itself. Each day's own evil is sufficient.

Judgement (7:1-6)

"Don't judge, so that you won't be judged. For with whatever judgement you judge, you will be judged; and with whatever measure you measure, it will be measured to you.

Why do you see the speck that is in your brother's eye, but don't consider the beam that is in your own eye? Or how will you tell your brother, 'Let me remove the speck from your eye,' and hinei, the beam is in your own eye? You hypocrite! First remove the beam out of your own eye, and then you can see clearly to remove the speck out of your brother's eye.

Don't give that which is holy to the dogs, neither throw your pearls before the pigs, lest perhaps they trample them under their feet, and turn and tear you to pieces.

Ask (7:7-12)

"Ask, and it will be given you. Seek, and you will find. Knock, and it will be opened for you. For everyone who asks receives. He who seeks finds. To him who knocks it will be opened. Or who is there among you who, if his son asks him for bread, will give him a stone? Or if he asks for a fish, who will give him a serpent? If you then, being evil, know how to give good gifts to your children, how much more will your Abba who is in heaven give good things to those who ask him!

Therefore, whatever you desire for men to do to you, you shall also do to them; for this is the Torah and the Prophets.

The Way (7:13-20)

"Enter in by the narrow gate; for the gate is wide and the way is broad that leads to destruction, and there are many who enter in by it. How narrow is the gate and the way is restricted that leads to life! There are few who find it.

Beware of false prophets, who come to you in sheep's clothing, but inwardly are ravening wolves. By their fruits you will know them. Do you gather grapes from thorns or figs from thistles? Even so, every good tree produces good fruit, but the corrupt tree produces evil fruit. A good tree can't produce evil fruit, neither can a corrupt tree produce good fruit. Every tree that doesn't grow good fruit is cut down and thrown into the fire. Therefore by their fruits you will know them.

Mashal: House (7:21-29)

"Not everyone who says to me, 'Master, Master,' will enter into my kingdom, but he who does the will of my Abba who is in heaven. Many will tell me in that day, 'Master, Master, didn't we prophesy in your name, in your name cast out shedim, and in your name do many miracles?' Then I will tell them, 'I never knew you. Depart from me, you who act without Torah!'

Everyone therefore who hears these words of mine and does them, I will liken him to a wise man who built his house on a rock. The rain came down, the floods came, and the winds blew and beat on that house; and it didn't fall, for it was founded on the rock. Everyone who hears these words of mine and doesn't do them will be like a foolish man who built his house on the sand. The rain came down, the floods came, and the winds blew and beat on that house; and it fell—and its fall was great."

When I had finished saying these things, the crowds were astonished at my torah, for I taught them with authority, and not like the scholars.

Leper (8:1-4)

When I came down from the mountain, great crowds followed me. Hinei! A leper came and bowed down to me, saying,

"Master, if you want to, you can make me clean." I stretched out my hand and touched him, saying, "I want to. Be made clean!" Immediately his leprosy was cleansed. I said to him, "See that you tell nobody; but go, show yourself to the kohen, and offer the gift that Moshe commanded, as a testimony to them."

Centurion (8:5-13)

When I came into Kfar-Nachum, a centurion came to me, asking me for help, saying, "Master, my servant lies in the house paralyzed, grievously tormented." I said to him, "I will come and heal him." The centurion answered, "Master, I'm not worthy for you to come under my roof. Just say the word, and my servant will be healed. For I am also a man under authority, having under myself soldiers. I tell this one, 'Go,' and he goes; and tell another, 'Come,' and he comes; and tell my servant, 'Do this,' and he does it."

When I heard it, I marvelled and said to those who followed, "Most certainly I tell you, I haven't found so great a faith, not even in Israel! I tell you that many will come from the east and the west, and will sit down with Avraham, Yitzchak, and Yaakov in the kingdom of Heaven, but the children of the kingdom will be thrown out into the outer darkness. There will be weeping and gnashing of teeth."

I said to the centurion, "Go your way. Let it be done for you as you have believed." His servant was healed in that hour.

Peter's House (8:14-17)

When I came into Peter's house, I saw his wife's eema lying sick with a fever. I touched her hand, and the fever left her. So she got up and served me.

When evening came, they brought to me many possessed with shedim. I cast out the spirits with a word, and healed all who were sick, that it might be fulfilled which was spoken through

Yeshaya the prophet, saying, "He took our infirmities and bore our diseases."

Storm (8:18-27)

Now when I saw great crowds around me, I gave the order to depart to the other side. A scholar came and said to me, "Rabbi, I will follow you wherever you go." I said to him, "The foxes have holes and the birds of the sky have nests but I, the Ben-Adam, have nowhere to lay my head."

Another of my talmidim said to me, "Master, allow me first to go and bury my abba." But I said to him, "Follow me, and leave the dead to bury their own dead."

When I got into a boat, my talmidim followed me. Hinei! A violent storm came up on the sea, so much that the boat was covered with the waves; but I was asleep. The talmidim came to me and woke me up, saying, "Save us, Master! We are dying!" I said to them, "Why are you fearful, you of little faith?" Then I got up, rebuked the wind and the sea, and there was a great calm. The men marvelled, saying, "What kind of man is this, that even the wind and the sea shema to him?"

Gadara (8:28-34)

When I came to the other side, into the country of Gadara, two people possessed by shedim met me there, coming out of the tombs, exceedingly fierce, so that nobody could pass that way. Hinei! They cried out, saying, "What do we have to do with you, Yeshua, Ben-Elohim? Have you come here to torment us before the moed?"

Now there was a herd of many pigs feeding far away from them. The shedim begged me, saying, "If you cast us out, permit us to go away into the herd of pigs." I said to them, "Go!" They came out and went into the herd of pigs, and hinei! The whole herd of pigs rushed down the cliff into the sea and died in the water.

Those who fed them fled and went away into the city and told everything, including what happened to those who were possessed with shedim. Hinei! All the city came out to meet me. When they saw me, they begged that I would depart from their borders.

Paralytic (9:1-8)

I entered into a boat and crossed over, and came into my own city. Hinei! They brought to me a man who was paralyzed, lying on a bed. Seeing their faith, I said to the paralytic, "Son, cheer up! Your sins are forgiven you."

Hinei! Some of the scholars said to themselves, "This man blasphemes." Knowing their thoughts, I said, "Why do you think evil in your hearts? For which is easier, to say, 'Your sins are forgiven;' or to say, 'Get up, and walk?' But that you may know that I, the Ben-Adam, have authority on earth to forgive sins—" (then I said to the paralytic), "Get up, and take up your mat, and go home." He arose and departed to his house.

But when the crowds saw it, they marvelled and praised God, who had given such authority to men.

Mattai (9:9-13)

As I passed by from there, I saw a man called Mattai sitting at the tax collection office. I said to him, "Follow me!" He got up and followed me.

As I sat in the house, hinei! Many tax collectors and sinners came and sat down with me and my talmidim. When the Prushim saw it, they said to my talmidim, "Why does your rabbi eat with tax collectors and sinners?" When I heard it, I said to them, "Those who are healthy have no need for a physician, but those who are sick do. But you go and learn what this means: 'I desire mercy, and not sacrifice,' for I came not to call the tzaddikim, but sinners—to return in teshuva."

Fasting (9:14-17)

Then Yochanan's talmidim came to me, saying, "Why do we and the Prushim fast often, but your talmidim don't fast?" I said to them, "Can the bnei-chuppah mourn as long as the chattan is with them? But the days will come when the chattan will be taken away from them, and then they will fast.

No one puts a piece of unshrunk cloth on an old garment; for the patch would tear away from the garment, and a worse hole is made. Neither do people put new wine into old wineskins, or else the skins would burst, and the wine be spilled, and the skins ruined. No, they put new wine into fresh wineskins, and both are preserved."

Official's Daughter (9:18-26)

While I told these things to them, hinei! An official came and bowed down to me, saying, "My daughter has just died, but come and lay your hand on her, and she will live." I got up and followed him, as did my talmidim.

Hinei! A woman who had a discharge of blood for twelve years came behind me, and touched the tzitzit of my garment; for she said within herself, "If I just touch his garment, I will be made well." But, turning around and seeing her, I said, "Daughter, cheer up! Your faith has made you well." And the woman was made well from that hour.

When I came into the official's house and saw the flute players and the crowd in noisy disorder, I said to them, "Make room, because the girl isn't dead, but sleeping." They were ridiculing me. But when the crowd was sent out, I entered in, took her by the hand, and the girl arose. The report of this went out into all that land.

Blind Men (9:27-31)

As I passed by from there, two blind men followed me, calling out and saying, "Have mercy on us, Ben-David!"

When I had come into the house, the blind men came to me. I said to them, "Do you believe that I am able to do this?" They told me, "Yes, Master." Then I touched their eyes, saying, "According to your faith be it done to you." Then their eyes were opened.

I strictly commanded them, saying, "See that no one knows about this." But they went out and spread abroad my fame in all that land.

Mute Man (9:32-38)

As they went out, hinei! A mute man who was possessed by a shed was brought to me. When the shed was cast out, the mute man spoke. The crowds marvelled, saying, "Nothing like this has ever been seen in Israel!" But the Prushim said, "By the prince of the shedim, he casts out shedim."

I went about all the cities and the villages, teaching in their shuls and proclaiming the besorah of the Kingdom, and healing every disease and every sickness among the people. But when I saw the crowds, I was moved with compassion for them because they were harassed and scattered, like sheep without a shepherd. Then I said to my talmidim, "The harvest indeed is plentiful, but the labourers are few. Pray therefore that the Master of the harvest will send out labourers into his harvest."

Twelve Called (10:1-4)

I called my twelve talmidim to myself, and gave them authority over unclean spirits, to cast them out, and to heal every disease and every sickness.

Now the names of the twelve shaliachs are these. The first, Shimon, who is called Peter; Andrew, his brother; Yaakov Ben-Zavdai; Yochanan, his brother; Philip; Bar-Talmai; Toma; Mattai the tax collector; Yaakov Ben-Chalfai; Labbai, who was also called Taddai; Shimon the Zealot; and Yehuda from Kriyot, who also betrayed me.

Twelve Sent (10:5-15)

I sent these twelve out and commanded them, saying, "Don't go among the goyim, and don't enter into any city of the Shomronim. Rather, go to the lost sheep of the house of Israel. As you go, proclaim, saying, 'The kingdom of Heaven is at hand!' Heal the sick, cleanse the lepers, and cast out shedim. Freely you received, so freely give.

Don't take any gold, silver, or brass in your money belts. Take no bag for your journey, neither two coats, nor sandals, nor staff: for the labourer is worthy of his food. Into whatever city or village you enter, find out who in it is worthy, and stay there until you go on. As you enter into the household, greet it. If the household is worthy, let your shalom come on it, but if it isn't worthy, let your shalom return to you.

Whoever doesn't receive you or shema to your words, as you go out of that house or that city, shake the dust off your feet. Most certainly I tell you, it will be more tolerable for the land of Sodom and Gomorrah on Yom HaDin than for that city!

Beware (10:16-25)

"Hinei! I send you out as sheep among wolves. Therefore be wise as serpents and harmless as doves. But beware of men, for they will deliver you up to sanhedrins, and in their synagogues they will scourge you. Yes, and you will be brought before governors and kings for my sake, for a testimony to them and to the goyim. But when they deliver you up, don't be anxious how or what you will say, for it will be given you in that hour what you will say.

For it is not you who speak, but your Abba's Ruach who speaks in you.

Brother will deliver up brother to death, and the abba his child. Children will rise up against parents and cause them to be put to death. You will be hated by all men for my name's sake, but he who endures to the end will be saved. But when they persecute you in this city, flee into the next, for most certainly I tell you, you will not have gone through the cities of Israel until I, the Ben-Adam, have come.

A talmid is not above his rabbi, nor a servant above his master. It is enough for the talmid that he be like his rabbi, and the servant like his master. If they have called the master of the house Baal-Zvuv, how much more those of his household!

Fear (10:26-36)

"Therefore don't be afraid of them, for there is nothing covered that will not be revealed, or hidden that will not be known. What I tell you in the darkness, speak in the light; and what you hear whispered in the ear, proclaim on the housetops. Don't be afraid of those who kill the body, but are not able to kill the soul. Rather, fear him who is able to destroy both soul and body in Hinnom Valley. Aren't two sparrows sold for a copper coin? Not one of them falls to the ground apart from your Abba's will. But the very hairs of your head are all numbered. Therefore don't be afraid. You are of more value than many sparrows.

Everyone therefore who confesses me before men, I will also confess him before my Abba who is in heaven. But whoever denies me before men, I will also deny him before my Abba who is in heaven.

Don't think that I came to send peace on the earth. I didn't come to send peace, but a sword. For I came to set a man at odds against his abba, and a daughter against her eema, and a daughter-in-law against her mother-in-law. A man's foes will be those of his own household.

Worthy (10:32-11:1)

"He who loves abba or eema more than me is not worthy of me; and he who loves son or daughter more than me isn't worthy of me. He who doesn't take his cross and follow after me isn't worthy of me. He who seeks his life will lose it; and he who loses his life for my sake will find it.

He who receives you receives me, and he who receives me receives him who sent me. He who receives a prophet in the name of a prophet will receive a prophet's reward. He who receives a tzaddik in the name of a tzaddik will receive a tzaddik's reward. Whoever gives one of these little ones just a cup of cold water to drink in the name of a talmid, most certainly I tell you, he will in no way lose his reward."

When I had finished directing my twelve talmidim, I departed from there to teach and proclaim in their cities.

Yochanan In Prison (11:2-15)

Now when Yochanan heard in the prison of my doings, he sent two of his talmidim and said to me, "Are you he who comes, or should we look for another?" I answered them, "Go and tell Yochanan the things which you hear and see: the blind receive their sight, the lame walk, the lepers are cleansed, the deaf hear, the dead are raised up, and the poor have the Besorah preached to them. Ashrei is he who finds no occasion for stumbling in me."

As these went their way, I began to say to the crowds concerning Yochanan, "What did you go out into the wilderness to see? A reed shaken by the wind? But what did you go out to see? A man in soft clothing? Hinei! Those who wear soft clothing are in kings' houses. But why did you go out? To see a prophet? Yes, I tell you, and much more than a prophet! For this is he, of whom it is written, 'Hinei! I send my messenger before your face, who will prepare your way before you.'

Most certainly I tell you, among those who are born of women there has not arisen anyone greater than Yochanan the Immerser; yet he who is least in my kingdom is greater than he. From the days of Yochanan the Immerser until now, my kingdom suffers violence, and the violent take it by force. For all the Prophets and the Torah prophesied until Yochanan. If you are willing to receive it, this is Eliyahu, who is to come. He who has ears to shema, let him shema.

This Generation (11:16-24)

But to what shall I compare this generation? It is like children sitting in the shuk, who call to their companions and say, 'We played the flute for you, and you didn't dance. We mourned for you, and you didn't lament.' For Yochanan came neither eating nor drinking, and they say, 'He has a shed!' I, the Ben-Adam, came eating and drinking, and they say, 'Hinei! A gluttonous man and a drunkard, a friend of tax collectors and sinners!' But wisdom is justified by her children."

Then I began to denounce the cities in which most of my miracles had been done, because they didn't return in teshuva. "Oy to you, Korazin! Oy to you, Beit-Tzaida! For if the miracles had been done in Tyre and Sidon which were done in you, they would have returned in teshuva long ago in sackcloth and ashes. But I tell you, it will be more tolerable for Tyre and Sidon on Yom HaDin than for you. You, Kfar-Nachum, who are exalted to heaven, you will go down to Sheol. For if the miracles had been done in Sodom which were done in you, it would have lasted until today. But I tell you that it will be more tolerable for the land of Sodom on Yom HaDin, than for you."

Come (11:25-30)

At that time, I answered, "Modeh ani, Abba, Master of heaven and earth, that you hid these things from the wise and understanding, and revealed them to infants. Yes, Abba, for so it was well-pleasing in your sight."

All things have been handed over to me by my Abba. No one knows me except my Abba; neither does anyone know my Abba except me, his Son, and he to whom I desire to reveal him.

Come to me, all you who labour and are heavily burdened, and I will give you rest. Take my yoke upon you and learn from me, for I am gentle and humble in heart; and you will find rest for your souls. For my yoke is easy, and my burden is light.

Grain Fields (12:1-8)

At that time, I went through the grain fields on Shabbat. My talmidim were hungry and began to pluck heads of grain and to eat. But the Prushim, when they saw it, said to me, "Hinei! Your talmidim do what is not lawful to do on Shabbat."

But I said to them, "Haven't you read what David did when he was hungry, and those who were with him: how he entered into God's house and ate the showbread, which was not lawful for him to eat, nor for those who were with him, but only for the kohanim? Or have you not read in the Torah that on Shabbat the kohanim in the Beit HaMikdash profane Shabbat and are guiltless? But I tell you that someone greater than the Beit HaMikdash is here. But if you had known what this means, 'I desire mercy, and not sacrifice,' you wouldn't have condemned the guiltless. For I, the Ben-Adam, am Master of Shabbat."

Withered Hand (12:9-21)

I departed from there and went into their shul, and hinei! There was a man with a withered hand. They asked me, "Is it lawful to heal on Shabbat?" so that they might accuse me. I said to them,

"What man is there among you who has one sheep, and if this one falls into a pit on Shabbat, won't he grab on to it and lift it out? Of how much more value then is a man than a sheep! Therefore it is lawful to do good on Shabbat." Then I told the man, "Stretch out your hand." He stretched it out; and it was restored whole, just like the other. But the Prushim went out and conspired against me, how they might destroy me.

Perceiving that, I withdrew from there. Great crowds followed me; and I healed them all, and commanded them that they should not make me known, that it might be fulfilled which was spoken through Yeshaya the prophet, saying, "Hinei! My servant whom I have chosen, my beloved in whom my soul is delighted. I will put my Ruach on him. He will proclaim justice to the goyim. He will not strive, nor shout, neither will anyone hear his voice in the streets. He won't break a bruised reed. He won't quench a smoking flax, until he leads justice to victory. In his name, the goyim will hope."

Blind & Mute Man (12:22-37)

Then someone possessed by a shed, blind and mute, was brought to me; and I healed him, so that the blind and mute man both spoke and saw. All the crowds were amazed, and said, "Can this be the Ben-David?" But when the Prushim heard it, they said, "This man does not cast out shedim except by Baal-Zvuv, the prince of the shedim."

Knowing their thoughts, I said to them, "Every kingdom divided against itself is brought to desolation, and every city or house divided against itself will not stand. If antagonist casts out antagonist, he is divided against himself. How then will his kingdom stand? If I by Baal-Zvuv cast out shedim, by whom do your children cast them out? Therefore they will be your judges. But if I by the Ruach-Elohim cast out shedim, then God's kingdom has come upon you. Or how can someone enter into the house of the strong man and plunder his goods, unless he first bind the strong man? Then he will plunder his house.

He who is not with me is mitnaged against me, and he who doesn't gather with me, scatters. Therefore I tell you, every sin and blasphemy will be forgiven men, but the blasphemy against the Ruach will not be forgiven men. Whoever speaks a word against me, the Ben-Adam, it will be forgiven him; but whoever speaks against Ruach HaKodesh, it will not be forgiven him, either in this olam, or in the olam to come.

Either make the tree good and its fruit good, or make the tree corrupt and its fruit corrupt; for the tree is known by its fruit. You offspring of vipers, how can you, being evil, speak good things? For out of the abundance of the heart, the mouth speaks. The good man out of his good treasure brings out good things, and the evil man out of his evil treasure brings out evil things. I tell you that every idle word that men speak, they will give account of it on Yom HaDin. For by your words you will be justified, and by your words you will be condemned."

Evil Generation (12:38-45)

Then certain of the scholars and Prushim answered, "Rabbi, we want to see a sign from you." But I answered them, "An evil and adulterous generation seeks after a sign, but no sign will be given to it but the sign of Yonah the prophet. For as Yonah was three days and three nights in the belly of the huge fish, so will I, the Ben-Adam, be three days and three nights in the heart of the earth.

The men of Nineveh will stand up in the judgement with this generation and will condemn it, for they returned in teshuva at the proclaiming of Yonah; and hinei! Someone greater than Yonah is here. The Queen of the South will rise up in the judgement with this generation and will condemn it, for she came from the ends of the earth to hear the wisdom of Shlomo; and hinei! Someone greater than Shlomo is here.

When an unclean spirit has gone out of a man, he passes through waterless places seeking rest, and doesn't find it. Then he says, 'I will return into my house from which I came;' and when he has come back, he finds it empty, swept, and put in order. Then he goes and takes with himself seven other spirits more evil than he is, and they enter in and dwell there. The last state of that man becomes worse than the first. Even so will it be also to this evil generation."

Eema & Brothers (12:46-50)

While I was yet speaking to the crowds, hinei! My eema and my brothers stood outside, seeking to speak to me. Someone said to me, "Hinei! Your eema and your brothers stand outside, seeking to speak to you." But I answered him who spoke to me, "Who is my eema? Who are my brothers?" I stretched out my hand towards my talmidim, and said, "Hinei! My eema and my brothers. For whoever does the will of my Abba who is in heaven, he is my brother, and sister, and eema."

Mashal: Farmer (13:1-9)

On that day I went out of the house and sat by the seaside. Great crowds gathered to me, so that I entered into a boat and sat; and all the crowd stood on the beach.

I spoke to them many things in mashalim, saying, "Hinei! A farmer went out to sow. As he sowed, some seeds fell by the roadside, and the birds came and devoured them. Others fell on rocky ground, where they didn't have much soil, and immediately they sprang up, because they had no depth of earth. When the sun had risen, they were scorched. Because they had no root, they withered away. Others fell among thorns. The thorns grew up and choked them. Others fell on good soil and yielded fruit: some one hundred times as much, some sixty, and some thirty. He who has ears to shema, let him shema."

Mashalim (13:10-17)

The talmidim came, and said to me, "Why do you speak to them in mashalim?" I answered them, "To you it is given to know the mysteries of my kingdom, but it is not given to them. For whoever has, to him will be given, and he will have abundance; but whoever doesn't have, from him will be taken away even that which he has.

Therefore I speak to them in mashalim, because seeing they don't see, and hearing, they don't hear, neither do they understand. In them the prophecy of Yeshaya is fulfilled, which says, 'By hearing you will hear, and will in no way understand; Seeing you will see, and will in no way perceive; for this people's heart has grown callous, their ears are dull of hearing, and they have closed their eyes; or else perhaps they might perceive with their eyes, hear with their ears, understand with their heart, and would turn again, and I would heal them.'

But blessed are your eyes, for they see; and your ears, for they hear! For most certainly I tell you that many prophets and tzaddikim desired to see the things which you see, and didn't see them; and to hear the things which you hear, and didn't hear them.

Farmer Explained (13:18-23)

"Shema, then, to the mashal of the farmer. When anyone hears the word of my kingdom and doesn't understand it, the evil one comes and snatches away that which has been sown in his heart. This is what was sown by the roadside. What was sown on the rocky places, this is he who hears the word and immediately receives it with joy; yet he has no root in himself, but endures for a while. When oppression or persecution arises because of the word, immediately he stumbles. What was sown among the thorns, this is he who hears the word, but the cares of this olam and the deceitfulness of riches choke the word, and he becomes unfruitful. What was sown on the good ground, this is he who hears the word and understands it, who most certainly bears fruit and produces, some one hundred times as much, some sixty, and some thirty."

Mashal: Darnel Weeds (13:24-30)

I set another mashal before them, saying, "My kingdom is like a man who sowed good seed in his field, but while people slept, his enemy came and sowed darnel weeds also among the wheat, and went away. But when the blade sprang up and produced grain, then the darnel weeds appeared also.

The servants of the householder came and said to him, 'Sir, didn't you sow good seed in your field? Where did these darnel weeds come from?' He said to them, 'An enemy has done this.' The servants asked him, 'Do you want us to go and gather them up?' But he said, 'No, lest perhaps while you gather up the darnel weeds, you root up the wheat with them. Let both grow together until the harvest, and in the harvest moed I will tell the reapers, "First, gather up the darnel weeds, and bind them in bundles to burn them; but gather the wheat into my barn."'"

Mashalim: Mustard Seed & Yeast (13:31-36)

I set another mashal before them, saying, "My kingdom is like a grain of mustard seed which a man took, and sowed in his field, which indeed is smaller than all seeds. But when it is grown, it is greater than the herbs and becomes a tree, so that the birds of the air come and nest in its branches."

I spoke another mashal to them. "My kingdom is like chametz which a woman took and hid in three measures of meal, until it was all leavened."

I spoke all these things in mashalim to the crowds; and without a mashal, I didn't speak to them, that it might be fulfilled which was spoken through the prophet, saying, "I will open my mouth in mashalim; I will utter things hidden from the foundation of the world."

Then I sent the crowds away, and went into the house.

Darnel Weeds Explained (13:36-43)

My talmidim came to me, saying, "Explain to us the mashal of the darnel weeds of the field." I answered them, "He who sows the good seed is me, the Ben-Adam; the field is the world; the good seeds are the children of my kingdom; and the darnel weeds are the children of the evil one. The enemy who sowed them is the accuser. The harvest is the end of this olam, and the reapers are messengers.

As therefore the darnel weeds are gathered up and burned with fire; so will it be at the end of this olam. I, the Ben-Adam, will send out my messengers, and they will gather out of my kingdom all things that cause stumbling and those who act without Torah, and will cast them into the furnace of fire. There will be weeping and gnashing of teeth. Then the tzaddikim will shine like the sun in the kingdom of their Abba. He who has ears to shema, let him shema.

Mashalim: Treasure, Merchant, Dragnet (13:44-52)

"Again, my kingdom is like treasure hidden in the field, which a man found and hid. In his joy, he goes and sells all that he has and buys that field.

Again, my kingdom is like a man who is a merchant seeking fine pearls, who having found one pearl of great price, he went and sold all that he had and bought it.

Again, my kingdom is like a dragnet that was cast into the sea and gathered some fish of every kind, which, when it was filled, fishermen drew up on the beach. They sat down and gathered the good into containers, but the bad they threw away. So it will be in the end of this olam. The messengers will come and separate the wicked from among the tzaddikim, and will cast them into the furnace of fire. There will be weeping and gnashing of teeth."

I said to them, "Have you understood all these things?" They answered me, "Yes, Master." I said to them, "Therefore every scholar who has been made a talmid in my kingdom is like a man who is a householder, who brings out of his treasure new and old things."

My Country (13:53-58)

When I had finished these mashalim, I departed from there. Coming into my own country, I taught them in their shul, so that they were astonished and said, "Where did this man get this wisdom and these miracles? Isn't this the carpenter's son? Isn't his eema called Miriam, and his brothers Yaakov, Yosi, Shimon, and Yehuda? Aren't all of his sisters with us? Where then did this man get all of these things?" They were offended by me. But I said to them, "A prophet is not without honour, except in his own country and in his own house." I didn't do many miracles there because of their unbelief.

Tetrarch (14:1-12)

At that time, Herod the tetrarch heard the report concerning me, and said to his servants, "This is Yochanan the Immerser. He is risen from the dead! That is why these powers work in him." For Herod had arrested Yochanan, bound him, and put him in prison for the sake of Herodias, his brother Philip's wife. For Yochanan said to him, "It is not lawful for you to have her." When he would have put him to death, he feared the crowd, because they counted him as a prophet.

But when Herod's birthday came, the daughter of Herodias danced among them and pleased Herod. Therefore he promised with an oath to give her whatever she should ask. She, being prompted by her mother, said, "Give me here on a platter the head of Yochanan the Immerser." The king was grieved, but for the sake of his oaths and of those who sat at the table with him, he commanded it to be given, and he sent and beheaded Yochanan in the prison. His head was brought on a platter and given to the young lady; and she brought it to her mother.

His talmidim came, took the body, and buried it. Then they went and told me.

Five Loaves (14:13-21)

Now when I heard this, I withdrew from there in a boat to a deserted place apart. When the crowds heard it, they followed me on foot from the cities. I went out, and I saw a great crowd. I had compassion on them and healed their sick.

When evening had come, my talmidim came to me, saying, "This place is deserted, and the hour is already late. Send the crowds away, that they may go into the villages, and buy themselves food." But I said to them, "They don't need to go away. You give them something to eat." They told me, "We only have here five loaves and two fish." I said, "Bring them here to me." I commanded the crowds to sit down on the grass; and I took the five loaves and the two fish, and looking up to heaven, I made the bracha, broke and gave the loaves to the talmidim; and the talmidim gave to the crowds. They all ate and were filled.

They took up twelve baskets full of that which remained left over from the broken pieces. Those who ate were about five thousand men, in addition to women and children.

Sea (14:22-36)

Immediately I made the talmidim get into the boat and go ahead of me to the other side, while I sent the crowds away. After I had sent the crowds away, I went up onto the mountain by myself to pray. When evening had come, I was there alone. But the boat was now in the middle of the sea, distressed by the waves, for the wind was contrary. In the fourth watch of the night, I came to them, walking on the sea. When the talmidim saw me walking on the sea, they were troubled, saying, "It's a ghost!" and they cried out for fear. But immediately I spoke to them, saying, "Cheer up! It's me! Don't be afraid."

Peter answered me and said, "Master, if it is you, command me to come to you on the waters." I said, "Come!" Peter stepped down from the boat and walked on the waters to come to me. But when he saw that the wind was strong, he was afraid, and beginning to sink, he cried out, saying, "Master, save me!" Immediately I stretched out my hand, took hold of him, and said to him, "You of little faith, why did you doubt?" When we got up into the boat, the wind ceased. Those who were in the boat came and bowed down to me, saying, "You are truly the Ben-Elohim!"

When we had crossed over, we came to the land of Ginesar. When the people of that place recognized me, they sent into all that surrounding region and brought to me all who were sick; and they begged me that they might just touch the tzitzit of my garment. As many as touched it were made whole.

Tradition (15:1-20)

Then Prushim and scholars came to me from Yerushalaim, saying, "Why do your talmidim disobey the tradition of the elders? For they don't do Netilat Yadaim when they eat bread." I answered them, "Why do you also disobey the mitzvah of God because of your tradition? For God commanded, 'Honour your father and your mother,' and, 'He who speaks evil of father or mother, let him be put to death.' But you say, 'Whoever may tell his abba or his eema, "Whatever help you might otherwise have gotten from me is a gift devoted to God," he shall not honour his abba or eema.' You have made the mitzvah of God void because of your tradition. You hypocrites! Well did Yeshaya prophesy of you, saying, 'These people draw near to me with their mouth, and honour me with their lips; but their heart is far from me. And they worship me in vain, teaching as doctrine rules made by men.'"

I summoned the crowd, and said to them, "Shema, and understand. That which enters into the mouth doesn't defile the man; but that which proceeds out of the mouth, this defiles the man." Then the talmidim came and said to me, "Do you know that the Prushim were offended when they heard this saying?" But I answered, "Every plant which my Abba in heaven didn't plant will be uprooted. Leave them alone. They are blind guides of the blind. If the blind guide the blind, both will fall into a pit."

Peter answered me, "Explain the mashal to us." So I said, "Do you also still not understand? Don't you understand that whatever goes into the mouth passes into the belly and then out of the body? But the things which proceed out of the mouth come out of the heart, and they defile the man. For out of the heart come evil thoughts, murders, adulteries, sexual sins, thefts, false testimony, and blasphemies. These are the things which defile the man; but to eat with unwashed hands doesn't defile the man."

Canaanite Woman (15:21-28)

I went out from there and withdrew into the region of Tyre and Sidon. Hinei! A Canaanite woman came out from those borders and cried, saying, "Have mercy on me, Master, Ben-David! My daughter is severely possessed by a shed!" But I answered her not a word. My talmidim came and begged me, saying, "Send her away; for she cries after us." But I answered, "I wasn't sent to anyone but the lost sheep of the house of Israel." But she came and bowed down to me, saying, "Master, help me." But I answered, "It is not appropriate to take the children's bread and throw it to the puppies." But she said, "Yes, Master, but even the puppies eat the crumbs which fall from their masters' table!" Then I answered her, "Woman, great is your faith! Be it done to you even as you desire." And her daughter was healed from that hour.

Seven Loaves (15:29-39)

I departed from there and came near to the Kinneret; and I went up on the mountain and sat there. Great crowds came to me, having with them the lame, blind, mute, maimed, and many others, and they put them down at my feet. I healed them, so that the crowd wondered when they saw the mute speaking, the injured healed, the lame walking, and the blind seeing—and they praised the God of Israel.

I summoned my talmidim and said, "I have compassion on the crowd, because they have continued with me now three days and have nothing to eat. I don't want to send them away fasting, or they might faint on the way." The talmidim said to me, "Where could we get so many loaves in a deserted place as to satisfy so great a crowd?" I said to them, "How many loaves do you have?" They said, "Seven, and a few small fish." I commanded the crowd to sit down on the ground; and I took the seven loaves and the fish. I made the bracha and broke them, and gave to the talmidim, and the talmidim to the crowds. They all ate and were filled.

They took up seven baskets full of the broken pieces that were left over. Those who ate were four thousand men, in addition to women and children. Then I sent away the crowds, got into the boat, and came into the borders of Magdala.

Prushim & Tzadukim (16:1-12)

The Prushim and Tzadukim came, and testing me, asked me to show them a sign from heaven. But I answered them, "When it is evening, you say, 'It will be fair weather, for the sky is red.' In the morning, 'It will be unclean weather today, for the sky is red and threatening.' Hypocrites! You know how to discern the appearance of the sky, but you can't discern the signs of the moadim! An evil and adulterous generation seeks after a sign, and there will be no sign given to it, except the sign of the prophet Yonah." I left them and departed.

The talmidim came to the other side and had forgotten to take bread. I said to them, "Take heed and beware of the chametz of the Prushim and Tzadukim!" They reasoned among themselves, saying, "We brought no bread." Perceiving it, I said, "Why do you reason among yourselves, you of little faith, because you have brought no bread? Don't you yet perceive or remember the five loaves for the five thousand, and how many baskets you took up, or the seven loaves for the four thousand, and how many baskets you took up? How is it that you don't perceive that I didn't speak to you concerning bread? But beware of the chametz of the Prushim and Tzadukim."

Then they understood that I didn't tell them to beware of the chametz of bread, but of the torah of the Prushim and Tzadukim.

Caesarea Philippi (16:13-28)

Now when I came into the parts of Caesarea Philippi, I asked my talmidim, saying, "Who do men say that I, the Ben-Adam, am?" They said, "Some say Yochanan the Immerser, some, Eliyahu, and others, Yirmiya or one of the prophets." I said to them, "But who do you say that I am?" Shimon Peter answered, "You are the Mashiach, the Son of the living God." I answered him, "Ashrei are you, Shimon Bar-Yonah, for flesh and blood has not revealed this to you, but my Abba who is in heaven. I also tell you that you are Peter, and on this rock I will build my kehilla, and the gates of Sheol will not prevail against it. I will give to you the keys of my kingdom, and whatever you forbid on earth will have been forbidden in heaven; and whatever you permit on earth will have been permitted in heaven." Then I commanded the talmidim that they should tell no one that I was the Mashiach.

From that time, I began to show my talmidim that I must go to Yerushalaim and suffer many things from the elders, chief kohanim, and scholars, and be killed, and the third day be raised up. Peter took me aside and began to be mochiach with me, saying, "Far be it from you, Master! This will never be done to you." But I turned and said to Peter, "Get behind me, antagonist! You are a stumbling block to me, for you are not setting your mind on the things of God, but on the things of men."

Then I said to my talmidim, "If anyone desires to come after me, let him deny himself, take up his cross, and follow me. For whoever desires to save his life will lose it, and whoever will lose his life for my sake will find it. For what will it profit a man if he gains the whole world and forfeits his life? Or what will a man give in exchange for his life? For I, the Ben-Adam, will come in the glory of my Abba with his messengers, and then I will render to everyone according to his deeds. Most certainly I tell you, there are some standing here who will in no way taste of death until they see me, the Ben-Adam, coming in my kingdom."

Moshe & Eliyahu (17:1-13)

After six days, I took with me Peter, Yaakov, and Yochanan his brother, and brought them up onto a high mountain by themselves. I was changed before them. My face shone like the sun, and my garments became as white as the light. Hinei! Moshe and Eliyahu appeared to them talking with me.

Peter answered and said to me, "Master, it is good for us to be here. If you want, let's make three sukkot here: one for you, one for Moshe, and one for Eliyahu." While he was still speaking, hinei! A bright cloud overshadowed them. Hinei! A Bat-Kol came out of the cloud, saying, "This is my beloved Son, with whom I am delighted. Shema to him!" When the talmidim heard it, they fell on their faces, and were very afraid. I came and touched them and said, "Get up, and don't be afraid." Lifting up their eyes, they saw no one, except me alone.

As they were coming down from the mountain, I commanded them, saying, "Don't tell anyone what you saw until I, the Ben-Adam, have risen from the dead." My talmidim asked me, saying, "Then why do the scholars say that Eliyahu must come first?" I answered them, "Eliyahu indeed comes first, and will restore all things; but I tell you that Eliyahu has come already, and they didn't recognize him, but did to him whatever they wanted to. Even so I, the Ben-Adam, will also suffer by them."

Then the talmidim understood that I spoke to them of Yochanan the Immerser.

Epileptic (17:14-23)

When we came to the crowd, a man came to me, kneeling down to me and saying, "Master, have mercy on my son, for he is epileptic and suffers grievously; for he often falls into the fire, and often into the water. So I brought him to your talmidim, and they could not cure him." I answered, "Faithless and perverse generation! How long will I be with you? How long will I bear with you? Bring him here to me." I rebuked the shed, and it went out of him, and the boy was cured from that hour.

Then the talmidim came to me privately, and said, "Why weren't we able to cast it out?" I said to them, "Because of your unbelief. For most certainly I tell you, if you have faith as a grain of mustard seed, you will tell this mountain, 'Move from here to there,' and it will move; and nothing will be impossible for you. But this kind doesn't go out except by tefillah and fasting."

While we were staying in the Galil, I said to them, "I, the Ben-Adam, am about to be handed over into the hands of men, and they will kill me, and the third day I will be raised up." They were exceedingly sorry.

Half-Shekel Tax (17:24-27)

When we had come to Kfar-Nachum, those who collected the half-shekel came to Peter, and said, "Doesn't your rabbi pay the half-shekel?" He said, "Yes." When he came into the house, I anticipated him, saying, "What do you think, Shimon? From whom do the kings of the earth receive toll or tribute? From their children, or from strangers?" Peter said to me, "From strangers." I said to him, "Therefore the children are exempt. But, lest we cause them to stumble, go to the sea, cast a hook, and take up the first fish that comes up. When you have opened its mouth, you will find a shekel. Take that, and give it to them for me and you."

Little Ones (18:1-14)

In that hour the talmidim came to me, saying, "Who then is greatest in the kingdom of Heaven?" I called a little child to myself, and set him in the middle of them and said, "Most certainly I tell you, unless you turn and become as little children, you will in no way enter into my kingdom. Whoever therefore humbles himself as this little child is the greatest in my kingdom.

Whoever receives one such little child in my name receives me, but whoever causes one of these little ones who believe in me to stumble, it would be better for him if a huge millstone were hung around his neck and that he were sunk in the depths of the sea. Oy to the world because of occasions of stumbling! For it must be that the occasions come, but oy to that person through whom the occasion comes! If your hand or your foot causes you to stumble, cut it off and cast it from you. It is better for you to enter into life maimed or crippled, rather than having two hands or two feet to be cast into the everlasting fire. If your eye causes you to stumble, pluck it out and cast it from you. It is better for you to enter into life with one eye, rather than having two eyes to be cast into the Hinnom Valley of fire.

See that you don't despise one of these little ones, for I tell you that in heaven their messengers always see the face of my Abba who is in heaven. For I, the Ben-Adam, came to save that which was lost. What do you think? If a man has one hundred sheep, and one of them goes astray, doesn't he leave the ninety-nine, go to the mountains, and seek that which has gone astray? If he finds it, most certainly I tell you, he rejoices over it more than over the ninety-nine which have not gone astray. Even so it is not the will of your Abba who is in heaven that one of these little ones should perish.

Sin (18:15-20)

"If your brother sins against you, go, be mochiach with him, between you and him alone. If he listens to you, you have gained back your brother. But if he doesn't shema, take one or two more with you, that at the mouth of two or three witnesses every word may be established. If he refuses to shema to them, tell it to the kehilla. If he refuses to shema to the kehilla also, let him be to you as a goy or a tax collector.

Most certainly I tell you, whatever things you forbid on earth will have been forbidden in heaven, and whatever things you permit on earth will have been permitted in heaven. Again, assuredly I tell you, that if two of you will agree on earth concerning anything that they will ask, it will be done for them by my Abba who is in heaven. For where two or three are gathered together in my name, there I am in the middle of them."

Forgiveness (18:21-35)

Then Peter came and said to me, "Master, how often shall my brother sin against me, and I forgive him? Until seven times?" I said to him, "I don't tell you until seven times, but, until seventy times seven!

Therefore my kingdom is like a certain king who wanted to settle accounts with his servants. When he had begun to settle, someone was brought to him who owed him ten thousand talents of silver. But because he couldn't pay, his master commanded him to be sold, with his wife, his children, and all that he had, and payment to be made. The servant therefore fell down and knelt before him, saying, 'Master, have patience with me, and I will repay you all!' The master of that servant, being moved with compassion, released him and forgave him the debt. But that servant went out and found one of his fellow servants who owed him one hundred days' wages, and he grabbed him and took him by the throat, saying, 'Pay me what you owe!' So his fellow servant fell down at his feet and begged him, saying, 'Have patience with me, and I will repay you!' He would not, but went and cast him into prison until he should pay back that which was due. So when his fellow servants saw what was done, they were exceedingly sorry, and came and told their master all that was done. Then his master called him in and said to him, 'You wicked servant! I forgave you all that debt because you begged me. Shouldn't you also have had mercy on your fellow servant, even as I had mercy on you?' His master was angry, and handed him over to the tormentors until he should pay all that was due to him.

So my Abba in heaven will also do to you, if you don't each forgive your brother from your hearts for his misdeeds."

Marriage (19:1-12)

When I had finished these words, I departed from the Galil and came into the borders of Judea beyond the Yarden. Great crowds followed me, and I healed them there.

Prushim came to me, testing me and saying, "Is it lawful for a man to divorce his wife for any reason?" I answered, "Haven't you read that he who made them from the beginning made them male and female, and said, 'For this cause a man shall leave his father and mother, and shall be joined to his wife; and the two shall become echad?' So that they are no more two, but echad.

What therefore God has joined together, don't let man tear apart." They asked me, "Why then did Moshe command us to give her a get and divorce her?" I said to them, "Moshe, because of the hardness of your hearts, allowed you to divorce your wives, but from the beginning it has not been so. I tell you that whoever divorces his wife, except for sexual immorality, and marries another, commits adultery; and he who marries her when she is divorced commits adultery."

My talmidim said to me, "If this is the case of the man with his wife, it is not expedient to marry." But I said to them, "Not all men can receive this saying, but those to whom it is given. For there are eunuchs who were born that way from their mother's womb, and there are eunuchs who were made eunuchs by men; and there are eunuchs who made themselves eunuchs for the kingdom of Heaven's sake. He who is able to receive it, let him receive it."

Children (19:13-15)

Then little children were brought to me that I should lay my hands on them and pray; and the talmidim rebuked them. But I said, "Allow the little children, and don't forbid them to come to me; for my kingdom belongs to such as these." I laid my hands on them, and departed from there.

Young Man (19:16-30)

Hinei! Someone came to me and said, "Good Rabbi, what good thing shall I do, that I may live forever?" I said to him, "Why do you call me good? No one is good but one, that is, God. But if you want to enter into life, keep the mitzvot." He said to me, "Which ones?" I said, "'You shall not murder.' 'You shall not commit adultery.' 'You shall not steal.' 'You shall not offer false testimony.' 'Honour your father and your mother.' And, 'You shall love your neighbour as yourself.'" The young man said to me, "All these things I have observed from my youth. What do I still lack?" I said to him, "If you want to be mature, go, sell what you have, and give to the poor, and you will have treasure in heaven; and come, follow me." But when the young man heard this, he went away sad, for he was someone who had great possessions.

I said to my talmidim, "Most certainly I say to you, a rich man will enter into my kingdom with difficulty. Again I tell you, it is easier for a camel to go through a needle's eye than for a rich man to enter into my kingdom." When the talmidim heard it, they were exceedingly astonished, saying, "Who then can be saved?" Looking at them, I said, "With men this is impossible, but with God all things are possible."

Then Peter answered, "Hinei! We have left everything and followed you. What then will we have?" I said to them, "Most certainly I tell you that you who have followed me, in the regeneration when I, the Ben-Adam, will sit on my glorious throne, you also will sit on twelve thrones, judging the twelve tribes of Israel. Everyone who has left houses, or brothers, or sisters, or abba, or eema, or wife, or children, or lands, for my name's sake, will receive one hundred times, and will live forever. But many will be last who are first, and first who are last.

Mashal: Labourers (20:1-16)

"For my kingdom is like a man who was the master of a household, who went out early in the morning to hire labourers for his vineyard. When he had agreed with the labourers for a day's wage, he sent them into his vineyard. He went out about the third hour, and saw others standing idle in the shuk. He said to them, 'You also go into the vineyard, and whatever is right I will give you.' So they went their way. Again he went out about the sixth and the ninth hour, and did likewise. About the eleventh hour he went out and found others standing idle. He said to them, 'Why do you stand here all day idle?' They said to him, 'Because no one has hired us.' He said to them, 'You also go into the vineyard, and you will receive whatever is right.'

When evening had come, the master of the vineyard said to his manager, 'Call the labourers and pay them their wages, beginning from the last to the first.' When those who were hired at about the eleventh hour came, they each received a day's wage. When the first came, they supposed that they would receive more; and they likewise each received a day's wage. When they received it, they murmured against the master of the household, saying, 'These last have spent one hour, and you have made them equal to us who have borne the burden of the day and the scorching heat!' But he answered one of them, 'Friend, I am doing you no wrong. Didn't you agree with me for a day's wage? Take that which is yours, and go your way. It is my desire to give to this last just as much as to you. Isn't it lawful for me to do what I want to with what I own? Or do you have ayin hara, because I am good?'

So the last will be first, and the first last. For many are called, but few are chosen."

Sons of Zavdai (20:17-28)

As I was going up to Yerushalaim, I took the twelve talmidim aside, and on the way I said to them, "Hinei! We are going up to Yerushalaim, and I, the Ben-Adam, will be handed over to the chief kohanim and scholars, and they will condemn me to death, and will hand me over to the goyim to mock, to scourge, and to crucify; and the third day I will be raised up."

Then the eema of the sons of Zavdai came to me with her sons, kneeling and asking a certain thing of me. I said to her, "What do you want?" She said to me, "Command that these, my two sons, may sit, one on your right hand and one on your left hand, in your kingdom." But I answered, "You don't know what you are asking. Are you able to drink the cup that I am about to drink, and be immersed with the mikvah that I am immersed with?"

They said to me, "We are able." I said to them, "You will indeed drink my cup, and be immersed with the mikvah that I am immersed with; but to sit at my right hand and on my left hand is not mine to give, but it is for whom it has been prepared by my Abba."

When the ten heard it, they were indignant with the two brothers. But I summoned them, and said, "You know that the rulers of the goyim lord it over them, and their great people exercise authority over them. It shall not be so among you; but whoever desires to become great among you shall be your servant. Whoever desires to be first among you shall be your bondservant, even as I, the Ben-Adam, came not to be served, but to serve, and to give my life as a ransom for many."

Blind Men (20:29-34)

As we went out from Jericho, a great crowd followed me. Hinei! Two blind men sitting by the road, when they heard that I was passing by, cried out, "Master, have mercy on us, Ben-David!" The crowd rebuked them, telling them that they should be quiet, but they cried out even more, "Master, have mercy on us, Ben-David!" I stood still and called them, and asked, "What do you want me to do for you?" They told me, "Master, that our eyes may be opened." Moved with compassion, I touched their eyes; and immediately their eyes received their sight, and they followed me.

Yerushalaim (21:1-11)

When we came near to Yerushalaim and came to Beit-Pagei, to the Hill of Olives, then I sent two talmidim, saying to them, "Go into the village that is opposite you, and immediately you will find a donkey tied, and a colt with her. Untie them and bring them to me. If anyone says anything to you, you shall say, 'The Master needs them,' and immediately he will send them."

All this was done that it might be fulfilled which was spoken through the prophet, saying, "Tell the Bat-Tzion, hinei! Your King comes to you, humble, and riding on a donkey, on a colt, the foal of a donkey."

The talmidim went and did just as I commanded them, and brought the donkey and the colt and laid their clothes on them; and I sat on them. A very great crowd spread their clothes on the road. Others cut branches from the trees and spread them on the road. The crowds who went in front of me, and those who followed, kept shouting, "Hoshia-na to the Ben-David! Blessed is he who comes in the name of Hashem! Hoshia-na in the highest!"

When I had come into Yerushalaim, all the city was stirred up, saying, "Who is this?" The crowds said, "This is the prophet, Yeshua, from Natzeret in the Galil."

Beit HaMikdash (21:12-17)

I entered into the Beit HaMikdash of God and drove out all of those who sold and bought in the Beit HaMikdash, and overthrew the money changers' tables and the seats of those who sold the doves. I said to them, "It is written, 'My house shall be called a house of tefillah,' but you have made it a den of robbers!"

The lame and the blind came to me in the Beit HaMikdash, and I healed them. But when the chief kohanim and the scholars saw the wonderful things that I did, and the children who were crying in the Beit HaMikdash and saying, "Hoshia-na to the Ben-David!" they were indignant, and said to me, "Do you hear what these are saying?" I said to them, "Yes. Did you never read, 'Out of the mouth of children and nursing babies, you have perfected praise?'"

I left them and went out of the city to Beit-Hini, and camped there.

Fig Tree (21:18-22)

Now in the morning, as I returned to the city, I was hungry. Seeing a fig tree by the road, I came to it and found nothing on it but leaves. I said to it, "Let there be no fruit from you forever!" Immediately the fig tree withered away.

When the talmidim saw it, they marvelled, saying, "How did the fig tree immediately wither away?" I answered them, "Most certainly I tell you, if you have faith and don't doubt, you will not only do what was done to the fig tree, but even if you told this mountain, 'Be taken up and cast into the sea,' it would be done. All things, whatever you ask in tefillah, believing, you will receive."

Smicha (21:23-32)

When I had come into the Beit HaMikdash, the chief kohanim and the elders of the people came to me as I was teaching, and said, "By what authority do you do these things? Who gave you smicha?" I answered them, "I also will ask you one question, which if you tell me, I likewise will tell you by what authority I do these things. The mikvah of Yochanan, where was it from? From heaven or from men?" They reasoned with themselves, saying, "If we say, 'From heaven,' he will ask us, 'Why then did you not believe him?' But if we say, 'From men,' we fear the crowd, for all hold Yochanan as a prophet." They answered me, and said, "We don't know." I also said to them, "Neither will I tell you by what authority I do these things.

But what do you think? A man had two sons, and he came to the first, and said, 'Son, go work today in my vineyard.' He answered, 'I will not,' but afterward he changed his mind, and went. He came to the second, and said the same thing. He answered, 'I'm going, sir,' but he didn't go. Which of the two did the will of his abba?" They said to me, "The first." I said to them, "Most certainly I tell you that the tax collectors and the prostitutes are entering into God's kingdom before you. For Yochanan came to you in the way of righteousness, and you didn't believe him; but the tax collectors and the prostitutes believed him. When you saw it, you didn't even return in teshuva afterward, that you might believe him.

Mashal: Vineyard (21:33-46)

"Shema to another mashal. There was a man who was a master of a household who planted a vineyard, set a hedge about it, dug a wine press in it, built a tower, leased it out to farmers, and went into another country. When the moed for the fruit came near, he sent his servants to the farmers to receive his fruit. The farmers took his servants, beat one, killed another, and stoned another. Again, he sent other servants more than the first; and they treated them the same way. But afterward he sent to them his son, saying, 'They will respect my son.' But the farmers, when they saw the son, said among themselves, 'This is the heir. Come, let's kill him and seize his inheritance.' So they took him and threw him out of the vineyard, then killed him.

When therefore the master of the vineyard comes, what will he do to those farmers?" They told me, "He will miserably destroy those miserable men, and will lease out the vineyard to other farmers who will give him the fruit in its moed." I said to them, "Did you never read in the Tanach, 'The stone which the builders rejected was made the head of the corner. This was from Hashem. It is marvellous in our eyes'? Therefore I tell you, God's kingdom will be taken away from you and will be given to a nation producing its fruit. He who falls on this stone will be broken to pieces, but on whomever it will fall, it will scatter him as dust."

When the chief kohanim and the Prushim heard my mashalim, they perceived that I spoke about them. When they sought to seize me, they feared the crowds, because they considered me to be a prophet.

Mashal: Chatunah (22:1-14)

I answered and spoke to them again in mashalim, saying, "The kingdom of Heaven is like a certain king, who made a chatunah for his son, and sent out his servants to call those who were invited to the chatunah, but they would not come. Again he sent out other servants, saying, 'Tell those who are invited, "Hinei! I have prepared my dinner. My cattle and my fatlings are killed, and all things are ready. Come to the chatunah!"' But they made light of it, and went their ways, one to his own farm, another to his merchandise; and the rest grabbed his servants, treated them shamefully, and killed them.

When the king heard that, he was angry, and sent his armies, destroyed those murderers, and burned their city. Then he said to his servants, 'The wedding is ready, but those who were invited weren't worthy. Go therefore to the intersections of the highways, and as many as you may find, invite to the chatunah.' Those servants went out into the highways and gathered together as many as they found, both bad and good. The wedding was filled with guests.

But when the king came in to see the guests, he saw there a man who didn't have on wedding clothing, and he said to him, 'Friend, how did you come in here not wearing wedding clothing?' He was speechless. Then the king said to the servants, 'Bind him hand and foot, take him away, and throw him into the outer darkness. That is where the weeping and grinding of teeth will be.'

For many are called, but few chosen."

Prushim & Herodians (22:15-22)

Then the Prushim went and took counsel how they might entrap me in my talk. They sent their talmidim to me, along with the Herodians, saying, "Rabbi, we know that you are honest, and teach the way of God in truth, no matter whom you teach; for you aren't partial to anyone. Tell us therefore, what do you think? Is it lawful to pay taxes to Caesar, or not?" But I perceived their wickedness, and said, "Why do you test me, you hypocrites? Show me the tax money." They brought to me a denarius coin. I asked them, "Whose is this image and inscription?" They said to me, "Caesar's." Then I said to them, "Give therefore to Caesar the things that are Caesar's, and to God the things that are God's." When they heard it, they marvelled, and left me and went away.

Tzadukim (22:23-33)

On that day Tzadukim (those who say that there is no resurrection) came to me. They asked me, saying, "Rabbi, Moshe said, 'If a man dies, having no children, his brother shall marry his wife and raise up offspring for his brother.' Now there were with us seven brothers. The first married and died, and having no offspring left his wife to his brother. In the same way, the second also, and the third, to the seventh. After them all, the woman died. In the resurrection therefore, whose wife will she be of the seven? For they all had her."

But I answered them, "You are mistaken, not knowing the Tanach, nor the power of God. For in the resurrection they neither marry nor are given in marriage, but are like God's messengers in heaven. But concerning the resurrection of the dead, haven't you read that which was spoken to you by God, saying, 'I am the God of Avraham, and the God of Yitzchak, and the God of Yaakov?' God is not the God of the dead, but of the living."

When the crowds heard it, they were astonished at my torah.

Greatest Mitzvah (22:34-40)

But the Prushim, when they heard that I had silenced the Tzadukim, gathered themselves together. One of them, a Torah expert, asked me a question, testing me. "Rabbi, which is the greatest mitzvah in the Torah?" I said to him, "'You shall love Hashem your God with all your heart, with all your soul, and with all your mind.' This is the first and greatest mitzvah. A second likewise is this, 'You shall love your neighbour as yourself.' The whole Torah and the Prophets depend on these two mitzvot."

Mashiach (22:41-46)

Now while the Prushim were gathered together, I asked them a question, saying, "What do you think of the Mashiach? Whose son is he?" They said to me, "Of David." I said to them, "How then does David in the Ruach call him Master, saying, 'Hashem said to my Master, sit at my right hand, until I make your enemies a footstool for your feet'? If then David calls him Master, how is he his son?"

No one was able to answer me a word, neither did any man dare ask me any more questions from that day forward.

Scholars & Prushim (23:1-39)

Then I spoke to the crowds and to my talmidim, saying, "The scholars and the Prushim sit on Moshe's seat. All things therefore whatever they tell you to observe, observe and do, but don't do what they do; for they say, and don't do! For they bind heavy burdens that are grievous to be borne, and lay them on men's shoulders; but they themselves will not lift a finger to help them.

But they do all their deeds to be seen by men. They make their tefillin broad and enlarge the tzitzit of their garments, and love the place of honour at feasts, the best seats at shul, the salutations in the shuk, and to be called 'Rabbi, Rabbi' by men. But you are not to be called 'Rabbi', for one is your Rabbi, the Mashiach, and all of you are brothers. Call no man on the earth your father, for one is your Abba, he who is in heaven. Neither be called masters, for one is your master, the Mashiach. But he who is greatest among you will be your servant. Whoever exalts himself will be humbled, and whoever humbles himself will be exalted.

Hypocrites (23:13-28)

"Oy to you, scholars and Prushim, hypocrites! For you devour widows' houses, and as a pretence you make long tefillot. Therefore you will receive greater condemnation.

But oy to you, scholars and Prushim, hypocrites! Because you shut up the kingdom of Heaven against men; for you don't enter in yourselves, neither do you allow those who are entering in to enter. Oy to you, scholars and Prushim, hypocrites! For you travel around by sea and land to make one proselyte; and when he becomes one, you make him twice as much a son of Hinnom Valley as yourselves.

Oy to you, you blind guides, who say, 'Whoever swears by the Mikdash, it is nothing; but whoever swears by the gold of the Mikdash, he is obligated.' You blind fools! For which is greater, the gold or the Mikdash that sanctifies the gold? And, 'Whoever swears by the altar, it is nothing; but whoever swears by the gift that is on it, he is obligated?' You blind fools! For which is greater, the gift, or the altar that sanctifies the gift? He therefore who swears by the altar, swears by it and by everything on it. He who swears by the Mikdash, swears by it and by him who is living in it. He who swears by heaven, swears by the throne of God and by him who sits on it.

Oy to you, scholars and Prushim, hypocrites! For you tithe mint, dill, and cumin, and have left undone the weightier matters of the Torah: justice, mercy, and faith. But you ought to have done these, and not to have left the others undone. You blind guides, who strain out a gnat, and swallow a camel!

Oy to you, scholars and Prushim, hypocrites! For you clean the outside of the cup and of the platter, but within they are full of extortion and unrighteousness. You blind Parush, first clean the inside of the cup and of the platter, that its outside may become clean also. Oy to you, scholars and Prushim, hypocrites! For you are like whitened tombs, which outwardly appear beautiful, but inwardly are full of dead men's bones and of all uncleanness. Even so you also outwardly appear righteous to men, but inwardly you are full of hypocrisy and without Torah.

Yerushalaim (23:29-39)

"Oy to you, scholars and Prushim, hypocrites! For you build the tombs of the prophets and decorate the tombs of the tzaddikim, and say, 'If we had lived in the days of our fathers, we wouldn't have been partakers with them in the blood of the prophets.' Therefore you testify to yourselves that you are children of those who killed the prophets. Fill up, then, the measure of your fathers. You serpents, you offspring of vipers, how will you escape the judgement of Hinnom Valley?

Therefore, hinei! I send to you prophets, wise men, and scholars. Some of them you will kill and crucify; and some of them you will scourge in your synagogues and persecute from city to city, that on you may come all the righteous blood shed on the earth, from the blood of righteous Hevel to the blood of Zecharya Ben-Berechya, whom you killed between the Mikdash and the altar. Most certainly I tell you, all these things will come upon this generation.

Yerushalaim, Yerushalaim, who kills the prophets and stones those who are sent to her! How often I would have gathered your children together, even as a hen gathers her chicks under her wings, and you would not. Hinei! Your house is left to you desolate. For I tell you, you will not see me from now on, until you say, 'Blessed is he who comes in the name of Hashem!'"

My Coming (24:1-14)

I went out from the Beit HaMikdash, and was going on my way. My talmidim came to me to show me the buildings of the Beit

HaMikdash. But I answered them, "You see all of these things, don't you? Most certainly I tell you, there will not be left here one stone on another, that will not be thrown down."

As I sat on the Hill of Olives, the talmidim came to me privately, saying, "Tell us, when will these things be? What is the sign of your coming, and of the end of this olam?" I answered them, "Be careful that no one leads you astray. For many will come in my name, saying, 'I am the Mashiach,' and will lead many astray. You will hear of wars and rumours of wars. See that you aren't troubled, for all this must happen, but the end is not yet. For nation will rise against nation, and kingdom against kingdom; and there will be famines, plagues, and earthquakes in various places. But all these things are the beginning of birth pains.

Then they will deliver you up to oppression and will kill you. You will be hated by all of the goyim for my name's sake. Then many will stumble, and will deliver up one another, and will hate one another. Many false prophets will arise and will lead many astray. Because the absence of Torah will increase, the love of many will grow cold. But he who endures to the end will be saved.

This Besorah of the Kingdom will be preached in the whole world for a testimony to all the goyim, and then the end will come.

Suffering (24:15-28)

"When, therefore, you see the abomination of desolation, which was spoken of through Daniel the prophet, standing in the holy place" (let the reader understand), "then let those who are in Judea flee to the mountains. Let him who is on the housetop not go down to take out the things that are in his house. Let him who is in the field not return back to get his clothes. But oy to those who are with child and to nursing mothers in those days! Pray that your flight will not be in the winter nor on Shabbat, for then there will be great suffering, such as has not been from the beginning of the world until now, no, nor ever will be. Unless those days had been shortened, no flesh would have been saved. But for the sake of the chosen, those days will be shortened.

Then if any man tells you, 'Hinei, here is the Mashiach!' or, 'There!' don't believe it. For false mashiachs and false prophets will arise, and they will show great signs and wonders, so as to lead astray, if possible, even the chosen. Hinei! I have told you beforehand. If therefore they tell you, 'Hinei! He is in the wilderness,' don't go out; or 'Hinei! He is in the inner rooms,' don't believe it. For as the lightning flashes from the east, and is seen even to the west, so will the coming of the Ben-Adam be. For wherever the carcass is, that is where the vultures gather together.

Gathering (24:29-35)

"But immediately after the suffering of those days, the sun will be darkened, the moon will not give its light, the stars will fall from the sky, and the powers of the heavens will be shaken; and then the sign of the Ben-Adam will appear in the sky. Then all the tribes of the earth will mourn, and they will see me, the Ben-Adam, coming on the clouds of the sky with power and great glory. I will send out my messengers with a great sound of a shofar, and they will gather together my chosen from the four winds, from one end of the sky to the other.

Now from the fig tree learn this mashal: When its branch has now become tender and produces its leaves, you know that the summer is near. Even so you also, when you see all these things, know that I am near, even at the doors.

Most certainly I tell you, this people will not pass away until all these things are accomplished. Heaven and earth will pass away, but my words will not pass away.

That Day (24:36-51)

"But no one knows of that day and hour, not even the messengers of heaven, but my Abba only. As the days of Noach were, so will the coming of the Ben-Adam be. For as in those days which were before the flood they were eating and drinking, marrying and giving in marriage, until the day that Noach entered into the ship, and they didn't know until the flood came and took them all away, so will the coming of the Ben-Adam be. Then two men will be in the field: one will be taken and one will be left. Two women will be grinding at the mill: one will be taken and one will be left.

Watch therefore, for you don't know in what hour your Master comes. But know this, that if the master of the house had known in what watch of the night the thief was coming, he would have watched, and would not have allowed his house to be broken into. Therefore also be ready, for in an hour that you don't expect, I, the Ben-Adam, will come.

Who then is the faithful and wise servant, whom his master has set over his household, to give them their food in due season? Ashrei is that servant whom his master finds doing so when he comes! Most certainly I tell you that he will set him over all that he has. But if that evil servant should say in his heart, 'My master is delaying his coming,' and begins to beat his fellow servants, and eat and drink with the drunkards, the master of that servant will come in a day when he doesn't expect it and in an hour when he doesn't know it, and will cut him in pieces and appoint his portion with the hypocrites. That is where the weeping and grinding of teeth will be.

Mashal: Ten Virgins (25:1-13)

"Then my kingdom will be like ten virgins who took their menorahs and went out to meet the chattan. Five of them were foolish, and five were wise. Those who were foolish, when they took their menorahs, took no oil with them, but the wise took oil in their vessels with their menorahs.

Now while the chattan delayed, they all slumbered and slept. But at midnight there was a cry, 'Hinei! The chattan is coming! Come out to meet him!' Then all those virgins arose, and trimmed their menorahs. The foolish said to the wise, 'Give us some of your oil, for our menorahs are going out.' But the wise answered, saying, 'What if there isn't enough for us and you? You go rather to those who sell, and buy for yourselves.'

While they went away to buy, the chattan came, and those who were ready went in with him to the chatunah, and the door was shut. Afterward the other virgins also came, saying, 'Master, Master, open to us.' But he answered, 'Most certainly I tell you, I don't know you.'

Watch therefore, for you don't know the day nor the hour in which I, the Ben-Adam, am coming.

Mashal: Talents (25:14-30)

"For it is like a man going into another country, who called his own servants and entrusted his goods to them. To one he gave five talents of silver, to another two, to another one, to each according to his own ability. Then he went on his journey. Immediately he who received the five talents went and traded with them, and made another five talents. In the same way, he also who got the two gained another two. But he who received the one talent went away and dug in the earth and hid his master's money.

Now after a long time the master of those servants came, and settled accounts with them. He who received the five talents came and brought another five talents, saying, 'Master, you handed over to me five talents. Hinei! I have gained another five talents in addition to them.' His master said to him, 'Well done, good and faithful servant. You have been faithful over a few things, I will set you over many things. Enter into the joy of your master.' He also who got the two talents came and said, 'Master, you handed over to me two talents. Hinei! I have gained another two talents in addition to them.' His master said to him, 'Well done, good and faithful servant. You have been faithful over a few things. I will set you over many things. Enter into the joy of your master.'

He also who had received the one talent came and said, 'Master, I knew you that you are a hard man, reaping where you didn't sow, and gathering where you didn't scatter. I was afraid, and went away and hid your talent in the earth. Hinei! You have what is yours.' But his master answered him, 'You wicked and slothful servant. You knew that I reap where I didn't sow, and gather where I didn't scatter. You ought therefore to have deposited my money with the bankers, and at my coming I should have received back my own with interest. Take away therefore the talent from him and give it to him who has the ten talents. For to everyone who has will be given, and he will have abundance, but from him who doesn't have, even that which he has will be taken away. Throw out the unprofitable servant into the outer darkness, where there will be weeping and gnashing of teeth.'

Mashal: Sheep & Goats (25:31-46)

"But when I, the Ben-Adam, come in my glory, and all the holy messengers with me, then I will sit on my glorious throne. Before me all the goyim will be gathered, and I will separate them one from another, as a shepherd separates the sheep from the goats. I will set the sheep on my right hand, but the goats on my left.

Then I, the King, will tell those on my right hand, 'Come, blessed of my Abba, inherit the kingdom prepared for you from the foundation of the world; for I was hungry and you gave me food to eat. I was thirsty and you gave me drink. I was a stranger and you took me in. I was naked and you clothed me. I was sick and you visited me. I was in prison and you came to me.' Then the tzaddikim will answer me, saying, 'Sir, when did we see you hungry and feed you, or thirsty and give you a drink? When did we see you as a stranger and take you in, or naked and clothe you? When did we see you sick or in prison and come to you?' I, the King, will answer them, 'Most certainly I tell you, because you did it to one of the least of these my brothers, you did it to me.'

Then I will say also to those on the left hand, 'Depart from me, you cursed, into the everlasting fire which is prepared for the accuser and his messengers; for I was hungry, and you didn't give me food to eat; I was thirsty, and you gave me no drink; I was a stranger, and you didn't take me in; naked, and you didn't clothe me; sick, and in prison, and you didn't visit me.' Then they will also answer, saying, 'Sir, when did we see you hungry, or thirsty, or a stranger, or naked, or sick, or in prison, and didn't help you?' Then I will answer them, saying, 'Most certainly I tell you, because you didn't do it to one of the least of these, you didn't do it to me.'

These will go away into everlasting punishment, but the tzaddikim will live forever."

Anointing (26:1-16)

When I had finished all these words, I said to my talmidim, "You know that after two days Pesach is coming and I, the Ben-Adam, will be handed over to be crucified." Then the chief kohanim, the scholars, and the elders of the people were gathered together in the court of the Kohen Gadol, who was called Kayafa. They took counsel together that they might take me by deceit and kill me. But they said, "Not during the Festival, lest a riot occur among the people."

Now when I was in Beit-Hini, in the house of Shimon the leper, a woman came to me having an alabaster jar of very expensive perfume, and she poured it on my head as I sat at the table. But when my talmidim saw this, they were indignant, saying, "Why this waste? For this perfume might have been sold for much and given to the poor." However, knowing this, I said to them, "Why do you trouble the woman? She has done a good deed for me. For you always have the poor with you, but you don't always have me. For in pouring this perfume on my body, she did it to prepare me for burial. Most certainly I tell you, wherever this Besorah is preached in the whole world, what this woman has done will also be spoken of as a memorial of her."

Then one of the Twelve, who was called Yehuda from Kriyot, went to the chief kohanim and said, "What are you willing to give me if I deliver him to you?" So they weighed out for him thirty pieces of silver. From that time he sought opportunity to betray me.

Pesach (26:17-29)

Now on the first day of Matzot, the talmidim came to me, saying to me, "Where do you want us to prepare for you to eat the Pesach?" I said, "Go into the city to a certain person, and tell him, 'The Rabbi says, "My moed is at hand. I will keep the Pesach at your house with my talmidim."'" The talmidim did as I commanded them, and they prepared the Pesach.

Now when evening had come, I was reclining at the table with the twelve talmidim. As we were eating, I said, "Most certainly I tell you that one of you will betray me." They were exceedingly sorrowful, and each began to ask me, "It isn't me, is it, Master?" I answered, "He who dipped his hand with me in the dish will betray me. I, the Ben-Adam, am going even as it is written of me, but oy to that man through whom I am betrayed! It would be better for that man if he had not been born." Yehuda, who betrayed me, answered, "It isn't me, is it, Rabbi?" I said to him, "You said it."

As we were eating, I took matzah, made the bracha for it, and broke it. I gave to the talmidim and said, "Take, eat; this is my body." I took the cup, made the bracha, and gave to them, saying, "All of you drink it, for this is my blood of the renewed brit, which is poured out for many for the forgiveness of sins. But I tell you that I will not drink of this 'pri ha'gafen' from now on, until that day when I drink it anew with you in my Abba's kingdom."

Hill of Olives (26:30-35)

When we had sung the Hallel, we went out to the Hill of Olives. Then I said to them, "All of you will be made to stumble because of me tonight, for it is written, 'I will strike the shepherd, and the sheep of the flock will be scattered.' But after I am raised up, I will go before you into the Galil."

But Peter answered me, "Even if all will be made to stumble because of you, I will never be made to stumble." I said to him, "Most certainly I tell you that tonight, before the rooster crows, you will deny me three times." Peter said to me, "Even if I must die with you, I will not deny you." All of the talmidim also said likewise.

Gat-Shemen (26:36-46)

Then I came with them to a place called Gat-Shemen, and said to my talmidim, "Sit here, while I go there and pray." I took with me Peter and the two sons of Zavdai, and began to be sorrowful and severely troubled. Then I said to them, "My soul is exceedingly sorrowful, even to death. Stay here and watch with me."

I went forward a little, fell on my face, and prayed, saying, "My Abba, if it is possible, let this cup pass away from me; nevertheless, not what I desire, but what you desire." I came to the talmidim and found them sleeping, and said to Peter, "What, couldn't you watch with me for one hour? Watch and pray, that you don't enter into temptation. The ruach indeed is willing, but the flesh is weak."

Again, a second time I went away and prayed, saying, "My Abba, if this cup can't pass away from me unless I drink it, your desire be done." I came again and found them sleeping, for their eyes were heavy. I left them again, went away, and prayed a third time, saying the same words. Then I came to my talmidim and said to them, "Are you still sleeping and resting? Hinei! The hour is at hand and I, the Ben-Adam, am betrayed into the hands of sinners. Arise, let's be going. Hinei! He who betrays me is at hand."

Betrayal (26:47-56)

While I was still speaking, hinei! Yehuda, one of the Twelve, came, and with him a great crowd with swords and clubs, from the chief kohanim and elders of the people. Now he who betrayed me had given them a sign, saying, "Whoever I kiss, he is the one. Seize him." Immediately he came to me, and said, "Greetings, Rabbi!" and kissed me. I said to him, "Friend, why are you here?" Then they came and laid hands on me, and took me.

Hinei! One of those who were with me stretched out his hand and drew his sword, and struck the servant of the Kohen Gadol, and cut off his ear. Then I said to him, "Put your sword back into its place, for all those who take the sword will die by the sword. Or do you think that I couldn't ask my Abba, and he would even now send me more than twelve legions of messengers? How then would the Scriptures be fulfilled that it must be so?"

In that hour I said to the crowds, "Have you come out as against a robber with swords and clubs to seize me? I sat daily in the Beit HaMikdash teaching, and you didn't arrest me. But all this has happened that the writings of the prophets might be fulfilled."

Then all the talmidim left me and fled.

Kohen Gadol (26:57-68)

Those who had taken me led me away to Kayafa the Kohen Gadol, where the scholars and the elders were gathered together. But Peter followed me from a distance to the court of the Kohen Gadol, and entered in and sat with the officers, to see the end.

Now the chief kohanim, the elders, and the whole Sanhedrin sought false testimony against me, that they might put me to death, and they found none. Even though many false witnesses came forward, they found none. But at last two false witnesses came forward and said, "This man said, 'I am able to destroy the Mikdash of God, and to build it in three days.'" The Kohen Gadol stood up and said to me, "Have you no answer? What is this that these testify against you?" But I stayed silent. The Kohen Gadol answered me, "I adjure you by the living God that you tell us whether you are the Mashiach, the Ben-Elohim." I said to him, "You have said so. Nevertheless, I tell you, after this you will see me, the Ben-Adam, sitting at the right hand of Power, and coming on the clouds of the sky."

Then the Kohen Gadol tore his clothing, saying, "He has spoken blasphemy! Why do we need any more witnesses? Hinei! Now you have heard his blasphemy. What do you think?" They answered, "He is worthy of death!"

Then they spat in my face and beat me with their fists, and some slapped me, saying, "Prophesy to us, you Mashiach! Who hit you?"

Peter's Denial (26:69-75)

Now Peter was sitting outside in the court, and a maid came to him, saying, "You were also with Yeshua, the Galilean!" But he denied it before them all, saying, "I don't know what you are talking about."

When he had gone out onto the porch, someone else saw him and said to those who were there, "This man also was with

Yeshua from Natzeret." Again he denied it with an oath, "I don't know the man."

After a little while those who stood by came and said to Peter, "Surely you are also one of them, for your speech makes you known." Then he began to curse and to swear, "I don't know the man!" Immediately the rooster crowed. Peter remembered the word which I had said to him, "Before the rooster crows, you will deny me three times."

Then he went out and wept bitterly.

Yehuda's Remorse (27:1-10)

Now when morning had come, all the chief kohanim and the elders of the people took counsel against me to put me to death. They bound me, led me away, and handed me over to Pontius Pilate, the governor.

Then Yehuda, who betrayed me, when he saw that I was condemned, felt remorse, and brought back the thirty pieces of silver to the chief kohanim and elders, saying, "I have sinned in that I betrayed innocent blood." But they said, "What is that to us? You see to it." He threw down the pieces of silver in the Mikdash and departed. Then he went away and hanged himself. The chief kohanim took the pieces of silver and said, "It's not lawful to put them into the treasury, since it is the price of blood." They took counsel, and bought the potter's field with them to bury strangers in. Therefore that field has been called "The Field of Blood" to this day.

Then that which was spoken through Yirmiya the prophet was fulfilled, saying, "They took the thirty pieces of silver, the price of him upon whom a price had been set, whom some of the Bnei-Israel priced, and they gave them for the potter's field, as Hashem commanded me."

Pilate (27:11-26)

Now I stood before the governor; and the governor asked me, saying, "Are you the King of the Jewish people?" I said to him, "So you say." When I was accused by the chief kohanim and elders, I answered nothing. Then Pilate said to me, "Don't you hear how many things they testify against you?" I gave him no answer, not even one word, so that the governor marvelled greatly.

Now at the Festival the governor was accustomed to release to the crowd one prisoner whom they desired. They had then a notable prisoner called Bar-Abba. When therefore they were gathered together, Pilate said to them, "Whom do you want me to release to you? Bar-Abba, or Yeshua who is called Mashiach?" For he knew that because of envy they had handed me over.

While he was sitting on the judgement seat, his wife sent to him, saying, "Have nothing to do with that righteous man, for I have suffered many things today in a dream because of him." Now the chief kohanim and the elders persuaded the crowds to ask for Bar-Abba and destroy me. But the governor answered them, "Which of the two do you want me to release to you?" They said, "Bar-Abba!" Pilate said to them, "What then shall I do to Yeshua who is called Mashiach?" They all said to him, "Let him be crucified!" But the governor said, "Why? What evil has he done?" But they cried out exceedingly, saying, "Let him be crucified!"

So when Pilate saw that nothing was being gained, but rather that a disturbance was starting, he took water and washed his hands before the crowd, saying, "I am innocent of the blood of this righteous person. You see to it." All the people answered, "May his blood be on us and on our children!" Then he released Bar-Abba to them, but me he flogged and handed over to be crucified.

Praetorium (27:27-31)

Then the governor's soldiers took me into the Praetorium, and gathered the whole garrison together against me. They stripped me and put a scarlet robe on me. They braided a crown of thorns and put it on my head, and a reed in my right hand; and they knelt down before me and mocked me, saying, "Hail, King of the Jewish people!" They spat on me, and took the reed and struck me on the head.

When they had mocked me, they took the robe off me, and put my clothes on me, and led me away to crucify me.

Crucifixion (27:32-44)

As we came out, they found a man of Cyrene, Shimon by name, and they compelled him to go with us, that he might carry my cross. When we came to a place called "Golgolta", that is to say, "The place of a skull," they gave me sour wine to drink mixed with gall. When I had tasted it, I would not drink.

When they had crucified me, they divided my clothing among them, casting lots, and they sat and watched me there. They set up over my head the accusation against me written, "THIS IS YESHUA, THE KING OF THE JEWISH PEOPLE."

Then there were two robbers crucified with me, one on my right hand and one on the left.

Those who passed by blasphemed me, wagging their heads and saying, "You who destroy the Mikdash and build it in three days, save yourself! If you are Ben-Elohim, come down from the cross!" Likewise the chief kohanim also mocking with the scholars, the Prushim, and the elders, said, "He saved others, but he can't save himself. If he is the Melech-Yisrael, let him come down from the cross now, and we will believe in him. He trusts in God. Let God deliver him now, if he wants him; for he said, 'I am Ben-Elohim.'"

The robbers also who were crucified with me cast on me the same reproach.

Death (27:45-56)

Now from the sixth hour there was darkness over all the land until the ninth hour. About the ninth hour I cried with a loud voice, saying, "Eli, Eli, lama sabachthani?" That is, "My God, my God, why have you forsaken me?" Some of them who stood there, when they heard it, said, "This man is calling Eliyahu." Immediately one of them ran and took a sponge, filled it with vinegar, put it on a reed, and gave me a drink. The rest said, "Let him be. Let's see whether Eliyahu comes to save him."

I cried again with a loud voice, and yielded up my ruach. Hinei! The veil of the Mikdash was torn in two from the top to the bottom. The earth quaked and the rocks were split. The tombs were opened, and many bodies of the holy people who had fallen asleep were raised; and coming out of the tombs after my resurrection, they entered into the Ir HaKodesh and appeared to many.

Now the centurion and those who were with him watching me, when they saw the earthquake and the things that were done, were terrified, saying, "Truly this was God's own son!"

Many women were there watching from afar, who had followed me from the Galil, serving me. Among them were Miriam from Magdala, Miriam the eema of Yaakov and Yosi, and the eema of the sons of Zavdai.

Burial (27:57-66)

When evening had come, a rich man from Ramatayim named Yosef, who himself was also a talmid of mine, came. This man went to Pilate and asked for my body. Then Pilate commanded the body to be given up. Yosef took the body and wrapped it in a clean linen cloth and laid it in his own new tomb, which he had cut out in the rock. Then he rolled a large stone against the door of the tomb, and departed. Miriam from Magdala was there, and the other Miriam, sitting opposite the tomb.

Now on the next day, which was the day after the Preparation Day, the chief kohanim and the Prushim were gathered together to Pilate, saying, "Sir, we remember what that deceiver said while he was still alive: 'After three days I will rise again.' Command therefore that the tomb be made secure until the third day, lest perhaps his talmidim come at night and steal him away, and tell the people, 'He is risen from the dead;' and the last deception will be worse than the first." Pilate said to them, "You have a guard. Go, make it as secure as you can." So they went with the guard and made the tomb secure, sealing the stone.

Dawn (28:1-10)

Now after Shabbat, as it began to dawn on the first day of the week, Miriam from Magdala and the other Miriam came to see the tomb.

Hinei! There was a great earthquake, for a messenger of Hashem descended from the sky and came and rolled away the stone from the door and sat on it. His appearance was like lightning, and his clothing white as snow. For fear of him, the guards shook, and became like dead men.

The messenger answered the women, "Don't be afraid, for I know that you seek Yeshua, who has been crucified. He is not here, for he has risen, just like he said. Come, see the place where the Master was lying. Go quickly and tell his talmidim, 'He has risen from the dead, and hinei! He goes before you into the Galil; there you will see him.' Hinei! I have told you."

They departed quickly from the tomb with fear and great joy, and ran to bring my talmidim word. As they went to tell my talmidim, hinei! I met them, saying, "Rejoice!" They came and took hold of my feet, and bowed down to me. Then I said to them, "Don't be afraid! Go tell my brothers that they should go into the Galil, and there they will see me."

Guards (28:11-15)

Now while they were going, hinei! Some of the guards came into the city and told the chief kohanim all the things that had happened. When they were assembled with the elders and had taken counsel, they gave a large amount of silver to the soldiers, saying, "Say that his talmidim came by night and stole him away while we slept. If this comes to the governor's ears, we will persuade him and make you free of worry." So they took the money and did as they were told.

This saying was spread abroad among the Judeans, and continues until today.

Eleven (28:16-20)

But the eleven talmidim went into the Galil, to the mountain where I had sent them. When they saw me, they bowed down to me; but some doubted.

I came to them and spoke to them, saying, "All authority has been given to me in heaven and on earth. Go and make talmidim of all the goyim, immersing them in the name of the Father and of the Son and of the Ruach HaKodesh, teaching them to observe all the things that I commanded you. Hinei! I am with you always, even to the end of the olam."

AS TOLD TO MARK

Breisheet (1:1-8)

The beginning of the Besorah about me: the Mashiach, Ben-Elohim.

As it is written in the Prophets, "Hinei! I send my messenger before your face, who will prepare your way before you: the voice of someone crying in the wilderness, 'Make ready the way of Hashem! Make his paths straight!'" Yochanan came immersing in the wilderness and proclaiming the mikvah of returning in teshuva for forgiveness of sins. All the country of Judea and all those of Yerushalaim went out to him. They were immersed by him in the Yarden river, confessing their sins.

Yochanan was clothed with camel's hair and a leather belt around his waist. He ate locusts and wild honey. He preached, saying, "After me comes he who is mightier than I, the thong of whose sandals I am not worthy to stoop down and loosen. I immersed you in water, but he will immerse you in Ruach HaKodesh."

Mikvah (1:9-13)

In those days, I came from Natzeret in the Galil, and was immersed by Yochanan in the Yarden. Immediately coming up from the water, I saw the heavens parting and the Ruach descending on me like a dove. A Bat-Kol came out of the sky, "You are my beloved Son, with whom I am delighted."

Immediately the Ruach drove me out into the wilderness. I was there in the wilderness forty days, tempted by the antagonist. I was with the chayot; and the messengers were ministering to me.

Fishermen (1:14-20)

Now after Yochanan was taken into custody, I came into the Galil, proclaiming the besorah of God's kingdom, and saying, "The moed is fulfilled, and God's kingdom is at hand! Return in teshuva, and believe in the Besorah."

Passing along by the Kinneret, I saw Shimon and Andrew, the brother of Shimon, casting a net into the sea, for they were fishermen. I said to them, "Come after me, and I will make you into fishers for men." Immediately they left their nets, and followed me.

Going on a little further from there, I saw Yaakov Ben-Zavdai, and Yochanan his brother, who were also in the boat doing tikkun on the nets. Immediately I called them, and they left their abba, Zavdai, in the boat with the hired servants, and went after me.

Unclean Spirit (1:21-28)

We went into Kfar-Nachum, and immediately on Shabbat I entered into the shul and taught. They were astonished at my torah, for I taught them as having authority, and not as the scholars.

Immediately there was in their shul a man with an unclean spirit, and he cried out, saying, "Ha! What do we have to do with you, Yeshua from Natzeret? Have you come to destroy us? I know who you are: the Holy One of God!" I rebuked him, saying, "Sheket, and come out of him!" The unclean spirit, convulsing him and crying with a loud voice, came out of him.

They were all amazed, so that they questioned among themselves, saying, "What is this? A new torah? For with authority he commands even the unclean spirits, and they shema to him!" The report of me went out immediately everywhere into all the region of the Galil and its surrounding area.

Shimon's House (1:29-39)

Immediately, when we had come out of the shul, we came into the house of Shimon and Andrew, with Yaakov and Yochanan. Now Shimon's wife's eema lay sick with a fever, and immediately they told me about her. I came and took her by the hand and raised her up. The fever left her immediately, and she served us.

At evening, when the sun had set, they brought to me all who were sick and those who were possessed by shedim. All the city was gathered together at the door. I healed many who were sick with various diseases and cast out many shedim. I didn't allow the shedim to speak, because they knew me.

Early in the morning, while it was still dark, I rose up and went out, and departed into a deserted place, and davened there. Shimon and those who were with him searched for me. They found me and told me, "Everyone is looking for you." I said to them, "Let's go elsewhere into the next towns, that I may proclaim there also, because I came out for this reason."

I went into their shuls throughout all the Galil, proclaiming and casting out shedim.

Leper (1:40-45)

A leper came to me, begging me, kneeling down to me, and saying to me, "If you want to, you can make me clean." Being moved with compassion, I stretched out my hand, and touched him, and said to him, "I want to. Be made clean." When I had said this, immediately the leprosy departed from him and he was made clean.

I strictly warned him and immediately sent him out, and said to him, "See that you say nothing to anybody, but go show yourself to the kohen and offer for your cleansing the things which Moshe commanded, for a testimony to them." But he went out, and began to proclaim it much, and to spread about the matter, so that I could no more openly enter into a city, but was outside in desert places. People came to me from everywhere.

Paralytic (2:1-12)

When I entered again into Kfar-Nachum after some days, it was heard that I was at home. Immediately many were gathered together, so that there was no more room, not even around the door; and I spoke the word to them.

Four people came, carrying a paralytic to me. When they could not come near to me for the crowd, they removed the roof where I was. When they had broken it up, they let down the mat that the paralytic was lying on. Seeing their faith, I said to the paralytic, "Son, your sins are forgiven you."

But there were some of the scholars sitting there and reasoning in their hearts, "Why does this man speak blasphemies like that? Who can forgive sins but God alone?" Immediately, perceiving in my ruach that they so reasoned within themselves, I said to them, "Why do you reason these things in your hearts? Which is easier, to tell the paralytic, 'Your sins are forgiven;' or to say, 'Arise, and take up your bed, and walk?' But that you may know that I, the Ben-Adam, have authority on earth to forgive sins"—I said to the paralytic— "I tell you, arise, take up your mat, and go home." He arose, and immediately took up the mat and went out in front of them all, so that they were all amazed and praised God, saying, "We never saw anything like this!"

Levi (2:13-17)

I went out again by the seaside. All the crowd came to me, and I taught them. As I passed by, I saw Levi Ben-Chalfai sitting at the tax office. I said to him, "Follow me." And he arose and followed me.

I was reclining at the table in his house, and many tax collectors and sinners sat down with me and my talmidim, for there were many, and they followed me. The scholars and the Prushim, when they saw that I was eating with the sinners and tax collectors, said to my talmidim, "Why is it that he eats and drinks with tax collectors and sinners?" When I heard it, I said to them, "Those who are healthy have no need for a physician, but those who are sick. I came not to call the tzaddikim, but sinners—to return in teshuva."

Fasting (2:18-22)

Yochanan's talmidim and the Prushim were fasting, and they came and asked me, "Why do Yochanan's talmidim and the talmidim of the Prushim fast, but your talmidim don't fast?" I said to them, "Can the bnei-chuppah fast while the chattan is with them? As long as they have the chattan with them, they can't fast. But the days will come when the chattan will be taken away from them, and then they will fast in that day.

No one sews a piece of unshrunk cloth on an old garment, or else the patch shrinks and the new tears away from the old, and a worse hole is made. No one puts new wine into old wineskins; or else the new wine will burst the skins, and the wine pours out, and the skins will be destroyed; but they put new wine into fresh wineskins."

Grain Fields (2:23-28)

I was going through the grain fields on Shabbat; and my talmidim began, as we went, to pluck the ears of grain. The Prushim said to me, "Hinei! Why do they do that which is not lawful on Shabbat?" I said to them, "Did you never read what David did when he had need and was hungry—he, and those who were with him? How he entered into God's house at the time of Evyatar the Kohen Gadol, and ate the showbread, which is not lawful to eat except for the kohanim, and gave also to those who were with him?"

I said to them, "Shabbat was made for man, not man for Shabbat. Therefore I, the Ben-Adam, am master even of Shabbat."

Withered Hand (3:1-6)

I entered again into the shul, and there was a man there whose hand was withered. They watched me, whether I would heal him on Shabbat, that they might accuse me. I said to the man whose hand was withered, "Stand up." I said to them, "Is it lawful on Shabbat to do good or to do harm? To save a life or to kill?" But they were silent. When I had looked around at them with anger, being grieved at the hardening of their hearts, I said to the man, "Stretch out your hand." He stretched it out, and his hand was restored as healthy as the other.

The Prushim went out, and immediately conspired with the Herodians against me, how they might destroy me.

Twelve (3:7-19)

I withdrew to the sea with my talmidim; and a great crowd followed me from the Galil, from Judea, from Yerushalaim, from Idumaea, beyond the Yarden, and those from around Tyre and Sidon. A great crowd, hearing what great things I did, came to me. I spoke to my talmidim that a little boat should stay near me because of the crowd, so that they wouldn't press on me. For I had healed many, so that as many as had diseases pressed on me that they might touch me. The unclean spirits, whenever they saw me, fell down before me and cried, "You are the Ben-Elohim!" I sternly warned them that they should not make me known.

I went up onto the mountain and called to myself those whom I wanted, and they came to me. I appointed twelve, that they might be with me, and that I might send them out to proclaim and to have authority to heal sicknesses and to cast out shedim: Shimon (to whom I gave the name Peter); Yaakov Ben-Zavdai; and Yochanan, the brother of Yaakov, (whom I called Bnei-Regesh, which means, Sons of Thunder); Andrew; Philip; Bar-Talmai; Mattai; Toma; Yaakov Ben-Chalfai; Taddai; Shimon the Zealot; and Yehuda from Kriyot, who also betrayed me.

Friends & Mishpacha (3:19-35)

Then I came into a house. The crowd came together again, so that we could not so much as eat bread. When my friends heard it, they went out to seize me; for they said, "He is insane."

The scholars who came down from Yerushalaim said, "He has Baal-Zvuv," and, "By the prince of the shedim he casts out the shedim." I summoned them and said to them in mashalim, "How can antagonist cast out antagonist? If a kingdom is divided against itself, that kingdom cannot stand. If a house is divided against itself, that house cannot stand. If an antagonist has risen up against himself, and is divided, he can't stand, but has an end. But no one can enter into the house of the strong man to plunder unless he first binds the strong man; then he will plunder his house. Most certainly I tell you, all sins of the Bnei-Adam will be forgiven, including their blasphemies with which they may blaspheme; but whoever may blaspheme against Ruach HaKodesh never has forgiveness, but is subject to everlasting condemnation." —because they said, "He has an unclean spirit."

My eema and my brothers came, and standing outside, they sent to me, calling me. A crowd was sitting around me, and they told me, "Hinei! Your eema, your brothers, and your sisters are outside looking for you." I answered them, "Who are my eema and my brothers?" Looking around at those who sat around me, I said, "Hinei! My eema and my brothers. For whoever does the will of God is my brother, my sister, and eema."

Mashal: Farmer (4:1-9)

Again I began to teach by the seaside. A great crowd was gathered to me, so that I entered into a boat in the sea and sat down. All the crowd were on the land by the sea.

I taught them many things in mashalim, and told them in my torah, "Shema! Hinei! The farmer went out to sow. As he sowed, some seed fell by the road, and the birds came and devoured it. Others fell on the rocky ground, where it had little soil, and immediately it sprang up, because it had no depth of soil. When the sun had risen, it was scorched; and because it had no root, it withered away. Others fell among the thorns, and the thorns grew up and choked it, and it yielded no fruit. Others fell into the good ground and yielded fruit, growing up and increasing. Some produced thirty times, some sixty times, and some one hundred times as much."

I said, "Whoever has ears to shema, let him shema!"

Farmer Explained (4:10-20)

When I was alone, those who were around me with the Twelve asked me about the mashalim. I said to them, "To you is given the mystery of my kingdom, but to those who are outside, all things are done in mashalim, that 'seeing they may see and not perceive, and hearing they may hear and not understand, lest perhaps they should return in teshuva, and their sins should be forgiven them.'"

I said to them, "Don't you understand this mashal? How will you understand all of the mashalim? The farmer sows the word. The ones by the road are the ones where the word is sown; and when they have heard, immediately the antagonist comes and takes away the word which has been sown in them. These in the same way are those who are sown on the rocky places, who, when they have heard the word, immediately receive it with joy. They have no root in themselves, but are short-lived. When oppression or persecution arises because of the word, immediately they stumble. Others are those who are sown among the thorns. These are those who have heard the word, and the cares of this olam, and the deceitfulness of riches, and the lusts of other things entering in choke the word, and it becomes unfruitful. Those which were sown on the good ground are those who shema to the word, accept it, and bear fruit, some thirty times, some sixty times, and some one hundred times."

Mashal: Menorah (4:21-25)

I said to them, "Is a menorah brought to be put under a basket or under a bed? Isn't it put on a stand? For there is nothing hidden except that it should be made known, neither was anything made secret but that it should come to light. If any man has ears to shema, let him shema!"

I said to them, "Take heed what you shema to. With whatever measure you measure, it will be measured to you; and more will be given to you who shema. For whoever has, to him more will be given; and he who doesn't have, even that which he has will be taken away from him."

Mashal: Seeds (4:26-34)

I said, "My kingdom is as if a man should cast seed on the earth, and should sleep and rise night and day, and the seed should spring up and grow, though he doesn't know how. For the earth bears fruit by itself: first the blade, then the ear, then the full grain in the ear. But when the fruit is ripe, immediately he puts in the sickle, because the harvest has come."

I said, "How will we liken my kingdom? Or with what mashal will we illustrate it? It's like a grain of mustard seed, which, when it is sown in the earth, though it is less than all the seeds that are on the earth, yet when it is sown, grows up and becomes greater than all the herbs, and puts out great branches, so that the birds of the sky can nest under its shadow."

With many such mashalim I spoke the word to them, as they were able to hear it. Without a mashal I didn't speak to them; but privately to my own talmidim I explained everything.

Storm (4:35-41)

On that day, when evening had come, I said to them, "Let's go over to the other side." Leaving the crowd, they took me with them, just as I was, in the boat. Other small boats were also with me. A big wind storm arose, and the waves beat into the boat, so much that the boat was already filled. I myself was in the stern, asleep on the cushion; and they woke me up and asked me, "Rabbi, don't you care that we are dying?" I awoke and rebuked the wind, and said to the sea, "Shalom! Be still!" The wind ceased and there was a great calm. I said to them, "Why are you so afraid? How is it that you have no faith?" They were greatly afraid and said to one another, "Who then is this, that even the wind and the sea shema to him?"

Gadara (5:1-20)

We came to the other side of the sea, into the country of Gadara. When I had come out of the boat, immediately a man with an unclean spirit met me out of the tombs. He lived in the tombs. Nobody could bind him anymore, not even with chains, because he had been often bound with fetters and chains, and the chains had been torn apart by him, and the fetters broken in pieces. Nobody had the strength to tame him. Always, night and day, in the tombs and in the mountains, he was crying out, and cutting himself with stones. When he saw me from afar, he ran and bowed down to me, and crying out with a loud voice, he said, "What have I to do with you, Yeshua, son of El-Elyon? I adjure you by God, don't torment me." For I said to him, "Come out of the man, you unclean spirit!"

I asked him, "What is your name?" He said to me, "My name is Legion, for we are many." He begged me much that I would not send them away out of the country. Now on the mountainside there was a great herd of pigs feeding. All the shedim begged me, saying, "Send us into the pigs, that we may enter into them." At once I gave them permission. The unclean spirits came out and entered into the pigs. The herd of about two thousand rushed down the steep bank into the sea, and they were drowned in the sea.

Those who fed the pigs fled, and told it in the city and in the country. The people came to see what it was that had happened. They came to me, and saw him who had been possessed by shedim sitting, clothed, and in his right mind, even him who had the legion; and they were afraid. Those who saw it declared to them what happened to him who was possessed by shedim, and about the pigs. They began to beg me to depart from their region.

As I was entering into the boat, he who had been possessed by shedim begged me that he might be with me. I didn't allow him, but said to him, "Go home, to your friends, and tell them what great things Hashem has done for you and how he had mercy on you." He went his way, and began to proclaim in Decapolis how I had done great things for him, and everyone marvelled.

Shul President (5:21-43)

When I had crossed back over in the boat to the other side, a great crowd was gathered to me; and I was by the sea. Hinei! The president of a shul, Yair by name, came; and seeing me, he fell at my feet and begged me much, saying, "My little daughter is at the point of death. Please come and lay your hands on her, that she may be made healthy, and live." I went with him, and a great crowd followed me, and they pressed upon me on all sides.

A certain woman who had a discharge of blood for twelve years, and had suffered many things by many physicians, and had spent all that she had, and was no better, but rather grew worse, having heard the things concerning me, came up behind me in the crowd and touched my clothes. For she said, "If I just touch his clothes, I will be made well." Immediately the flow of her blood was dried up, and she felt in her body that she was healed of her affliction.

Immediately, perceiving in myself that the power had gone out from me, I turned around in the crowd and asked, "Who touched my clothes?" My talmidim said to me, "You see the crowd pressing against you, and you say, 'Who touched me?'" I looked around to see her who had done this thing. But the woman, fearing and trembling, knowing what had been done to her, came and fell down before me, and told me all the truth. I said to her, "Daughter, your faith has made you well. Go in shalom, and be cured of your disease."

While I was still speaking, people came from the shul president's house, saying, "Your daughter is dead. Why bother the Rabbi anymore?" But, when I heard the message spoken, I immediately said to the president of the shul, "Don't be afraid, only believe." I allowed no one to follow me except Peter, Yaakov, and Yochanan the brother of Yaakov.

I came to the shul president's house, and I saw an uproar, weeping, and great wailing. When I had entered in, I said to them, "Why do you make an uproar and weep? The child is not dead, but is asleep!" They ridiculed me. But, having put them all out, I took the child's abba, her eema, and those who were with me, and went in where the child was lying. Taking the child by the hand, I said to her, "Talitha kumi!" which means, being translated, "Girl, I tell you, get up!" Immediately the girl rose up and walked, for she was twelve years old. They were amazed with great amazement. I strictly ordered them that no one should know this, and commanded that something should be given to her to eat.

My Country (6:1-6)

I went out from there. I came into my own country, and my talmidim followed me. When Shabbat had come, I began to teach in the shul, and many hearing me were astonished, saying, "Where did this man get these things?" and, "What is the wisdom that is given to this man, that such miracles come about by his hands? Isn't this the carpenter, the son of Miriam and brother of Yaakov, Yosi, Yehuda, and Shimon? Aren't his sisters here with us?" So they were offended at me. I said to them, "A prophet is not without honour, except in his own country, and among his own mishpacha, and in his own house."

I could do no miracle there, except that I laid my hands on a few sick people and healed them. I marvelled because of their unbelief.

Twelve Sent (6:7-13)

I went around the villages teaching. I called to myself the Twelve, and began to send them out two by two; and I gave them authority over the unclean spirits.

I commanded them that they should take nothing for their journey, except a staff only: no bread, no wallet, no money in their purse, but to wear sandals, and not put on two tunics. I said to them, "Wherever you enter into a house, stay there until you depart from there. Whoever will not receive you nor shema to you, as you depart from there, shake off the dust that is under your feet for a testimony against them. Assuredly, I tell you, it will be more tolerable for Sodom and Gomorrah on Yom HaDin than for that city!"

They went out and preached that people should return in teshuva. They cast out many shedim, and anointed many with oil who were sick and healed them.

Herod (6:14-29)

King Herod heard this, for my name had become known, and he said, "Yochanan the Immerser has risen from the dead, and therefore these powers are at work in him." But others said, "He is Eliyahu." Others said, "He is a prophet, or like one of the prophets." But Herod, when he heard this, said, "This is Yochanan, whom I beheaded. He has risen from the dead!"

For Herod himself had sent out and arrested Yochanan and bound him in prison for the sake of Herodias, his brother Philip's wife, for he had married her. For Yochanan had said to Herod, "It is not lawful for you to have your brother's wife." Herodias set herself against him and desired to kill him, but she couldn't, for Herod feared Yochanan, knowing that he was a tzaddik and a holy man, and kept him safe. When he heard him, he did many things, and he heard him gladly.

Then a convenient day came when Herod on his birthday made a banquet for his nobles, the high officers, and the chief men of the Galil. When the daughter of Herodias herself came in and danced, she pleased Herod and those sitting with him. The king said to the young lady, "Ask me whatever you want, and I will give it to you." He swore to her, "Whatever you ask of me, I will give you, up to half of my kingdom." She went out and said to her mother, "What shall I ask?" She said, "The head of Yochanan the Immerser." She came in immediately with haste to the king and requested, "I want you to give me right now the head of Yochanan the Immerser on a platter." The king was exceedingly sorry, but for the sake of his oaths and of his dinner guests, he didn't wish to refuse her. Immediately the king sent out a soldier of his guard and commanded to bring Yochanan's head; and he went and beheaded him in the prison, and brought his head on a platter, and gave it to the young lady; and the young lady gave it to her mother.

When his talmidim heard this, they came and took up his corpse and laid it in a tomb.

Five Loaves (6:30-44)

The shaliachs gathered themselves together to me, and they told me all things, whatever they had done, and whatever they had taught. I said to them, "Come away into a deserted place, and rest awhile." For there were many coming and going, and we had no leisure so much as to eat. We went away in the boat to a deserted place by ourselves.

They saw us going, and many recognized me and ran there on foot from all the cities. They arrived before us and came together to me. I came out, saw a great crowd, and I had compassion on them because they were like sheep without a shepherd; and I began to teach them many things.

When it was late in the day, my talmidim came to me and said, "This place is deserted, and it is late in the day. Send them away, that they may go into the surrounding country and villages and buy themselves bread, for they have nothing to eat." But I answered them, "You give them something to eat." They asked me, "Shall we go and buy two hundred days' wages worth of bread and give them something to eat?" I said to them, "How many loaves do you have? Go see." When they knew, they said, "Five, and two fish." I commanded them that everyone should sit down in groups on the green grass. They sat down in ranks, by hundreds and by fifties. I took the five loaves and the two fish; and looking up to heaven, I made the bracha and broke the loaves, and I gave to my talmidim to set before them, and I divided the two fish among them all. They all ate and were filled.

They took up twelve baskets full of broken pieces and also of the fish. Those who ate the loaves were five thousand men.

Ginesar (6:45-56)

Immediately I made my talmidim get into the boat and go ahead to the other side, to Beit-Tzaida, while I myself sent the crowd away. After I had taken leave of them, I went up the mountain to pray.

When evening had come, the boat was in the middle of the sea, and I was alone on the land. Seeing them distressed in rowing, for the wind was contrary to them, about the fourth watch of the night I came to them, walking on the sea; and I would have passed by them, but they, when they saw me walking on the sea, supposed that it was a ghost, and cried out; for they all saw me and were troubled. But I immediately spoke with them and said to them, "Cheer up! It's me! Don't be afraid." I got into the boat with them; and the wind ceased, and they were very amazed among themselves, and marvelled; for they hadn't understood about the loaves, but their hearts were hardened.

When we had crossed over, we came to land at Ginesar and moored to the shore. When we had come out of the boat, immediately the people recognized me, and ran around that whole region, and began to bring those who were sick on their mats to where they heard I was. Wherever I entered—into villages, or into cities, or into the country—they laid the sick in the shuk and begged me that they might just touch the tzitzit of my garment; and as many as touched me were made well.

Tradition (7:1-23)

Then the Prushim and some of the scholars gathered together to me, having come from Yerushalaim. Now when they saw some of my talmidim eating bread with defiled, that is unwashed, hands, they found fault. (For the Prushim and all the Jewish people don't eat unless they wash their hands and forearms, holding to the tradition of the elders. They don't eat when they come from the shuk unless they bathe themselves, and there are many other things which they have received to hold to: washings of cups, pitchers, and bronze vessels.)

The Prushim and the scholars asked me, "Why don't your talmidim walk according to the tradition of the elders, but eat their bread with unwashed hands?" I answered them, "Well did Yeshaya prophesy of you hypocrites, as it is written, 'This people honours me with their lips, but their heart is far from me. They worship me in vain, teaching as doctrines the commandments of men.' For you set aside the mitzvah of God, and hold tightly to the tradition of men—the washing of pitchers and cups, and you do many other such things."

I said to them, "Full well do you reject the mitzvah of God, that you may keep your tradition. For Moshe said, 'Honour your father and your mother;' and, 'He who speaks evil of father or mother, let him be put to death.' But you say, 'If a man tells his abba or his eema, "Whatever profit you might have received from me is Corban,"'" that is to say, given to God, "then you no longer allow him to do anything for his abba or his eema, making void the word of God by your tradition which you have handed down. You do many things like this."

I called all the crowd to myself and said to them, "Shema to me, all of you, and understand. There is nothing from outside of the man that going into him can defile him; but the things which proceed out of the man are those that defile the man. If anyone has ears to shema, let him shema!"

When I had entered into a house away from the crowd, my talmidim asked me about the mashal. I said to them, "Are you also without understanding? Don't you perceive that whatever goes into the man from outside can't defile him, because it doesn't go into his heart, but into his stomach, then into the latrine, purging all foods?" I said, "That which proceeds out of the man, that defiles the man. For from within, out of the hearts of men, proceed evil thoughts, adulteries, sexual sins, murders, thefts, covetings, wickedness, deceit, lustful desires, ayin hara, blasphemy, pride, and foolishness. All these evil things come from within and defile the man."

Greek Woman (7:24-30)

From there I arose and went away into the borders of Tyre and Sidon. I entered into a house and didn't want anyone to know it, but I couldn't escape notice. For a woman whose little daughter had an unclean spirit, having heard of me, came and fell down at my feet. Now the woman was a Greek, a Syrophoenician by race. She begged me that I would cast the shed out of her daughter. But I said to her, "Let the children be filled first, for it is not appropriate to take the children's bread and throw it to the puppies." But she answered me, "Yes, sir. Yet even the puppies under the table eat the children's crumbs." I said to her, "For this saying, go your way. The shed has gone out of your daughter." She went away to her house, and found the child having been laid on the bed, with the shed gone out.

Deaf Man (7:31-37)

Again I departed from the borders of Tyre and Sidon, and came to the Kinneret through the middle of the region of Decapolis. They brought to me someone who was deaf and had an impediment in his speech. They begged me to lay my hand on him. I took him aside from the crowd privately and put my fingers into his ears; and I spat and touched his tongue. Looking up to heaven, I sighed, and said to him, "Ephphatha!" that is, "Be opened!" Immediately his ears were opened, and the impediment of his tongue was released, and he spoke clearly.

I commanded them that they should tell no one, but the more I commanded them, so much the more widely they proclaimed it. They were astonished beyond measure, saying, "He has done all things well. He makes even the deaf hear and the mute speak!"

Seven Loaves (8:1-9)

In those days, when there was a very great crowd, and they had nothing to eat, I called my talmidim to myself and said to them, "I have compassion on the crowd, because they have stayed with me now three days and have nothing to eat. If I send them away fasting to their home, they will faint on the way, for some of them have come a long way." My talmidim answered me, "From where could anyone satisfy these people with bread here in a deserted place?" I asked them, "How many loaves do you have?" They said, "Seven."

I commanded the crowd to sit down on the ground, and I took the seven loaves. Having made the bracha, I broke them and gave them to my talmidim to serve, and they served the crowd. They also had a few small fish. Having made the bracha, I said to serve these also. They ate and were filled.

They took up seven baskets of broken pieces that were left over. Those who had eaten were about four thousand. Then I sent them away.

Magdala (8:10-21)

Immediately I entered into the boat with my talmidim and came into the region of Magdala. The Prushim came out and began to question me, seeking from me a sign from heaven and testing me. I sighed deeply in my ruach and said, "Why does this generation seek a sign? Most certainly I tell you, no sign will be given to this generation."

I left them, and again entering into the boat, departed to the other side. They forgot to take bread; and we didn't have more than one loaf in the boat with us. I warned them, saying, "Take heed: beware of the chametz of the Prushim and the chametz of Herod!" They reasoned with one another, saying, "It's because we have no bread." Perceiving it, I said to them, "Why do you reason that it's because you have no bread? Don't you perceive yet or understand? Is your heart still hardened? Having eyes, don't you see? Having ears, don't you hear? Don't you remember? When I broke the five loaves among the five thousand, how many baskets full of broken pieces did you take up?" They told me, "Twelve." "When the seven loaves fed the four thousand, how many baskets full of broken pieces did you take up?" They told me, "Seven." I asked them, "Don't you understand yet?"

Blind Man (8:22-26)

I came to Beit-Tzaida. They brought a blind man to me and begged me to touch him. I took hold of the blind man by the hand, and brought him out of the village. When I had spat on his eyes, and laid my hands on him, I asked him if he saw anything. He looked up, and said, "I see men, but I see them like walking trees." Then again I laid my hands on his eyes. He looked intently, and was restored, and saw everyone clearly. I sent him away to his house, saying, "Don't enter into the village, nor tell anyone in the village."

Caesarea Philippi (8:27-9:1)

I went out, with my talmidim, into the villages of Caesarea Philippi. On the way I asked my talmidim, "Who do men say that I am?" They told me, "Yochanan the Immerser, and others say Eliyahu, but others, one of the prophets." I said to them, "But who do you say that I am?" Peter answered, "You are the Mashiach." I commanded them that they should tell no one about me.

I began to teach them that I, the Ben-Adam, must suffer many things, and be rejected by the elders, the chief kohanim, and the scholars, and be killed, and after three days rise again. I spoke to them openly. Peter took me and began to be mochiach with me. But, turning around and seeing my talmidim, I rebuked Peter, and said, "Get behind me, antagonist! For you have in mind not the things of God, but the things of men."

I called the crowd to myself with my talmidim and said to them, "Whoever wants to come after me, let him deny himself, and take up his cross, and follow me. For whoever wants to save his life will lose it; and whoever will lose his life for my sake and the sake of the Besorah will save it. For what does it profit a man to gain the whole world and forfeit his life? For what will a man give in exchange for his life? For whoever will be ashamed of me and of my words in this adulterous and sinful generation, I, the Ben-Adam, also will be ashamed of him when I come in my Abba's glory with the holy messengers."

I said to them, "Most certainly I tell you, there are some standing here who will in no way taste death until they see my kingdom come with power."

Moshe & Eliyahu (9:2-13)

After six days I took with me Peter, Yaakov, and Yochanan, and brought them up onto a high mountain privately by themselves, and I was changed into another form in front of them. My clothing became glistening, exceedingly white, like snow, such as no launderer on earth can whiten them. Eliyahu and Moshe appeared to them, and they were talking with me.

Peter answered me, "Rabbi, it is good for us to be here. Let's make three sukkot: one for you, one for Moshe, and one for Eliyahu." For he didn't know what to say, for they were very afraid. A cloud came, overshadowing them, and a Bat-Kol came out of the cloud, "This is my beloved Son. Shema to him!" Suddenly looking around, they saw no one with us anymore, except me only.

As we were coming down from the mountain, I commanded them that they should tell no one what things they had seen until after I, the Ben-Adam, had risen from the dead. They kept this saying to themselves, questioning what the "rising from the dead" meant. They asked me, saying, "Why do the scholars say that Eliyahu must come first?" I said to them, "Eliyahu indeed comes first, and restores all things. How is it written about me, the Ben-Adam, that I should suffer many things and be despised? But I tell you that Eliyahu has come, and they have also done to him whatever they wanted to, even as it is written about him."

Epileptic (9:14-29)

Coming to the talmidim, I saw a great crowd around them, and scholars questioning them. Immediately all the crowd, when they saw me, were greatly amazed, and running to me, greeted me. I asked the scholars, "What are you asking them?" One of the crowd answered, "Rabbi, I brought to you my son, who has a mute spirit; and wherever it seizes him, it throws him down; and he foams at the mouth, grinds his teeth, and becomes rigid. I asked your talmidim to cast it out, and they weren't able." I answered him, "Unbelieving generation, how long shall I be with you? How long shall I bear with you? Bring him to me."

They brought him to me, and when I saw him, immediately the spirit convulsed him and he fell on the ground, wallowing and foaming at the mouth. I asked his abba, "How long has it been since this has been happening to him?" He said, "From childhood. Often it has cast him both into the fire and into the water to destroy him. But if you can do anything, have compassion on us and help us." I said to him, "If you can believe, all things are possible to him who believes." Immediately the child's abba cried out with tears, "I believe. Help my unbelief!"

When I saw that a crowd came running together, I rebuked the unclean spirit, saying to him, "You mute and deaf spirit, I command you, come out of him, and never enter him again!" After crying out and convulsing him greatly, it came out of him. The boy became like someone dead, so much that most of them said, "He is dead." But I took him by the hand and raised him up; and he arose.

When I had come into the house, my talmidim asked me privately, "Why couldn't we cast it out?" I said to them, "This kind can come out by nothing but by tefillah and fasting."

Greatest (9:30-50)

We went out from there and passed through the Galil. I didn't want anyone to know it, for I was teaching my talmidim, and said to them, "I, the Ben-Adam, am being handed over into the hands of men, and they will kill me; and when I am killed, on the third day I will rise again." But they didn't understand the saying, and were afraid to ask me.

I came to Kfar-Nachum, and when I was in the house I asked them, "What were you arguing among yourselves on the way?" But they were silent, for they had disputed with one another on the way about who was the greatest. I sat down and called the Twelve; and I said to them, "If any man wants to be first, he shall be last of all, and servant of all." I took a little child and set him in the middle of them. Taking him in my arms, I said to them, "Whoever receives one such little child in my name receives me; and whoever receives me, doesn't receive me, but him who sent me."

Yochanan said to me, "Rabbi, we saw someone who doesn't follow us casting out shedim in your name; and we forbade him, because he doesn't follow us." But I said, "Don't forbid him, for there is no one who will do a miracle in my name and be able quickly to speak evil of me. For whoever is not mitnaged against us is on our side. For whoever will give you a cup of water to drink in my name because you are mine, most certainly I tell you, he will in no way lose his reward.

Whoever will cause one of these little ones who believe in me to stumble, it would be better for him if he were thrown into the sea with a millstone hung around his neck. If your hand causes you to stumble, cut it off. It is better for you to enter into life maimed, rather than having your two hands to go into Hinnom Valley, into the unquenchable fire, 'where their worm doesn't die, and the fire is not quenched.' If your foot causes you to stumble, cut it off. It is better for you to enter into life lame, rather than having your two feet to be cast into Hinnom Valley, into the fire that will never be quenched— 'where their worm doesn't die, and the fire is not quenched.' If your eye causes you to stumble, throw it out. It is better for you to enter into my kingdom with one eye, rather than having two eyes to be cast into the Hinnom Valley of fire, 'where their worm doesn't die, and the fire is not quenched.'

For everyone will be salted with fire, and every sacrifice will be seasoned with salt. Salt is good, but if the salt has lost its saltiness, with what will you do tikkun on it? Have salt in yourselves, and be in shalom with one another."

Marriage (10:1-12)

I arose from there and came into the borders of Judea and beyond the Yarden. Crowds came together to me again. As I usually did, I was again teaching them.

Prushim came to me testing me, and asked me, "Is it lawful for a man to divorce his wife?" I answered, "What did Moshe command you?" They said, "Moshe allowed a get to be written, and to divorce her." But I said to them, "For your hardness of heart, he wrote you this mitzvah. But from the beginning of the creation, God made them male and female. For this cause a man will leave his abba and eema, and will join to his wife, and the two will become echad, so that they are no longer two, but echad. What therefore God has joined together, let no man separate."

In the house, my talmidim asked me again about the same matter. I said to them, "Whoever divorces his wife and marries another commits adultery against her. If a woman herself divorces her husband and marries another, she commits adultery."

Children (10:13-16)

They were bringing to me little children, that I should touch them, but the talmidim rebuked those who were bringing them. But when I saw it, I was moved with indignation and said to them, "Allow the little children to come to me! Don't forbid them, for my kingdom belongs to such as these. Most certainly I tell you, whoever will not receive my kingdom like a little child, he will in no way enter into it." I took them in my arms and blessed them, laying my hands on them.

Rich Man (10:17-31)

As I was going out into the way, someone ran to me, knelt before me, and asked me, "Good Rabbi, what shall I do that I may live forever?" I said to him, "Why do you call me good? No one is good except one—God. You know the mitzvot: 'Do not murder,' 'Do not commit adultery,' 'Do not steal,' 'Do not give false testimony,' 'Do not defraud,' 'Honour your father and mother.'" He said to me, "Rabbi, I have observed all these things from my youth." Looking at him, I loved him, and said to him, "One thing you lack. Go, sell whatever you have and give to the poor, and you will have treasure in heaven; and come, follow me, taking up the cross." But his face fell at that saying, and he went away sorrowful, for he was someone who had great possessions.

I looked around and said to my talmidim, "How difficult it is for those who have riches to enter into my kingdom!" The talmidim were amazed at my words. But I answered again, "My sons, how hard it is for those who trust in riches to enter into my kingdom! It is easier for a camel to go through a needle's eye than for a rich man to enter into my kingdom." They were exceedingly astonished, saying to me, "Then who can be saved?" Looking at them, I said, "With men it is impossible, but not with God, for all things are possible with God."

Peter began to tell me, "Hinei! We have left all and have followed you." I said, "Most certainly I tell you, there is no one who has left house, or brothers, or sisters, or abba, or eema, or wife, or children, or land, for my sake, and for the sake of the Besorah, but he will receive one hundred times more now in this time: houses, brothers, sisters, eemas, children, and land—with persecutions; and in the olam to come life forever. But many who are first will be last, and the last first."

Sons of Zavdai (10:32-45)

We were on the way, going up to Yerushalaim; and I was going in front of them, and they were amazed; and those who followed were afraid. I again took the Twelve, and began to tell them the things that were going to happen to me. "Hinei! We are going up to Yerushalaim. I, the Ben-Adam, will be handed over to the chief kohanim and the scholars. They will condemn me to death, and will deliver me to the goyim. They will mock me, spit on me, scourge me, and kill me. On the third day I will rise again."

Yaakov and Yochanan, the sons of Zavdai, came near to me, saying, "Rabbi, we want you to do for us whatever we will ask." I said to them, "What do you want me to do for you?" They said to me, "Grant to us that we may sit, one at your right hand and one at your left hand, in your glory." But I said to them, "You don't know what you are asking. Are you able to drink the cup that I drink, and to be immersed with the mikvah that I am immersed with?" They said to me, "We are able." I said to them, "You shall indeed drink the cup that I drink, and you shall be immersed with the mikvah that I am immersed with; but to sit at my right hand and at my left hand is not mine to give, but for whom it has been prepared."

When the ten heard it, they began to be indignant towards Yaakov and Yochanan. I summoned them and said to them, "You know that they who are recognized as rulers over the goyim lord it over them, and their great people exercise authority over them. But it shall not be so among you, but whoever wants to become great among you shall be your servant. Whoever of you wants to become first among you shall be bondservant of all. For I, the Ben-Adam, also came not to be served but to serve, and to give my life as a ransom for many."

Blind Beggar (10:46-52)

We came to Jericho. As I went out from Jericho with my talmidim and a great crowd, a son of Timai, Bar-Timai, a blind beggar, was sitting by the road. When he heard that it was me, Yeshua of Natzeret, he began to cry out and say, "Yeshua, Ben-David, have mercy on me!" Many rebuked him, that he should be quiet, but he cried out much more, "Ben-David, have mercy on me!" I stood still and said, "Call him." They called the blind man, saying to him, "Cheer up! Get up. He is calling you!" He, casting away his cloak, sprang up, and came to me. I asked him, "What do you want me to do for you?" The blind man said to me, "Ribboni, that I may see again." I said to him, "Go your way. Your faith has made you well." Immediately he received his sight and followed me on the way.

Yerushalaim (11:1-11)

When we came near to Yerushalaim, to Beit-Pagei and Beit-Hini, at the Hill of Olives, I sent two of my talmidim and said to them, "Go your way into the village that is opposite you. Immediately as you enter into it, you will find a young donkey tied, on which no one has sat. Untie him and bring him. If anyone asks you, 'Why are you doing this?' say, 'The Master needs him;' and immediately he will send him back here." They went away, and found a young donkey tied at the door outside in the open street, and they untied him. Some of those who stood there asked them, "What are you doing, untying the young donkey?" They said to them just as I had said, and they let them go.

They brought the young donkey to me and threw their garments on it, and I sat on it. Many spread their garments on the way, and others were cutting down branches from the trees and spreading them on the road. Those who went in front and those who followed cried out, "Hoshia-na! Blessed is he who comes in the name of Hashem! Blessed is the kingdom of our father David that is coming in the name of Hashem! Hoshia-na in the highest!"

I entered into the Beit HaMikdash in Yerushalaim. When I had looked around at everything, it being now evening, I went out to Beit-Hini with the Twelve.

Fig Tree (11:12-26)

The next day, when we had come out from Beit-Hini, I was hungry. Seeing a fig tree afar off having leaves, I came to see if perhaps I might find anything on it. When I came to it, I found nothing but leaves, for it was not the season for figs. I told it, "May no one ever eat fruit from you again!" and my talmidim heard it.

We came to Yerushalaim, and I entered into the Beit HaMikdash and began to throw out those who sold and those who bought in the Beit HaMikdash, and overthrew the money changers' tables and the seats of those who sold the doves. I would not allow anyone to carry a container through the Beit HaMikdash. I taught, saying to them, "Isn't it written, 'My house will be called a house of tefillah for all the goyim?' But you have made it a den of robbers!" The chief kohanim and the scholars heard it, and sought how they might destroy me. For they feared me, because all the crowd was astonished at my torah.

When evening came, I went out of the city. As we passed by in the morning, we saw the fig tree withered away from the roots. Peter, remembering, said to me, "Rabbi, hinei! The fig tree which you cursed has withered away." I answered them, "Have faith in God. For most certainly I tell you, whoever may tell this mountain, 'Be taken up and cast into the sea,' and doesn't doubt in his heart, but believes that what he says is happening, he shall have whatever he says. Therefore I tell you, all things whatever you daven and ask for, believe that you have received them, and you shall have them.

Whenever you stand davening, forgive, if you have anything against anyone; so that your Abba, who is in heaven, may also forgive you your transgressions. But if you do not forgive, neither will your Abba in heaven forgive your transgressions."

Smicha (11:27-33)

We came again to Yerushalaim, and as I was walking in the Beit HaMikdash, the chief kohanim, the scholars, and the elders came to me, and they began saying to me, "By what authority do you do these things? Or who gave you smicha to do these things?" I said to them, "I will ask you one question. Answer me, and I will tell you by what authority I do these things. The mikvah of Yochanan—was it from heaven, or from men? Answer me." They reasoned with themselves, saying, "If we should say, 'From heaven;' he will say, 'Why then did you not believe him?' If we should say, 'From men'"—they feared the people, for all held Yochanan to really be a prophet. They answered me, "We don't know." I said to them, "Neither will I tell you by what authority I do these things."

Mashal: Vineyard (12:1-12)

I began to speak to them in mashalim. "A man planted a vineyard, put a hedge around it, dug a pit for the wine press, built a tower, rented it out to a farmer, and went into another country.

When it was time, he sent a servant to the farmer to get from the farmer his share of the fruit of the vineyard. They took him, beat him, and sent him away empty. Again, he sent another servant to them; and they threw stones at him, wounded him in the head, and sent him away shamefully treated. Again he sent another, and they killed him, and many others, beating some, and killing some. Therefore still having one, his dearly loved son, he sent him last to them, saying, 'They will respect my son.' But those farmers said among themselves, 'This is the heir. Come, let's kill him, and the inheritance will be ours!' They took him, killed him, and cast him out of the vineyard.

What therefore will the master of the vineyard do? He will come and destroy the farmers, and will give the vineyard to others. Haven't you even read this Scripture: 'The stone which the builders rejected was made the head of the corner. This was from Hashem. It is marvellous in our eyes'?"

They tried to seize me, but they feared the crowd; for they perceived that I spoke the mashal against them. They left me and went away.

Prushim & Herodians (12:13-17)

They sent some of the Prushim and the Herodians to me, that they might trap me with words. When they had come, they asked me, "Rabbi, we know that you are honest, and don't defer to anyone; for you aren't partial to anyone, but truly teach the way of God. Is it lawful to pay taxes to Caesar, or not? Shall we give, or shall we not give?" But, knowing their hypocrisy, I said to them, "Why do you test me? Bring me a denarius coin, that I may see it." They brought it. I said to them, "Whose is this image and inscription?" They said to me, "Caesar's." I answered them, "Render to Caesar the things that are Caesar's, and to God the things that are God's." They marvelled greatly at me.

Tzadukim (12:18-27)

Some Tzadukim, who say that there is no resurrection, came to me. They asked me, saying, "Rabbi, Moshe wrote to us, 'If a man's brother dies and leaves a wife behind him, and leaves no children, that his brother should take his wife and raise up offspring for his brother.' There were seven brothers. The first took a wife, and dying left no offspring. The second took her, and died, leaving no children behind him. The third likewise; and the seven took her and left no children. Last of all the woman also died. In the resurrection, when they rise, whose wife will she be of them? For the seven had her as a wife."

I answered them, "Isn't this because you are mistaken, not knowing the Tanach nor the power of God? For when they will rise from the dead, they neither marry nor are given in marriage, but are like messengers in heaven. But about the dead, that they are raised, haven't you read in the Sefer-Moshe about the Bush, how God spoke to him, saying, 'I am the God of Avraham, the God of Yitzchak, and the God of Yaakov? He is not the God of the dead, but of the living. You are therefore badly mistaken."

Greatest Mitzvah (12:28-34)

One of the scholars came and heard them questioning together, and knowing that I had answered them well, asked me, "Which mitzvah is the greatest of all?" I answered, "The greatest is: 'Shema Yisrael, Adonai Eloheinu, Adonai echad. You shall love Adonai your God with all your heart, with all your soul, with all your mind, and with all your strength.' This is the first mitzvah. The second is like this: 'You shall love your neighbour as yourself.' There is no other mitzvah greater than these."

The scholar said to me, "Truly, Rabbi, you have said well that he is echad, and there is none other but he; and to love him with all the heart, with all the understanding, all the soul, and with all the strength, and to love his neighbour as himself, is more important than all whole burned offerings and sacrifices." When I saw that he answered wisely, I said to him, "You are not far from God's kingdom."

No one dared ask me any question after that.

Scholars (12:35-40)

I responded, as I taught in the Beit HaMikdash, "How is it that the scholars say that the Mashiach is the Ben-David? For David himself said in Ruach HaKodesh, 'Hashem said to my Master, "Sit at my right hand, until I make your enemies the footstool of your feet."' Therefore David himself calls him Master, so how can he be his son?" The common people heard me gladly.

In my teaching I said to them, "Beware of the scholars, who like to walk in long robes, and to get greetings in the shuk, and to get the best seats at shul and the best places at feasts, those who devour widows' houses, and for a pretence make long tefillot. These will receive greater condemnation."

Widow (12:41-44)

I sat down opposite the treasury and saw how the crowd cast money into the treasury. Many who were rich cast in much. A poor widow came and cast in two tiny coins, which equal a small copper coin. I called my talmidim to myself and said to them, "Most certainly I tell you, this poor widow gave more than all those who are giving into the treasury, for they all gave out of their abundance, but she, out of her poverty, gave all that she had to live on."

The End (13:1-13)

As I went out of the Beit HaMikdash, one of my talmidim said to me, "Rabbi, see what kind of stones and what kind of buildings!" I said to him, "Do you see these great buildings? There will not be left here one stone on another, which will not be thrown down."

As I sat on the Hill of Olives opposite the Beit HaMikdash, Peter, Yaakov, Yochanan, and Andrew asked me privately, "Tell us, when will these things be? What is the sign that these things are all about to be fulfilled?" Answering, I began to tell them, "Be careful that no one leads you astray. For many will come in my name, saying, 'I am he!' and will lead many astray. When you hear of wars and rumours of wars, don't be troubled. For those must happen, but the end is not yet. For nation will rise against nation, and kingdom against kingdom. There will be earthquakes in various places. There will be famines and troubles. These things are the beginning of birth pains.

But watch yourselves, for they will deliver you up to sanhedrins. You will be beaten in synagogues. You will stand before rulers and kings for my sake, for a testimony to them. The Besorah must first be preached to all the goyim. When they lead you away and deliver you up, don't be anxious beforehand or premeditate what you will say, but say whatever will be given you in that hour. For it is not you who speak, but Ruach HaKodesh. Brother will deliver up brother to death, and the abba his child. Children will rise up against parents and cause them to be put to death. You will be hated by all men for my name's sake, but he who endures to the end will be saved.

Oppression (13:14-23)

"But when you see the abomination of desolation, spoken of by Daniel the prophet, standing where it ought not" (let the reader understand), "then let those who are in Judea flee to the mountains, and let him who is on the housetop not go down, nor enter in, to take anything out of his house. Let him who is in the field not return back to take his cloak.

But oy to those who are with child and to those who nurse babies in those days! Pray that your flight won't be in the winter. For in those days there will be oppression, such as there has not been the like from the beginning of the creation which God created until now, and never will be. Unless Hashem had shortened the days, no flesh would have been saved; but for the sake of the chosen, whom he picked out, he shortened the days.

Then if anyone tells you, 'Hinei, here is the Mashiach!' or, 'Hinei, there!' don't believe it. For false mashiachs and false prophets will arise and will show signs and wonders, that they may lead astray, if possible, even the chosen. But you watch!

Hinei! I have told you all things beforehand.

My Coming (13:24-31)

"But in those days, after that oppression, the sun will be darkened, the moon will not give its light, the stars will be falling from the sky, and the powers that are in the heavens will be shaken. Then they will see me, the Ben-Adam, coming in clouds with great power and glory. Then I will send out my messengers, and will gather together my chosen from the four winds, from the ends of the earth to the ends of the sky.

Now from the fig tree, learn this mashal. When the branch has now become tender and produces its leaves, you know that the summer is near; even so you also, when you see these things coming to pass, know that it is near, at the doors. Most certainly I say to you, this people will not pass away until all these things happen. Heaven and earth will pass away, but my words will not pass away.

Watch (13:32-37)

"But of that day or that hour no one knows—not even the messengers in heaven, nor I the Son, but only my Abba.

Watch, keep alert, and daven; for you don't know when the moed is. It is like a man travelling to another country, having left his house and given authority to his servants, and to each one his work, and also commanded the doorkeeper to keep watch. Watch therefore, for you don't know when the master of the house is coming—whether at evening, or at midnight, or when the rooster crows, or in the morning; lest, coming suddenly, he might find you sleeping.

What I tell you, I tell all: Watch!"

Anointing (14:1-11)

It was now two days before Pesach and the Festival of Matzot, and the chief kohanim and the scholars sought how they might seize me by deception and kill me. For they said, "Not during the Festival, because there might be a riot among the people."

While I was at Beit-Hini, in the house of Shimon the leper, as I sat at the table, a woman came having an alabaster jar of perfume of pure nard—very costly. She broke the jar and poured it over my head. But there were some who were indignant among themselves, saying, "Why has this perfume been wasted? For this might have been sold for more than three hundred days' wages and given to the poor." So they grumbled against her. But I said, "Leave her alone. Why do you trouble her? She has done a good deed for me. For you always have the poor with you, and whenever you want to, you can do them good; but you will not always have me. She has done what she could. She has anointed my body beforehand for the burying. Most certainly I tell you, wherever this Besorah may be preached throughout the whole world, that which this woman has done will also be spoken of for a memorial of her."

Yehuda from Kriyot, who was one of the Twelve, went away to the chief kohanim, that he might deliver me to them. They, when they heard it, were glad, and promised to give him money. He sought how he might conveniently deliver me.

Pesach (14:12-25)

On the first day of Matzot, when they sacrificed the Pesach, my talmidim asked me, "Where do you want us to go and prepare that you may eat the Pesach?" I sent two of my talmidim and said to them, "Go into the city, and there a man carrying a pitcher of water will meet you. Follow him, and wherever he enters in, tell the master of the house, 'The Rabbi says, "Where is the guest room, where I may eat the Pesach with my talmidim?"' He will himself show you a large upper room furnished and ready. Get ready for us there." My talmidim went out, and came into the city, and found things as I had said to them, and they prepared the Pesach.

When it was evening I came with the Twelve. As we sat and were eating, I said, "Most certainly I tell you, one of you will betray me—he who eats with me." They began to be sorrowful, and to ask me one by one, "Surely not I?" And Acher said, "Surely not I?" I answered them, "It is one of the Twelve, he who dips with me in the dish. For I, the Ben-Adam, am going as it is written about me, but oy to that man by whom I am betrayed! It would be better for that man if he had not been born."

As we were eating, I took matzah, and when I had made the bracha, I broke it and gave to them, and said, "Take, eat. This is my body."

I took the cup, and when I had made the bracha, I gave to them. They all drank of it. I said to them, "This is my blood of the renewed brit, which is poured out for many. Most certainly I tell you, I will no more drink of the 'pri ha'gafen' until that day when I drink it anew in my kingdom."

Hill of Olives (14:26-31)

When we had sung the Hallel, we went out to the Hill of Olives. I said to them, "All of you will be made to stumble because of me tonight, for it is written, 'I will strike the shepherd, and the sheep will be scattered.' However, after I am raised up, I will go before you into the Galil."

But Peter said to me, "Although all will stumble, yet I will not." I said to him, "Most certainly I tell you that you today, even this night, before the rooster crows twice, you will deny me three times." But he spoke all the more, "If I must die with you, I will not deny you!"

They all said the same thing.

Gat-Shemen (14:32-42)

We came to a place which was named Gat-Shemen. I said to my talmidim, "Sit here while I pray." I took with me Peter, Yaakov, and Yochanan, and began to be greatly troubled and distressed. I said to them, "My soul is exceedingly sorrowful, even to death. Stay here and watch."

I went forward a little, and fell on the ground, and prayed that if it were possible, the hour might pass away from me. I said, "Abba, Father, all things are possible to you. Please remove this cup from me. However, not what I desire, but what you desire." I came and found them sleeping, and said to Peter, "Shimon, are you sleeping? Couldn't you watch one hour? Watch and pray, that you may not enter into temptation. The ruach indeed is willing, but the flesh is weak." Again I went away and prayed, saying the same words.

Again I returned and found them sleeping, for their eyes were very heavy; and they didn't know what to answer me. I came the third time and said to them, "Sleep on now, and take your rest. It is enough. The hour has come. Hinei! I, the Ben-Adam, am betrayed into the hands of sinners. Arise! Let's get going. Hinei! He who betrays me is at hand."

Betrayal (14:43-52)

Immediately, while I was still speaking, Yehuda, one of the Twelve, came—and with him a crowd with swords and clubs, from the chief kohanim, the scholars, and the elders. Now he who betrayed me had given them a sign, saying, "Whomever I will kiss, that is he. Seize him, and lead him away safely." When he had come, immediately he came to me and said, "Rabbi! Rabbi!" and kissed me.

They laid their hands on me and seized me. But a certain one of those who stood by drew his sword and struck the servant of the Kohen Gadol, and cut off his ear.

I answered them, "Have you come out, as against a robber, with swords and clubs to seize me? I was daily with you in the Beit HaMikdash teaching, and you didn't arrest me. But this is so that the Scriptures might be fulfilled." They all left me, and fled.

A certain young man followed me, having a linen cloth thrown around himself over his naked body. The young men grabbed him, but he left the linen cloth and fled from them naked.

Kohen Gadol (14:53-65)

They led me away to the Kohen Gadol. All the chief kohanim, the elders, and the scholars came together with him. (Peter had followed me from a distance, until he came into the court of the Kohen Gadol. He was sitting with the officers, and warming himself in the light of the fire.)

Now the chief kohanim and the whole Sanhedrin sought witnesses against me to put me to death, and found none. For many gave false testimony against me, and their testimony didn't agree with each other. Some stood up and gave false testimony against me, saying, "We heard him say, 'I will destroy this

Mikdash that is made with hands, and in three days I will build another made without hands.'" Even so, their testimony didn't agree.

The Kohen Gadol stood up in the middle, and asked me, "Have you no answer? What is it which these testify against you?" But I stayed quiet, and answered nothing. Again the Kohen Gadol asked me, "Are you the Mashiach, the Son of HaMevorach?" I said, "I am. You will see me, the Ben-Adam, sitting at the right hand of Power, and coming with the clouds of the sky."

The Kohen Gadol tore his clothes and said, "What further need have we of witnesses? You have heard the blasphemy! What do you think?" They all condemned me to be worthy of death. Some began to spit on me, and to cover my face, and to beat me with fists, and to tell me, "Prophesy!" The officers struck me with the palms of their hands.

Peter's Denial (14:66-72)

As Peter was in the courtyard below, one of the maids of the Kohen Gadol came, and seeing Peter warming himself, she looked at him and said, "You were also with Yeshua from Natzeret!" But he denied it, saying, "I neither know nor understand what you are saying." He went out on the porch, and the rooster crowed.

The maid saw him and began again to tell those who stood by, "This is one of them." But he again denied it. After a little while again those who stood by said to Peter, "You truly are one of them, for you are a Galilean, and your speech shows it." But he began to curse and to swear, "I don't know this man of whom you speak!" The rooster crowed the second time.

Peter remembered the words that I said to him, "Before the rooster crows twice, you will deny me three times." He fell down and wept.

Pilate (15:1-15)

Immediately in the morning the chief kohanim, with the elders, scholars, and the whole Sanhedrin, held a consultation, bound me, carried me away, and handed me over to Pilate. Pilate asked me, "Are you the King of the Jewish people?" I answered, "So you say." The chief kohanim accused me of many things. Pilate again asked me, "Have you no answer? See how many things they testify against you!" But I made no further answer, so that Pilate marvelled.

Now at the Festival he used to release to them one prisoner, whomever they asked of him. There was one called Bar-Abba, bound with his fellow insurgents, men who in the insurrection had committed murder. The crowd, crying aloud, began to ask him to do as he always did for them. Pilate answered them, saying, "Do you want me to release to you the King of the Jewish people?" For he perceived that for envy the chief kohanim had handed me over. But the chief kohanim stirred up the crowd, that he should release Bar-Abba to them instead.

Pilate again asked them, "What then should I do to him whom you call the King of the Jewish people?" They cried out again, "Crucify him!" Pilate said to them, "Why, what evil has he done?" But they cried out exceedingly, "Crucify him!" Pilate, wishing to please the crowd, released Bar-Abba to them, and handed me over, when he had flogged me, to be crucified.

Praetorium (15:16-20)

The soldiers led me away within the court, which is the Praetorium; and they called together the whole cohort. They clothed me with purple; and weaving a crown of thorns, they put it on me. They began to salute me, "Hail, King of the Jewish people!" They struck my head with a reed and spat on me, and bowing their knees, did homage to me.

When they had mocked me, they took the purple cloak off me, and put my own garments on me.

Crucifixion (15:20-32)

They led me out to crucify me. They compelled someone passing by, coming from the country, Shimon of Cyrene, the abba of Alexander and Rufus, to go with us that he might bear my cross.

They brought me to the place called Golgolta, which is, being translated, "The place of a skull." They offered me wine mixed with myrrh to drink, but I didn't take it. Crucifying me, they parted my garments among them, casting lots on them, what each should take. It was the third hour when they crucified me. The superscription of my accusation was written over me: "THE KING OF THE JEWISH PEOPLE."

With me they crucified two robbers, one on my right hand, and one on my left. The Scripture was fulfilled which says, "He was counted with transgressors."

Those who passed by blasphemed me, wagging their heads and saying, "Ha! You who destroy the Mikdash and build it in three days, save yourself, and come down from the cross!" Likewise, also the chief kohanim mocking among themselves with the scholars said, "He saved others. He can't save himself. Let the Mashiach, the Melech-Yisrael, now come down from the cross, that we may see and believe him." Those who were crucified with me also insulted me.

Death (15:33-41)

When the sixth hour had come, there was darkness over the whole land until the ninth hour. At the ninth hour I cried with a loud voice, saying, "Eloi, Eloi, lama sabachthani?" which is, being translated, "My God, my God, why have you forsaken me?" Some of those who stood by, when they heard it, said, "Hinei! He is calling Eliyahu." Someone ran, and filling a sponge full of vinegar, put it on a reed and gave it to me to drink, saying, "Let him be. Let's see whether Eliyahu comes to take him down."

I cried out with a loud voice, and gave up the ruach. The veil of the Mikdash was torn in two from the top to the bottom. When the centurion, who stood by opposite me, saw that I cried out like this and breathed my last, he said, "Truly this man was a son of God!"

There were also women watching from afar, among whom were both Miriam from Magdala and Miriam the eema of the younger Yaakov and of Yosi, and Shlomit; who, when I was in the Galil, followed me and served me; and many other women who came up with me to Yerushalaim.

Burial (15:42-47)

When evening had now come, because it was the Preparation Day, that is, the day before Shabbat, Yosef of Ramatayim, a prominent Sanhedrin member who also himself was looking for God's kingdom, came. He boldly went in to Pilate, and asked for my body. Pilate was surprised to hear that I was already dead; and summoning the centurion, he asked him whether I had been dead long. When he found out from the centurion, he granted the body to Yosef. He bought a linen cloth, and taking me down, wound me in the linen cloth and laid me in a tomb which had been cut out of a rock. He rolled a stone against the door of the tomb.

Miriam from Magdala and Miriam the eema of Yosi, saw where I was laid.

Dawn (16:1-8)

When Shabbat was past, Miriam from Magdala, and Miriam the eema of Yaakov, and Shlomit bought spices, that they might come and anoint me.

Very early on the first day of the week, they came to the tomb when the sun had risen. They were saying among themselves, "Who will roll away the stone from the door of the tomb for us?" for it was very big. Looking up, they saw that the stone was rolled back. Entering into the tomb, they saw a young man sitting on the right side, dressed in a white robe; and they were amazed. He said to them, "Don't be amazed. You seek Yeshua of Natzeret, who has been crucified. He has risen! He is not here. See the place where they laid him! But go, tell his talmidim and Peter, 'He goes before you into the Galil. There you will see him, as he said to you.'"

They went out, and fled from the tomb, for trembling and astonishment had come on them. They said nothing to anyone; for they were afraid.

Eleven (16:9-20)

Now when I had risen early on the first day of the week, I appeared first to Miriam from Magdala, from whom I had cast out seven shedim. She went and told those who had been with me, as they mourned and wept. When they heard that I was alive and had been seen by her, they disbelieved. After these things I was revealed in another form to two of them as they walked, on their way into the country. They went away and told it to the rest. They didn't believe them, either.

Afterward I was revealed to the Eleven themselves as they sat at the table; and I rebuked them for their unbelief and hardness of heart, because they didn't believe those who had seen me after I had risen. I said to them, "Go into all the world and proclaim the Besorah to the whole creation! He who believes and is immersed will be saved; but he who disbelieves will be condemned. These signs will accompany those who believe: in my name they will cast out shedim; they will speak with new languages; they will take up serpents; and if they drink any deadly thing, it will in no way hurt them; they will lay hands on the sick, and they will recover."

So then, after I had spoken to them, I was received up into heaven and sat down at the right hand of God. They went out and preached everywhere, while I worked with them and confirmed the word by the signs that followed.

AS TOLD TO LUKE

Zecharya & Elisheva (1:1-25)

Since many had undertaken to set in order a narrative concerning those matters which had been fulfilled among them, even as those who from the beginning were eyewitnesses and servants of the word handed them over to them, it seemed good to Luke also, having traced the course of all things accurately from the first, to write to his excellence Theophilus in order; that he might know the certainty concerning the things in which he had been instructed.

There was in the days of Herod, the king of Judea, a certain kohen named Zecharya, of the priestly division of Aviya. He had a wife of the Bnot-Aharon, and her name was Elisheva. They were both tzaddikim before God, walking blamelessly in all the mitzvot and ordinances of Hashem. But they had no child, because Elisheva was barren, and they both were well advanced in years.

Now while he executed the kohen's office before God in the order of his division according to the custom of the kohen's office, his lot was to enter into the Mikdash of Hashem and burn incense. The whole crowd of the people were davening outside at the hour of incense. A messenger of Hashem appeared to him, standing on the right side of the altar of incense. Zecharya was troubled when he saw him, and fear fell upon him.

But the messenger said to him, "Don't be afraid, Zecharya, because your request has been heard. Your wife, Elisheva, will bear you a son, and you shall call his name Yochanan. You will have joy and gladness, and many will rejoice at his birth. For he will be great in the sight of Hashem, and he will drink no wine nor strong drink. He will be filled with Ruach HaKodesh, even from his eema's womb. He will turn many of the Bnei-Israel to Hashem their God. He will go before him in the ruach and power of Eliyahu, 'to turn the hearts of the fathers to the children,' and the disobedient to the mindset of the tzaddikim; to prepare a people prepared for Hashem."

Zecharya said to the messenger, "How can I be sure of this? For I am an old man, and my wife is well advanced in years." The messenger answered him, "I am Gavriel, who stands in the presence of God. I was sent to speak to you and to bring you this besorah. Hinei! You will be silent and not able to speak until the day that these things will happen, because you didn't believe my words, which will be fulfilled in their proper moed."

The people were waiting for Zecharya, and they marvelled that he delayed in the Mikdash. When he came out, he could not speak to them. They perceived that he had seen a vision in the Mikdash. He continued making signs to them, and remained mute.

When the days of his service were fulfilled, he departed to his house. After these days Elisheva his wife conceived, and she hid herself five months, saying, "Thus has Hashem done to me in the days in which he looked at me, to take away my reproach among men."

Gavriel (1:26-38)

Now in the sixth month, the messenger Gavriel was sent from God to a city in the Galil named Natzeret, to a virgin pledged to be married to a man whose name was Yosef, of David's house. The virgin's name was Miriam.

Having come in, the messenger said to her, "Rejoice, you highly favoured person! Hashem is with you. Ashrei are you among women!" But when she saw him, she was greatly troubled at the saying, and considered what kind of salutation this might be. The messenger said to her, "Don't be afraid, Miriam, for you have found favour with God. Hinei! You will conceive in your womb and give birth to a son, and shall name him 'Yeshua.' He will be great and will be called Ben-Elyon. Hashem God will give him the throne of his father David, and he will reign over the house of Yaakov forever. There will be no end to his kingdom."

Miriam said to the messenger, "How can this be, seeing I am a virgin?" The messenger answered her, "Ruach HaKodesh will come on you, and the power of Elyon will overshadow you. Therefore also the holy one who is born from you will be called Ben-Elohim. Hinei! Elisheva your relative also has conceived a son in her old age; and this is the sixth month with her who was called barren. For nothing spoken by God is impossible." Miriam said, "Hinei! The servant of Hashem; let it be done to me according to your word." Then the messenger departed from her.

Miriam & Elisheva (1:39-56)

Miriam arose in those days and went into the hill country with haste, into a city of Judah, and entered into the house of Zecharya and greeted Elisheva. When Elisheva heard Miriam's greeting, the baby leapt in her womb; and Elisheva was filled with Ruach HaKodesh. She called out with a loud voice and said, "Ashrei are you among women, and ashrei is the fruit of your womb! Why am I so favoured, that the eema of my Master should come to me? For hinei! When the voice of your greeting came into my ears, the baby leaped in my womb for joy! Ashrei is she who believed, for there will be a fulfilment of the things which have been spoken to her from Hashem!"

Miriam said, "My soul magnifies Hashem. My ruach has rejoiced in God my Saviour, for he has looked at the humble state of his servant. For hinei! From now on, all generations will call me blessed. For he who is mighty has done great things for me. Holy is his name. His mercy is for generations and generations on those who fear him. He has shown strength with his arm. He has scattered the proud in the imagination of their hearts. He has put down princes from their thrones, and has exalted the lowly. He has filled the hungry with good things. He has sent the rich away empty. He has given help to Israel, his servant, that he might remember mercy, as he spoke to our fathers, to Avraham and his offspring forever."

Miriam stayed with her about three months, and then returned to her house.

Yochanan's Birth (1:57-80)

Now the time that Elisheva should give birth was fulfilled, and she gave birth to a son. Her neighbours and her mishpacha heard that Hashem had magnified his mercy towards her, and they rejoiced with her.

On the eighth day, they came to circumcise the child; and they would have called him Zecharya, after the name of his abba. His eema answered, "Not so; but he will be called Yochanan." They said to her, "There is no one among your mishpacha who is called by this name." They made signs to his abba, what he would have him called. He asked for a writing tablet, and wrote, "His name is Yochanan." They all marvelled. His mouth was opened immediately and his tongue freed, and he spoke, blessing God. Fear came on all who lived around them, and all these sayings were talked about throughout all the hill country of Judea. All who heard them laid them up in their heart, saying, "What then will this child be?" The hand of Hashem was with him.

His abba Zecharya was filled with Ruach HaKodesh, and prophesied, saying, "Baruch Hashem, the God of Israel, for he has visited and redeemed his people; and has raised up a horn of yeshua for us in the house of his servant David (as he spoke by the mouth of his holy prophets who have been from of old), yeshua from our enemies and from the hand of all who hate us; to show mercy towards our fathers, to remember his holy covenant, the oath which he swore to Avraham our father, to grant to us that we, being delivered out of the hand of our enemies, should serve him without fear, in holiness and righteousness before him all the days of our life. And you, child, will be called a prophet of Elyon; for you will go before the face of Hashem to prepare his ways, to give knowledge of yeshua to his people by the forgiveness of their sins, because of the tender mercy of our God, by which the dawn from on high will visit us, to shine on those who sit in darkness and the shadow of death; to guide our feet into the way of shalom."

The child was growing and becoming strong in ruach, and was in the desert until the day of his public appearance to Israel.

My Birth (2:1-7)

Now in those days, a decree went out from Caesar Augustus that all the world should be enrolled. This was the first enrollment made when Quirinius was governor of Syria. All went to enroll themselves, everyone to his own city. Yosef also went up from the Galil, out of the city of Natzeret, into Judea, to David's city, which is called Beit-Lechem, because he was of the house and family of David, to enroll himself with Miriam, who was pledged to be married to him as wife, being pregnant. While they were there, the day had come for her to give birth. She gave birth to me, her firstborn son. She wrapped me in bands of cloth and laid me in a feeding trough, because there was no room for us in the inn.

Shepherds (2:8-20)

There were shepherds in the same country staying in the field, and keeping watch by night over their flock. Hinei! A messenger of Hashem stood by them, and the glory of Hashem shone around them, and they were terrified. The messenger said to them, "Don't be afraid, for hinei! I bring you besorah of great joy which will be to all the people. For there is born to you today, in David's city, a Saviour, who is Mashiach the Master. This is the sign to you: you will find a baby wrapped in strips of cloth, lying in a feeding trough." Suddenly, there was with the messenger a crowd of the heavenly army praising God and saying, "Glory to God in the highest, on earth shalom, good will towards men."

When the messengers went away from them into the sky, the shepherds said to one another, "Let's go to Beit-Lechem, now, and see this thing that has happened, which Hashem has made known to us." They came with haste and found both Miriam and Yosef, and me lying in the feeding trough. When they saw it, they publicized widely the saying which was spoken to them about me. All who heard it wondered at the things which were spoken to them by the shepherds. But Miriam kept all these sayings, pondering them in her heart.

The shepherds returned, glorifying and praising God for all the things that they had heard and seen, just as it was told them.

Bris (2:21-24)

When eight days were fulfilled for my bris, my name was called Yeshua, which was given by the messenger before I was conceived in the womb.

When the days of their purification according to the Torah of Moshe were fulfilled, they brought me up to Yerushalaim to present me to Hashem (as it is written in the Torah of Hashem, "Every male who opens the womb shall be called holy to Hashem"), and to offer a sacrifice according to that which is said in the Torah of Hashem, "A pair of turtledoves, or two young pigeons."

Shimon (2:25-35)

Hinei! There was a man in Yerushalaim whose name was Shimon. This man was a tzaddik and a chasid, looking for the Nechemat-Yisrael, and Ruach HaKodesh was on him. It had been revealed to him by Ruach HaKodesh that he should not see death before he had seen Hashem's Mashiach.

He came in the Ruach into the Beit HaMikdash. When my parents brought me in, that they might do concerning me according to the requirement of the Torah, then he received me into his arms and blessed God, and said, "Now you are releasing your servant, Hashem, according to your word, in shalom; for my eyes have seen your yeshua, which you have prepared before the face of all peoples; a light for revelation to the goyim, and the glory of your people Israel."

Yosef and my eema were marvelling at the things which were spoken concerning me. Shimon blessed them, and said to Miriam, my eema, "Hinei! This child is appointed for the falling and the rising of many in Israel, and for a sign which is spoken against. Yes, a sword will pierce through your own soul, that the thoughts of many hearts may be revealed."

Chana (2:36-39)

There was a certain Chana Bat-Penuel, a prophetess, of the tribe of Asher. She was of a great age, having lived with a husband seven years from her virginity, and she had been a widow for about eighty-four years. She didn't depart from the Beit HaMikdash, worshipping with fastings and petitions night and day. Coming up at that very hour, she gave thanks to Hashem, and spoke of me to all those who were looking for the Geulat-Yerushalaim.

When they had accomplished all things that were according to the Torah of Hashem, they returned into the Galil, to our own city, Natzeret.

Twelve Years Old (2:40-52)

I was growing, and was becoming strong in ruach, being filled with wisdom, and the grace of God was upon me.

My parents went every year to Yerushalaim at the Festival of Pesach. When I was twelve years old, they went up to Yerushalaim according to the custom of the Festival; and when they had fulfilled the days, as they were returning, I stayed behind in Yerushalaim. Yosef and my eema didn't know it, but supposing me to be in the company, they went a day's journey; and they looked for me among their mishpacha and acquaintances. When they didn't find me, they returned to Yerushalaim, looking for me.

After three days they found me in the Beit HaMikdash, sitting in the middle of the teachers, both listening to them and asking them questions. All who heard me were amazed at my understanding and my answers. When they saw me, they were astonished; and my eema said to me, "Son, why have you treated us this way? Hinei! Your abba and I were anxiously looking for you." I said to them, "Why were you looking for me? Didn't you know that I must be in my Abba's house?" They didn't understand the saying which I spoke to them.

I went down with them and came to Natzeret. I was subject to them, and my eema kept all these sayings in her heart. And I increased in wisdom and stature, and in favour with God and men.

Yochanan (3:1-20)

Now in the fifteenth year of the reign of Tiberius Caesar, Pontius Pilate being governor of Judea, and Herod being tetrarch of the Galil, and his brother Philip tetrarch of the region of Ituraea and Trachonitis, and Lysanias tetrarch of Abilene, during the high priesthood of Chanan and Kayafa, the word of God came to Yochanan Ben-Zecharya, in the wilderness. He came into all the region around the Yarden, proclaiming the mikvah of returning in teshuva for forgiveness of sins. As it is written in the sefer of the words of Yeshaya the prophet, "The voice of someone crying in the wilderness, 'Make ready the way of Hashem. Make his paths straight. Every valley will be filled. Every mountain and hill will be brought low. The crooked will become straight, and the rough ways smooth. All flesh will see God's yeshua.'"

He said therefore to the crowds who went out to be immersed by him, "You offspring of vipers, who warned you to flee from the wrath to come? Therefore produce fruits worthy of returning in teshuva, and don't begin to say among yourselves, 'We have Avraham for our father;' for I tell you that God is able to raise up Bnei-Avraham from these stones! Even now the axe also lies at the root of the trees. Every tree therefore that doesn't produce good fruit is cut down and thrown into the fire."

The crowds asked him, "What then must we do?" He answered them, "He who has two coats, let him give to him who has none. He who has food, let him do likewise." Tax collectors also came to be immersed, and they said to him, "Rabbi, what must we do?" He said to them, "Collect no more than that which is appointed to you." Soldiers also asked him, saying, "What about us? What must we do?" He said to them, "Extort from no one by violence, neither accuse anyone wrongfully. Be content with your wages."

As the people were in expectation, and all men reasoned in their hearts concerning Yochanan, whether perhaps he was the Mashiach, Yochanan answered them all, "I indeed immerse you with water, but he comes who is mightier than I, the strap of whose sandals I am not worthy to loosen. He will immerse you in Ruach HaKodesh and fire. His winnowing fan is in his hand, and he will thoroughly cleanse his threshing floor, and will gather the wheat into his barn; but he will burn up the chaff with unquenchable fire."

Then with many other words he was mochiach with the people and preached the Besorah to them, but Herod the tetrarch, being reproved by him for Herodias, his brother's wife, and for all the evil things which Herod had done, added this also to them all, that he shut up Yochanan in prison.

Mikvah (3:21-22)

Now when all the people were immersed, I also had been immersed and was davening. The sky was opened, and Ruach HaKodesh descended in a bodily form like a dove on me; and a Bat-Kol came out of the sky, saying, "You are my beloved Son. In you I am delighted!"

I myself, when I began to teach, was about thirty years old, being the son (as was supposed) of Yosef, Ben-Eli, Ben-Matthat, Ben-Levi, Ben-Malki, Ben-Yannai, Ben-Yosef, Ben-Matitya, Ben-Amotz, Ben-Nahum, Ben-Chesli, Ben-Nagai, Ben-Machat, Ben-Matitya, Ben-Shimi, Ben-Yosef, Ben-Yoda, Ben-Yochanan, Ben-Reisha, Ben-Zerubavel, Ben-Shealtiel, Ben-Neri, Ben-Melki, Ben-Adi, Ben-Kosam, Ben-Elmodad, Ben-Er, Ben-Yosi, Ben-Elazar, Ben-Yorim, Ben-Matat, Ben-Levi, Ben-Shimon, Ben-Yehuda, Ben-Yosef, Ben-Yonam, Ben-Elyakim, Ben-Mala, Ben-Mana, Ben-Matata, Ben-Natan, Ben-David, Ben-Yishai, Ben-Oved, Ben-Boaz, Ben-Salmon, Ben-Nachshon, Ben-Amminadav, Ben-Ram, Ben-Chetzron, Ben-Peretz, Ben-Yehuda, Ben-Yaakov, Ben-Yitzchak, Ben-Avraham, Ben-Terach, Ben-Nachor, Ben-Serug, Ben-Reu, Ben-Peleg, Ben-Ever, Ben-Shelach, Ben-Kenan, Ben-Arpachshad, Ben-Shem, Ben-Noach, Ben-Lamech, Ben-Metushelach, Ben-Chanoch, Ben-Yared, Ben-Mahalalel, Ben-Kenan, Ben-Enosh, Ben-Shet, Ben-Adam, Ben-Elohim.

Wilderness (4:1-13)

Full of Ruach HaKodesh, I returned from the Yarden and was led by the Ruach into the wilderness for forty days, being tempted by the accuser. I ate nothing in those days. Afterward, when they were completed, I was hungry. The accuser said to me, "If you are Ben-Elohim, command this stone to become bread." I answered him, saying, "It is written, 'Man shall not live by bread alone, but by every word of God.'"

The accuser, leading me up on a high mountain, showed me all the kingdoms of the world in a moment of time. The accuser said to me, "I will give you all this authority and their glory, for it has been handed over to me, and I give it to whomever I want. If you therefore will worship before me, it will all be yours." I answered him, "Get behind me, antagonist! For it is written, 'You shall worship Hashem your God, and you shall serve him only.'"

He led me to Yerushalaim and set me on the pinnacle of the Beit HaMikdash, and said to me, "If you are the Ben-Elohim, cast yourself down from here, for it is written, 'He will put his messengers in charge of you, to guard you;' and, 'On their hands they will bear you up, lest perhaps you dash your foot against a stone.'" Answering, I said to him, "It has been said, 'You shall not tempt Hashem your God.'"

When the accuser had completed every temptation, he departed from me until another time.

Natzeret (4:16-30)

I returned in the power of the Ruach into the Galil, and news about me spread through all the surrounding area. I taught in their shuls, being praised by all.

I came to Natzeret, where I had been brought up. I entered, as was my custom, into the shul on Shabbat, and stood up to read. The sefer of the prophet Yeshaya was handed to me. I opened the sefer, and found the place where it was written, "Hashem's Ruach is on me, because he has anointed me to proclaim besorah to the poor. He has sent me to heal the broken hearted, to proclaim release to the captives, recovering of sight to the blind, to deliver those who are crushed, and to proclaim the year of

Hashem's acceptance." I closed the sefer, gave it back to the Chazan, and sat down. The eyes of all in the shul were fastened on me. I began to tell them, "Today, this Haftarah has been fulfilled in your hearing."

All testified about me and wondered at the gracious words which proceeded out of my mouth; and they said, "Isn't this Yosef's son?" I said to them, "Doubtless you will tell me this proverb, 'Physician, heal yourself! Whatever we have heard done at Kfar-Nachum, do also here in your hometown.'" I said, "Most certainly I tell you, no prophet is acceptable in his hometown. But truly I tell you, there were many widows in Israel in the days of Eliyahu, when the sky was shut up three years and six months, when a great famine came over all the land. Eliyahu was sent to none of them, except to Zarephath, in the land of Sidon, to a woman who was a widow. There were many lepers in Israel in the time of Elisha the prophet, yet not one of them was cleansed, except Naaman, the Syrian."

They were all filled with wrath in the shul as they heard these things. They rose up, threw me out of the city, and led me to the brow of the hill that their city was built on, that they might throw me off the cliff. But, passing through the middle of them, I went my way.

Unclean Spirit (4:31-37)

I came down to Kfar-Nachum, a city of the Galil. I was teaching them on Shabbat, and they were astonished at my torah, for my word was with authority.

In the shul there was a man who had a spirit of an unclean shed; and he cried out with a loud voice, saying, "Ah! what have we to do with you, Yeshua from Natzeret? Have you come to destroy us? I know who you are: the Holy One of God!" I rebuked him, saying, "Sheket and come out of him!" When the shed had thrown him down in the middle of them, he came out of him, having done him no harm.

Amazement came on all and they spoke together, one with another, saying, "What is this word? For with authority and power he commands the unclean spirits, and they come out!" News about me went out into every place of the surrounding region.

Shimon's House (4:38-44)

I rose up from the shul and entered into Shimon's house. Shimon's mother-in-law was afflicted with a great fever, and they begged me to help her. I stood over her and rebuked the fever, and it left her. Immediately she rose up and served us.

When the sun was setting, all those who had any sick with various diseases brought them to me; and I laid my hands on every one of them, and healed them. Shedim also came out of many, crying out and saying, "You are the Mashiach, the Ben-Elohim!" Rebuking them, I didn't allow them to speak, because they knew that I was the Mashiach.

When it was day, I departed and went into an uninhabited place and the crowds looked for me, and came to me, and held on to me, so that I wouldn't go away from them. But I said to them, "I must proclaim the besorah of God's kingdom to the other cities also. For this reason I have been sent."

I was proclaiming in the shuls of the Galil.

Fishermen (5:1-11)

Now while the crowd pressed on me and heard the word of God, I was standing by the lake of Ginesar. I saw two boats standing by the lake, but the fishermen had gone out of them and were washing their nets. I entered into one of the boats, which was Shimon's, and asked him to put out a little from the land. I sat down and taught the crowds from the boat.

When I had finished speaking, I said to Shimon, "Put out into the deep and let down your nets for a catch." Shimon answered me, "Sir, we worked all night and caught nothing; but at your word I will let down the net." When they had done this, they caught a great crowd of fish, and their net was breaking. They beckoned to their partners in the other boat, that they should come and help them. They came and filled both boats, so that they began to sink.

But Shimon Peter, when he saw it, fell down at my knees, saying, "Depart from me, for I am a sinful man, sir!" For he was amazed, and all who were with him, at the catch of fish which they had caught; and so also were Yaakov and Yochanan, sons of Zavdai, who were partners with Shimon. I said to Shimon, "Don't be afraid. From now on you will be catching people!"

When they had brought their boats to land, they left everything, and followed me.

Leper (5:12-16)

While I was in one of the cities, hinei! There was a man full of leprosy. When he saw me, he fell on his face and begged me, saying, "Master, if you want to, you can make me clean." I stretched out my hand and touched him, saying, "I want to. Be made clean." Immediately the leprosy left him. I commanded him to tell no one, "But go your way and show yourself to the kohen, and offer for your cleansing according to what Moshe commanded, for a testimony to them."

But the report concerning me spread much more, and great crowds came together to hear and to be healed by me of their infirmities. But I withdrew myself into the desert and davened.

Paralytic (5:17-26)

On one of those days, I was teaching; and there were Prushim and teachers of the Torah sitting by who had come out of every village of the Galil, Judea, and Yerushalaim. The power of Hashem was with me to heal them.

Hinei! Men brought a paralyzed man on a cot, and they sought to bring him in to lay before me. Not finding a way to bring him in because of the crowd, they went up to the housetop and let him down through the tiles with his cot into the middle before me. Seeing their faith, I said to him, "Man, your sins are forgiven you."

The scholars and the Prushim began to reason, saying, "Who is this who speaks blasphemies? Who can forgive sins, but God alone?" Perceiving their thoughts, I answered them, "Why are you reasoning so in your hearts? Which is easier to say, 'Your sins are forgiven you,' or to say, 'Arise and walk?' But that you may know that I, the Ben-Adam, have authority on earth to forgive sins," I said to the paralyzed man, "I tell you, arise, take up your cot, and go home." Immediately he rose up before them, and took up that which he was laying on, and departed to his house, praising God.

Amazement took hold on all, and they praised God. They were filled with fear, saying, "We have seen strange things today."

Levi (5:27-39)

After these things I went out and saw a tax collector named Levi sitting at the tax office, and said to him, "Follow me!" He left everything, and rose up and followed me.

Levi made a great feast for me in his house. There was a great crowd of tax collectors and others who were reclining with us. The scholars and the Prushim murmured against my talmidim, saying, "Why do you eat and drink with the tax collectors and sinners?" I answered them, "Those who are healthy have no need for a physician, but those who are sick do. I have not come to call the tzaddikim, but sinners, to return in teshuva."

They said to me, "Why do Yochanan's talmidim often fast and daven, likewise also the talmidim of the Prushim, but yours eat and drink?" I said to them, "Can you make the bnei-chuppah fast while the chattan is with them? But the days will come when the chattan will be taken away from them. Then they will fast in those days."

I also told a mashal to them. "No one puts a piece from a new garment on an old garment, or else he will tear the new, and also the piece from the new will not match the old. No one puts new wine into old wineskins, or else the new wine will burst the skins, and it will be spilled and the skins will be destroyed. But new wine must be put into fresh wineskins, and both are preserved. No man having drunk old wine immediately desires new, for he says, 'The old is better.'"

Grain Fields (6:1-5)

Now on the second Shabbat after the first, I was going through the grain fields. My talmidim plucked the heads of grain and ate, rubbing them in their hands. But some of the Prushim said to them, "Why do you do that which is not lawful to do on Shabbat?" Answering them, I said, "Haven't you read what David did when he was hungry, he and those who were with him, how he entered into God's house, and took and ate the showbread, and gave also to those who were with him, which is not lawful to eat except for the kohanim alone?"

I said to them, "I, the Ben-Adam, am master of Shabbat."

Withered Hand (6:6-11)

It also happened on another Shabbat that I entered into the shul and taught. There was a man there, and his right hand was withered. The scholars and the Prushim watched me, to see whether I would heal on Shabbat, that they might find an accusation against me. But I knew their thoughts; and I said to the man who had the withered hand, "Rise up and stand in the middle." He arose and stood. Then I said to them, "I will ask you something: Is it lawful on Shabbat to do good, or to do harm? To save a life, or to kill?" I looked around at them all, and said to the man, "Stretch out your hand." He did, and his hand was restored as sound as the other.

But they were filled with rage, and talked with one another about what they might do to me.

Twelve (6:12-19)

In these days, I went out to the mountain to daven, and I continued all night in tefillah to God. When it was day, I called my talmidim, and from them I chose twelve, whom I also named shaliachs: Shimon, whom I also named Peter; Andrew, his brother; Yaakov; Yochanan; Philip; Bar-Talmai; Mattai; Toma; Yaakov Ben-Chalfai; Shimon who was called the Zealot; Yehuda brother of Yaakov; and Yehuda from Kriyot, who also became a traitor.

I came down with them and stood on a plain, with a crowd of my talmidim and a great number of the people from all Judea and Yerushalaim and the sea coast of Tyre and Sidon, who came to hear me and to be healed of their diseases, as well as those who were troubled by unclean spirits; and they were being healed. All the crowd sought to touch me, for power came out of me and healed them all.

Ashrei (6:20-26)

I lifted up my eyes to my talmidim, and said: "Ashrei are you who are poor, for my kingdom is yours. Ashrei are you who hunger now, for you will be filled. Ashrei are you who weep now, for you will laugh. Ashrei are you when men hate you, and when they exclude and mock you, and throw out your name as evil, for the Ben-Adam's sake. Rejoice in that day and leap for joy, for hinei! Your reward is great in heaven, for their fathers did the same thing to the prophets.

But oy to you who are rich! For you have received your consolation. Oy to you, you who are full now, for you will be hungry. Oy to you who laugh now, for you will mourn and weep. Oy, when men speak well of you, for their fathers did the same thing to the false prophets!

Your Abba (6:27-36)

"But I tell you who hear: love your enemies, do good to those who hate you, bless those who curse you, and pray for those who mistreat you. To him who strikes you on the cheek, offer also the other; and from him who takes away your cloak, don't withhold your coat also. Give to everyone who asks you, and don't ask him who takes away your goods to give them back again. As you would like people to do to you, do exactly so to them.

If you love those who love you, what credit is that to you? For even sinners love those who love them. If you do good to those who do good to you, what credit is that to you? For even sinners do the same. If you lend to those from whom you hope to receive, what credit is that to you? Even sinners lend to sinners, to receive back as much. But love your enemies, and do good, and lend, expecting nothing back; and your reward will be great, and you will be Bnei-Elyon; for he is kind towards the unthankful and evil. Therefore be merciful, even as your Abba is also merciful.

Your Rabbi (6:37-45)

"Don't judge, and you won't be judged. Don't condemn, and you won't be condemned. Set free, and you will be set free. Give, and it will be given to you: good measure, pressed down, shaken together, and running over, will be given to you. For with the same measure you measure it will be measured back to you."

I spoke a mashal to them. "Can the blind guide the blind? Won't they both fall into a pit? A talmid is not above his rabbi, but everyone when he has fully received tikkun will be like his rabbi.

Why do you see the speck of chaff that is in your brother's eye, but don't consider the beam that is in your own eye? Or how can you tell your brother, 'Brother, let me remove the speck of chaff that is in your eye,' when you yourself don't see the beam that is in your own eye? You hypocrite! First remove the beam from your own eye, and then you can see clearly to remove the speck of chaff that is in your brother's eye.

For there is no good tree that produces rotten fruit, nor again a rotten tree that produces good fruit. For each tree is known by its own fruit. For people don't gather figs from thorns, nor do they gather grapes from a bramble bush. The good man out of the good treasure of his heart brings out that which is good, and the evil man out of the evil treasure of his heart brings out that which is evil, for out of the abundance of the heart, his mouth speaks.

Mashal: House (6:46-49)

"Why do you call me, 'Master, Master,' and don't do the things which I say? Everyone who comes to me, and hears my words and does them, I will show you who he is like. He is like a man building a house, who dug and went deep and laid a foundation on the rock. When a flood arose, the stream broke against that house, and could not shake it, because it was founded on the rock. But he who hears and doesn't do, is like a man who built a house on the earth without a foundation, against which the stream broke, and immediately it fell; and the ruin of that house was great."

Centurion (7:1-10)

After I had finished speaking in the hearing of the people, I entered into Kfar-Nachum. A certain centurion's servant, who was dear to him, was sick and at the point of death. When he heard about me, he sent to me Jewish elders, asking me to come and save his servant. When they came to me, they begged me earnestly, saying, "He is worthy for you to do this for him, for he loves our nation, and he built our shul for us." I went with them.

When I was now not far from the house, the centurion sent friends to me, saying to me, "Master, don't trouble yourself, for I am not worthy for you to come under my roof. Therefore I didn't even think myself worthy to come to you; but say the word, and my servant will be healed. For I also am a man placed under authority, having under myself soldiers. I tell this one, 'Go!' and he goes; and to another, 'Come!' and he comes; and to my servant, 'Do this,' and he does it."

When I heard these things, I marvelled at him, and turned and said to the crowd who followed me, "I tell you, I have not found such great faith, no, not in Israel!" Those who were sent, returning to the house, found that the servant who had been sick was well.

Widow's Son (7:11-17)

Soon afterwards, I went to a city called Naim. Many of my talmidim, along with a great crowd, went with me. Now when I came near to the gate of the city, hinei! Someone who was dead was carried out, the only son of his eema, and she was a widow. Many people of the city were with her. When I saw her, I had compassion on her and said to her, "Don't cry." I came near and touched the coffin, and the bearers stood still. I said, "Young man, I tell you, arise!" He who was dead sat up and began to speak. Then I gave him to his eema.

Fear took hold of all, and they praised God, saying, "A great prophet has arisen among us!" and, "God has visited his people!" This report went out concerning me in the whole of Judea and in all the surrounding region.

Yochanan's Messengers (7:18-35)

The talmidim of Yochanan told him about all these things. Yochanan, calling to himself two of his talmidim, sent them to me, saying, "Are you the one who is coming, or should we look for another?" When the men had come to me, they said, "Yochanan the Immerser has sent us to you, saying, 'Are you he who comes, or should we look for another?'" In that hour I cured many of diseases and plagues and evil spirits; and to many who were blind I gave sight. I answered them, "Go and tell Yochanan the things which you have seen and heard: that the blind receive their sight, the lame walk, the lepers are cleansed, the deaf hear, the dead are raised up, and the poor have the Besorah preached to them. Ashrei is he who finds no occasion for stumbling in me."

When Yochanan's messengers had departed, I began to tell the crowds about Yochanan, "What did you go out into the wilderness to see? A reed shaken by the wind? But what did you go out to see? A man clothed in soft clothing? Hinei! Those who are gorgeously dressed and live delicately are in kings' courts. But what did you go out to see? A prophet? Yes, I tell you, and much more than a prophet. This is he of whom it is written, 'Hinei! I send my messenger before your face, who will prepare your way before you.' For I tell you, among those who are born of women there is not a greater prophet than Yochanan the Immerser; yet he who is least in my kingdom is greater than he."

When all the people and the tax collectors heard this, they declared God to be just, having been immersed with Yochanan's mikvah. But the Prushim and the Torah experts rejected the counsel of God, not being immersed by him themselves.

"To what then should I compare the people of this generation? What are they like? They are like children who sit in the shuk and call to one another, saying, 'We piped to you, and you didn't dance. We mourned, and you didn't weep.' For Yochanan the Immerser came neither eating bread nor drinking wine, and you say, 'He has a shed.' I, the Ben-Adam, have come eating and drinking, and you say, 'Hinei! A glutton and a drunkard, a friend of tax collectors and sinners!' Wisdom is justified by all her children."

Parush's House (7:36-50)

One of the Prushim invited me to eat with him. I entered into the Parush's house and sat at the table. Hinei! A woman in the city who was a sinner, when she knew that I was reclining in the Parush's house, brought an alabaster jar of perfume. Standing behind at my feet weeping, she began to wet my feet with her tears, and she wiped them with the hair of her head, kissed my feet, and anointed them with the perfume.

Now when the Parush who had invited me saw it, he said to himself, "This man, if he were a prophet, would have perceived who and what kind of woman this is who touches him, that she is a sinner." I answered him, "Shimon, I have something to tell you." He said, "Rabbi, say on." "A certain lender had two debtors. The one owed five hundred days' wages, and the other fifty. When they couldn't pay, he forgave them both. Which of them therefore will love him most?" Shimon answered, "He, I suppose, to whom he forgave the most." I said to him, "You have judged correctly."

Turning to the woman, I said to Shimon, "Do you see this woman? I entered into your house, and you gave me no water for my feet, but she has wet my feet with her tears, and wiped them with the hair of her head. You gave me no kiss, but she, since the time I came in, has not ceased to kiss my feet. You didn't anoint my head with oil, but she has anointed my feet with perfume. Therefore I tell you, her sins, which are many, are forgiven, for she loved much. But anyone to whom little is forgiven, loves little."

I said to her, "Your sins are forgiven." Those who sat at the table with me began to say to themselves, "Who is this who even forgives sins?" I said to the woman, "Your faith has saved you. Go in shalom."

Healed Women (8:1-3)

Soon afterwards, I went about through cities and villages, proclaiming and bringing the besorah of God's kingdom. With me were the Twelve, and certain women who had been healed of evil spirits and infirmities: Miriam who was called Magdalit, from whom seven shedim had gone out; and Yochana, the wife of Kuza, Herod's steward; Shoshana; and many others who served us from their possessions.

Mashal: Farmer (8:4-15)

When a great crowd came together and people from every city were coming to me, I spoke by a mashal: "The farmer went out to sow his seed. As he sowed, some fell along the road, and it was trampled under foot, and the birds of the sky devoured it. Other seed fell on the rock, and as soon as it grew, it withered away, because it had no moisture. Other fell amid the thorns, and the thorns grew with it and choked it. Other fell into the good ground and grew and produced one hundred times as much fruit." As I said these things, I called out, "He who has ears to shema, let him shema!"

Then my talmidim asked me, "What does this mashal mean?" I said, "To you it is given to know the mysteries of my kingdom, but to the rest it is given in mashalim, that 'seeing they may not see, and hearing they may not understand.'

Now the mashal is this: The seed is the word of God. Those along the road are those who hear; then the accuser comes and takes away the word from their heart, that they may not believe and be saved. Those on the rock are they who, when they hear, receive the word with joy; but these have no root. They believe for a while, then fall away in time of temptation. What fell among the thorns, these are those who have heard, and as they go on their way they are choked with cares, riches, and pleasures of life; and they bring no fruit to maturity. Those in the good ground, these are those who with an honest and good heart, having heard the word, hold it tightly, and produce fruit with perseverance.

Mashal: Menorah (8:16-18)

"No one, when he has lit a menorah, covers it with a container or puts it under a bed; but puts it on a stand, that those who enter in may see the light. For nothing is hidden that will not be revealed, nor anything secret that will not be known and come to light.

Be careful therefore how you shema. For whoever has, to him will be given; and whoever doesn't have, from him will be taken away even that which he thinks he has."

Eema & Brothers (8:19-21)

My eema and brothers came to me, and they could not come near me for the crowd. Some people told me, "Your eema and your brothers stand outside, desiring to see you." But I answered them, "My eema and my brothers are these who shema to the word of God and do it."

Storm (8:22-25)

Now on one of those days, I entered into a boat, myself and my talmidim, and I said to them, "Let's go over to the other side of the lake." So we launched out. But as we sailed, I fell asleep. A wind storm came down on the lake, and we were taking on dangerous amounts of water. They came to me and awoke me, saying, "Master, Master, we are dying!" I awoke and rebuked the wind and the raging of the water; then they ceased, and it was calm. I said to them, "Where is your faith?" Being afraid, they marvelled, saying to one another, "Who is this then, that he commands even the winds and the water, and they shema to him?"

Gadara (8:26-39)

Then we arrived at the country of Gadara, which is opposite the Galil. When I stepped ashore, a certain man out of the city who had shedim for a long time met me. He wore no clothes, and didn't live in a house, but in the tombs. When he saw me, he cried out and fell down before me, and with a loud voice said, "What do I have to do with you, Yeshua, son of El-Elyon? I beg you, don't torment me!" For I was commanding the unclean spirit to come out of the man. For the unclean spirit had often seized the man. He was kept under guard and bound with chains and fetters. Breaking the bonds apart, he was driven by the shed into the desert.

I asked him, "What is your name?" He said, "Legion," for many shedim had entered into him. They begged me that I would not command them to go into the abyss. Now there was there a herd of many pigs feeding on the mountain, and they begged me that I would allow them to enter into those. Then I allowed them. The shedim came out of the man and entered into the pigs, and the herd rushed down the steep bank into the lake and were drowned.

When those who fed them saw what had happened, they fled and told it in the city and in the country. People went out to see what had happened. They came to me and found the man from whom the shedim had gone out, sitting at my feet, clothed and in his right mind; and they were afraid. Those who saw it told them how he who had been possessed by shedim was healed. All the people of the surrounding country of Gadara asked me to depart from them, for they were very much afraid. Then I entered into the boat and returned.

But the man from whom the shedim had gone out begged me that he might go with me, but I sent him away, saying, "Return home, and declare what great things God has done for you." He went his way, proclaiming throughout the whole city what great things I had done for him.

Shul President (8:40-56)

When I returned, the crowd welcomed me, for they were all waiting for me. Hinei! A man named Yair came. He was the president of the shul. He fell down at my feet and begged me to come into his house, for he had an only daughter, about twelve years of age, and she was dying.

But as I went, the crowds pressed against me. A woman who had a flow of blood for twelve years, who had spent all her living on physicians and could not be healed by any, came behind me and touched the tzitzit of my cloak. Immediately the flow of her blood stopped. I said, "Who touched me?" When all denied it, Peter and those with me said, "Master, the crowds press and jostle you, and you say, 'Who touched me?'" But I said, "Someone did touch me, for I perceived that power had gone out of me." When the woman saw that she was not hidden, she came trembling; and falling down before me declared to me in the presence of all the people the reason why she had touched me, and how she was healed immediately. I said to her, "Daughter, cheer up. Your faith has made you well. Go in shalom."

While I still spoke, someone from the shul president's house came, saying to him, "Your daughter is dead. Don't trouble the Rabbi." But hearing it, I answered him, "Don't be afraid. Only believe, and she will be healed." When I came to the house, I didn't allow anyone to enter in, except Peter, Yochanan, Yaakov, the child's abba, and her eema. All were weeping and mourning her, but I said, "Don't weep. She isn't dead, but sleeping." They were ridiculing me, knowing that she was dead. But I put them all outside, and taking her by the hand, I called, saying, "Child, arise!" Her ruach returned, and she rose up immediately. I commanded that something be given to her to eat. Her parents were amazed, but I commanded them to tell no one what had been done.

Twelve Sent (9:1-9)

I called the Twelve together and gave them power and authority over all shedim, and to cure diseases. I sent them out to proclaim God's kingdom and to heal the sick. I said to them, "Take nothing for your journey—no staffs, nor wallet, nor bread, nor money. Don't have two tunics each. Into whatever house you enter, stay there, and depart from there. As many as don't receive you, when you depart from that city, shake off even the dust from your feet for a testimony against them." They departed and went throughout the villages, proclaiming the Besorah and healing everywhere.

Now Herod the tetrarch heard of all that was done by me; and he was very perplexed, because it was said by some that Yochanan had risen from the dead, and by some that Eliyahu had appeared, and by others that one of the old prophets had risen again. Herod said, "I beheaded Yochanan, but who is this about whom I hear such things?" He sought to see me.

Five Loaves (9:10-17)

The shaliachs, when they had returned, told me what things they had done. I took them and withdrew apart to a desert region of a city called Beit-Tzaida.

But the crowds, perceiving it, followed me. I welcomed them, spoke to them of God's kingdom, and cured those who needed healing. The day began to wear away; and the Twelve came and said to me, "Send the crowd away, that they may go into the surrounding villages and farms and lodge and get food, for we are here in a deserted place." But I said to them, "You give them something to eat." They said, "We have no more than five loaves and two fish, unless we should go and buy food for all these people." For they were about five thousand men. I said to my talmidim, "Make them sit down in groups of about fifty each." They did so, and made them all sit down. I took the five loaves and the two fish, and looking up to the sky, I made the bracha, broke them, and gave them to the talmidim to set before the crowd. They ate and were all filled.

They gathered up twelve baskets of broken pieces that were left over.

Mashiach (9:18-27)

As I was davening alone, the talmidim were near me, and I asked them, "Who do the crowds say that I am?" They answered, "'Yochanan the Immerser,' but others say, 'Eliyahu,' and others, that one of the old prophets has risen again." I said to them, "But who do you say that I am?" Peter answered, "God's Mashiach." But I warned them and commanded them to tell this to no one, saying, "I, the Ben-Adam, must suffer many things, and be rejected by the elders, chief kohanim, and scholars, and be killed, and the third day be raised up."

I said to all, "If anyone desires to come after me, let him deny himself, take up his cross, and follow me. For whoever desires to save his life will lose it, but whoever will lose his life for my sake will save it. For what does it profit a man if he gains the whole world, and loses or forfeits his own self? For whoever will be ashamed of me and of my words, of him will I, the Ben-Adam, be ashamed when I come in my glory, and the glory of my Abba, and of the holy messengers. But I tell you the truth: There are some of those who stand here who will in no way taste of death until they see my kingdom."

Moshe & Eliyahu (9:28-36)

About eight days after these sayings, I took with me Peter, Yochanan, and Yaakov, and went up onto the mountain to daven. As I was davening, the appearance of my face was altered, and my clothing became white and dazzling. Hinei! Two men were talking with me, who were Moshe and Eliyahu, who appeared in glory and spoke of my departure, which I was about to accomplish at Yerushalaim.

Now Peter and those who were with him were heavy with sleep, but when they were fully awake, they saw my glory, and the two men who stood with me. As they were parting from me, Peter said to me, "Master, it is good for us to be here. Let's make three sukkot: one for you, one for Moshe, and one for Eliyahu," not knowing what he said. While he said these things, a cloud came and overshadowed them, and they were afraid as they entered into the cloud. A Bat-Kol came out of the cloud, saying, "This is my beloved Son. Shema to him!" When the Bat-Kol came, I was found alone.

They were silent, and told no one in those days any of the things which they had seen.

Epileptic (9:37-45)

On the next day, when we had come down from the mountain, a great crowd met me. Hinei! A man from the crowd called out, saying, "Rabbi, I beg you to look at my son, for he is my only child. Hinei! A spirit takes him, he suddenly cries out, and it convulses him so that he foams; and it hardly departs from him, bruising him severely. I begged your talmidim to cast it out, and they couldn't." I answered, "Faithless and perverse generation, how long shall I be with you and bear with you? Bring your son here." While he was still coming, the shed threw him down and convulsed him violently. But I rebuked the unclean spirit, healed the boy, and gave him back to his abba.

They were all astonished at the majesty of God. But while all were marvelling at all the things which I did, I said to my talmidim, "Let these words sink into your ears, for I, the Ben-

Adam, will be handed over into the hands of men." But they didn't understand this saying. It was concealed from them, that they should not perceive it, and they were afraid to ask me about this saying.

Greatest (9:46-50)

An argument arose among them about which of them was the greatest. Perceiving the reasoning of their hearts, I took a little child, and set him by my side, and said to them, "Whoever receives this little child in my name receives me. Whoever receives me receives him who sent me. For whoever is least among you all, this one will be great." Yochanan answered, "Master, we saw someone casting out shedim in your name, and we forbade him, because he doesn't follow with us." I said to him, "Don't forbid him, for he who is not mitnaged against us is for us."

Shomronim (9:51-56)

It came to pass, when the days were near that I should be taken up, I intently set my face to go to Yerushalaim and sent messengers before my face. They went and entered into a village of the Shomronim, so as to prepare for me. They didn't receive me, because I was travelling with my face set towards Yerushalaim. When my talmidim, Yaakov and Yochanan, saw this, they said, "Master, do you want us to command fire to come down from the sky and destroy them, just as Eliyahu did?" But I turned and rebuked them, "You don't know of what kind of ruach you are. For I, the Ben-Adam, didn't come to destroy men's lives, but to save them."

Follow (9:56-62)

We went to another village. As we went on the way, a certain man said to me, "I want to follow you wherever you go, Master." I said to him, "The foxes have holes and the birds of the sky have nests but I, the Ben-Adam, have no place to lay my head."

I said to another, "Follow me!" But he said, "Master, allow me first to go and bury my abba." But I said to him, "Leave the dead to bury their own dead, but you go and announce God's kingdom."

Another also said, "I want to follow you, Master, but first allow me to say good-bye to those who are at my house." But I said to him, "No one, having put his hand to the plough and looking back, is fit for my kingdom."

Seventy Sent (10:1-16)

Now after these things, I also appointed seventy others, and sent them two by two ahead of me into every city and place where I was about to come. Then I said to them, "The harvest is indeed plentiful, but the labourers are few. Pray therefore to the Master of the harvest, that he may send out labourers into his harvest.

Go your ways. Hinei! I send you out as lambs among wolves. Carry no purse, nor wallet, nor sandals. Greet no one on the way. Into whatever house you enter, first say, 'Shalom be to this house.' If a ben-shalom is there, your shalom will rest on him; but if not, it will return to you. Stay in that same house, eating and drinking the things they give, for the labourer is worthy of his wages. Don't go from house to house. Into whatever city you enter and they receive you, eat the things that are set before you. Heal the sick who are there and tell them, 'God's kingdom has come near to you.'

But into whatever city you enter and they don't receive you, go out into its streets and say, 'Even the dust from your city that clings to us, we wipe off against you. Nevertheless know this, that God's kingdom has come near to you.' I tell you, it will be more tolerable in that day for Sodom than for that city. Oy to you, Korazin! Oy to you, Beit-Tzaida! For if the miracles had been done in Tyre and Sidon which were done in you, they would have returned in teshuva long ago, sitting in sackcloth and ashes.

But it will be more tolerable for Tyre and Sidon in the judgement than for you. You, Kfar-Nachum, who are exalted to heaven, will be brought down to Sheol.

Whoever listens to you listens to me, and whoever rejects you rejects me. Whoever rejects me rejects him who sent me."

Seventy Return (10:17-24)

The seventy returned with joy, saying, "Master, even the shedim are subject to us in your name!" I said to them, "I saw the antagonist having fallen like lightning from heaven. Hinei! I give you authority to tread on serpents and scorpions, and over all the power of the enemy. Nothing will in any way hurt you. Nevertheless, don't rejoice in this, that the spirits are subject to you, but rejoice that your names are written in heaven."

In that same hour, I rejoiced in Ruach HaKodesh, and said, "Modeh ani, Abba, Master of heaven and earth, that you have hidden these things from the wise and understanding, and revealed them to little children. Yes, Abba, for so it was well-pleasing in your sight."

Turning to the talmidim, I said, "All things have been handed over to me by my Abba. No one knows who I am, except my Abba, and who my Abba is, except me his Son, and he to whomever I desire to reveal him."

Turning to the talmidim, I said privately, "Ashrei are the eyes which see the things that you see, for I tell you that many prophets and kings desired to see the things which you see, and didn't see them, and to hear the things which you hear, and didn't hear them."

Mashal: Shomroni (10:25-37)

Hinei! A certain Torah expert stood up and tested me, saying, "Rabbi, what shall I do to live forever?" I said to him, "What is written in the Torah? How do you read it?" He answered, "You shall love Hashem your God with all your heart, with all your soul, with all your strength, and with all your mind; and your neighbour as yourself." I said to him, "You have answered correctly. Do this, and you will live."

But he, desiring to justify himself, asked me, "Who is my neighbour?" I answered, "A certain man was going down from Yerushalaim to Jericho, and he fell among robbers, who both stripped him and beat him, and departed, leaving him half dead. By chance a certain kohen was going down that way. When he saw him, he passed by on the other side. In the same way a Levite also, when he came to the place and saw him, passed by on the other side. But a certain Shomroni, as he travelled, came where he was. When he saw him, he was moved with compassion, came to him, and bound up his wounds, pouring on oil and wine. He set him on his own animal, brought him to an inn, and took care of him. On the next day, when he departed, he took out two days' wages, gave them to the host, and said to him, 'Take care of him. Whatever you spend beyond that, I will repay you when I return.'

Now which of these three do you think seemed to be a neighbour to him who fell among the robbers?" He said, "He who showed mercy on him." Then I said to him, "Go and do likewise."

Marta & Miriam (10:38-42)

As we went on our way, I entered into a certain village, and a certain woman named Marta received me into her house. She had a sister called Miriam, who also sat at my feet and heard my word. But Marta was distracted with much serving, and she came up to me, and said, "Master, don't you care that my sister left me to serve alone? Ask her therefore to help me." I answered her, "Marta, Marta, you are anxious and troubled about many things, but one thing is necessary. Miriam has chosen the good part, which will not be taken away from her."

Tefillah (11:1-13)

When I finished davening in a certain place, one of my talmidim said to me, "Master, teach us to daven, just as Yochanan also taught his talmidim." I said to them, "When you daven, say, 'Our Abba in heaven, may your name be kept holy. May your kingdom come. May your will be done on earth, as it is in heaven. Give us day by day our daily bread. Forgive us our sins, for we ourselves also forgive everyone who is indebted to us. Bring us not into temptation, but deliver us from the evil one.'"

I said to them, "Which of you, if you go to a friend at midnight and tell him, 'Friend, lend me three loaves of bread, for a friend of mine has come to me from a journey, and I have nothing to set before him,' and he from within will answer and say, 'Don't bother me! The door is now shut, and my children are with me in bed. I can't get up and give it to you'? I tell you, although he will not rise and give it to him because he is his friend, yet because of his persistence, he will get up and give him as many as he needs.

I tell you, keep asking, and it will be given you. Keep seeking, and you will find. Keep knocking, and it will be opened to you. For everyone who asks receives. He who seeks finds. To him who knocks it will be opened. Which of you abbas, if your son asks for bread, will give him a stone? Or if he asks for a fish, he won't give him a snake instead of a fish, will he? Or if he asks for an egg, he won't give him a scorpion, will he? If you then, being evil, know how to give good gifts to your children, how much more will your Abba in heaven give Ruach HaKodesh to those who ask him?"

Mute Shed (11:14-28)

I was casting out a shed, and it was mute. When the shed had gone out, the mute man spoke; and the crowds marvelled. But some of them said, "He casts out shedim by Baal-Zvuv, the prince of the shedim." Others, testing me, sought from me a sign from heaven. But, knowing their thoughts, I said to them, "Every kingdom divided against itself is brought to desolation. A house divided against itself falls. If an antagonist also is divided against himself, how will his kingdom stand? For you say that I cast out shedim by Baal-Zvuv. But if I cast out shedim by Baal-Zvuv, by whom do your children cast them out? Therefore they will be your judges. But if I by God's finger cast out shedim, then God's kingdom has come to you.

When the strong man, fully armed, guards his own dwelling, his goods are safe. But when someone stronger attacks him and overcomes him, he takes from him his whole armour in which he trusted, and divides his plunder. He who is not with me is mitnaged against me. He who doesn't gather with me scatters. The unclean spirit, when he has gone out of the man, passes through dry places, seeking rest; and finding none, he says, 'I will turn back to my house from which I came out.' When he returns, he finds it swept and put in order. Then he goes and takes seven other spirits more evil than himself, and they enter in and dwell there. The last state of that man becomes worse than the first."

It came to pass, as I said these things, a certain woman out of the crowd lifted up her voice and said to me, "Ashrei is the womb that bore you, and the breasts which nursed you!" But I said, "On the contrary, ashrei are those who shema to the word of God, and keep it."

Evil Generation (11:29-36)

When the crowds were gathering together to me, I began to say, "This is an evil generation. It seeks after a sign. No sign will be given to it but the sign of Yonah the prophet. For even as Yonah became a sign to the Ninevites, so I, the Ben-Adam, will also be to this generation.

The Queen of the South will rise up in the judgement with the men of this generation and will condemn them, for she came from the ends of the earth to hear the wisdom of Shlomo; and hinei! Someone greater than Shlomo is here. The men of Nineveh will stand up in the judgement with this generation, and will condemn it, for they returned in teshuva at the proclaiming of Yonah; and hinei! Someone greater than Yonah is here.

No one, when he has lit a menorah, puts it in a cellar or under a basket, but on a stand, that those who come in may see the light. The menorah of the body is the eye. Therefore when you have an ayin tov, your whole body is also full of light; but when it is an ayin hara, your body also is full of darkness. Therefore see whether the light that is in you isn't darkness. If therefore your whole body is full of light, having no part dark, it will be wholly full of light, as when the menorah with its bright shining gives you light."

Prushim (11:37-54)

Now as I spoke, a certain Parush asked me to dine with him. I went in and sat at the table. When the Parush saw it, he marvelled that I had not first immersed myself before dinner. I said to him, "Now you Prushim cleanse the outside of the cup and of the platter, but your inward part is full of extortion and wickedness. You fools, didn't he who made the outside make the inside also? But give as tzedakah those things which are within, and hinei! All things will be clean to you.

But oy to you Prushim! For you tithe mint and rue and every herb, but you bypass justice and God's love. You ought to have done these, and not to have left the others undone.

Oy to you Prushim! For you love the best seats at shul and the greetings in the shuk.

Oy to you, scholars and Prushim, hypocrites! For you are like hidden graves, and the men who walk over them don't know it."

Torah Experts (11:45-54)

One of the Torah experts answered me, "Rabbi, in saying this you insult us also." I said, "Oy to you Torah experts also! For you load men with burdens that are difficult to carry, and you yourselves won't even lift one finger to help carry those burdens.

Oy to you! For you build the tombs of the prophets, and your fathers killed them. So you testify and consent to the actions of your fathers. For they killed them, and you build their tombs. Therefore also the wisdom of God said, 'I will send to them prophets and shaliachs; and some of them they will kill and persecute, that the blood of all the prophets, which was shed from the foundation of the world, may be required of this generation, from the blood of Hevel to the blood of Zecharya, who perished between the altar and the Mikdash.' Yes, I tell you, it will be required of this generation.

Oy to you Torah experts! For you took away the key of knowledge. You didn't enter in yourselves, and those who were entering in, you hindered."

As I said these things to them, the scholars and the Prushim began to be terribly angry, and to draw many things out of me, lying in wait for me, and seeking to catch me in something I might say, that they might accuse me.

Fear (12:1-12)

Meanwhile, when a crowd of many thousands had gathered together, so much so that they trampled on each other, I began to tell my talmidim first of all, "Beware of the chametz of the Prushim, which is hypocrisy. But there is nothing covered up that will not be revealed, nor hidden that will not be known. Therefore whatever you have said in the darkness will be heard in the light. What you have spoken in the ear in the inner rooms will be proclaimed on the housetops.

I tell you, my friends, don't be afraid of those who kill the body, and after that have no more that they can do. But I will warn you whom you should fear. Fear him who, after he has killed, has power to cast into Hinnom Valley. Yes, I tell you, fear him! Aren't five sparrows sold for two copper coins? Not one of them is forgotten by God. But the very hairs of your head are all counted. Therefore don't be afraid. You are of more value than many sparrows.

I tell you, everyone who confesses me before men, I, the Ben-Adam, will also confess before the messengers of God; but he who denies me in the presence of men will be denied in the presence of God's messengers. Everyone who speaks a word against me, the Ben-Adam, will be forgiven, but those who blaspheme against Ruach HaKodesh will not be forgiven.

When they bring you before the synagogues, the rulers, and the authorities, don't be anxious how or what you will answer or what you will say; for Ruach HaKodesh will teach you in that same hour what you must say."

Mashal: Rich Man (12:13-21)

One of the crowd said to me, "Rabbi, tell my brother to divide the inheritance with me." But I said to him, "Man, who made me a judge or an arbitrator over you?" I said to them, "Beware! Keep yourselves from covetousness, for a man's life doesn't consist of the abundance of the things which he possesses."

I spoke a mashal to them, saying, "The ground of a certain rich man produced abundantly. He reasoned within himself, saying, 'What will I do, because I don't have room to store my crops?' He said, 'This is what I will do. I will pull down my barns, build bigger ones, and there I will store all my grain and my goods. I will tell my soul, "Soul, you have many goods laid up for many years. Take your ease, eat, drink, and be merry."' But God said to him, 'You fool, tonight your soul is required of you. The things which you have prepared—whose will they be?' So is he who lays up treasure for himself, and is not rich towards God."

Anxiety (12:22-34)

I said to my talmidim, "Therefore I tell you, don't be anxious for your life, what you will eat, nor yet for your body, what you will wear. Life is more than food, and the body is more than clothing. Consider the ravens: they don't sow, they don't reap, they have no warehouse or barn, and God feeds them. How much more valuable are you than birds!

Which of you by being anxious can add a cubit to his height? If then you aren't able to do even the least things, why are you anxious about the rest? Consider the lilies, how they grow. They don't toil, neither do they spin; yet I tell you, even Shlomo in all his glory was not arrayed like one of these. But if this is how God clothes the grass in the field, which today exists and tomorrow is cast into the oven, how much more will he clothe you, you of little faith?

Don't seek what you will eat or what you will drink; neither be anxious. For the goyim of the world seek after all of these things, but your Abba knows that you need these things. But seek God's kingdom, and all these things will be added to you.

Don't be afraid, little flock, for it is your Abba's good pleasure to give you the Kingdom! Sell what you have and give tzedakah to the needy. Make for yourselves purses which don't grow old, a treasure in the heavens that doesn't fail, where no thief approaches and no moth destroys. For where your treasure is, there will your heart be also.

Mashal: Steward (12:35-48)

"Let your waist be dressed and your menorahs burning. Be like men watching for their master when he returns from the chatunah, that when he comes and knocks, they may immediately open to him. Ashrei are those servants whom the master will find watching when he comes. Most certainly I tell you that he will dress himself, make them recline, and will come and serve them. They will be blessed if he comes in the second or third watch and finds them so. But know this, that if the master of the house had known in what hour the thief was coming, he would have watched and not allowed his house to be broken into. Therefore be ready also for I, the Ben-Adam, am coming in an hour that you don't expect me."

Peter said to me, "Master, are you telling this mashal to us, or to everybody?" I said, "Who then is the faithful and wise steward, whom his master will set over his household, to give them their portion of food at the right times? Ashrei is that servant whom his master will find doing so when he comes. Truly I tell you that he will set him over all that he has. But if that servant says in his heart, 'My master delays his coming,' and begins to beat the menservants and the maidservants, and to eat and drink and to be drunken, then the master of that servant will come in a day when he isn't expecting him and in an hour that he doesn't know, and will cut him in two, and place his portion with the unfaithful.

That servant who knew his master's will, and didn't prepare nor do what he wanted, will be beaten with many stripes, but he who didn't know, and did things worthy of stripes, will be beaten with few stripes. To whomever much is given, of him will much be required; and to whom much was entrusted, of him more will be asked.

Division (12:49-59)

"I came to throw fire on the earth. I wish it were already kindled! But I have a mikvah to be immersed with, and how distressed I am until it is accomplished!

Do you think that I have come to give peace on the earth? I tell you, no, but rather division. For from now on, there will be five in one house divided, three against two, and two against three. They will be divided, abba against son, and son against abba; eema against daughter, and daughter against her eema; mother-in-law against her daughter-in-law, and daughter-in-law against her mother-in-law."

I said to the crowds also, "When you see a cloud rising from the west, immediately you say, 'A shower is coming,' and so it happens. When a south wind blows, you say, 'There will be a scorching heat,' and it happens. You hypocrites! You know how to interpret the appearance of the earth and the sky, but how is it that you don't interpret this moed?

Why don't you judge for yourselves what is right? For when you are going with your adversary before the magistrate, try diligently on the way to be released from him, lest perhaps he drag you to the judge, and the judge deliver you to the officer, and the officer throw you into prison. I tell you, you will by no means get out of there until you have paid the very last penny."

Return (13:1-5)

Now there were some present at the same time who told me about the Galileans whose blood Pilate had mixed with their sacrifices. I answered them, "Do you think that these Galileans were worse sinners than all the other Galileans, because they suffered such things? I tell you, no, but unless you return in teshuva, you will all perish in the same way. Or those eighteen on whom the tower in Shiloach fell and killed them—do you think that they were worse offenders than all the men who dwell in Yerushalaim? I tell you, no, but, unless you return in teshuva, you will all perish in the same way."

Mashal: Fig Tree (13:6-9)

I spoke this mashal. "A certain man had a fig tree planted in his vineyard, and he came seeking fruit on it and found none. He said to the vine dresser, 'Hinei! These three years I have come looking for fruit on this fig tree, and found none. Cut it down! Why does it waste the soil?' He answered, 'Master, leave it alone this year also, until I dig around it and fertilize it. If it bears fruit, fine; but if not, after that, you can cut it down.'"

Bound Woman (13:10-17)

I was teaching in one of the shuls on Shabbat. Hinei! There was a woman who had a spirit of infirmity eighteen years. She was bent over and could in no way straighten herself up. When I saw her, I called her and said to her, "Woman, you are freed from your infirmity." I laid my hands on her, and immediately she stood up straight and praised God.

The president of the shul, being indignant because I had healed on Shabbat, said to the crowd, "There are six days in which men ought to work. Therefore come on those days and be healed, and not on Shabbat!" Therefore I answered him, "You hypocrites! Doesn't each one of you free his ox or his donkey from the stall on Shabbat and lead him away to water? Ought not this woman, being a Bat-Avraham whom the antagonist had bound eighteen long years, be freed from this bondage on Shabbat?"

As I said these things, all my adversaries were put to shame; and all the crowd rejoiced for all the glorious things that were done by me.

Mashalim: Mustard Seed & Yeast (13:18-21)

I said, "What is my kingdom like? To what shall I compare it? It is like a grain of mustard seed which a man took and put in his own garden. It grew and became a large tree, and the birds of the sky lived in its branches."

Again I said, "To what shall I compare my kingdom? It is like chametz, which a woman took and hid in three measures of flour, until it was all leavened."

Few Saved (13:22-30)

I went on my way through cities and villages, teaching, and travelling on to Yerushalaim.

Someone said to me, "Master, are they few who are saved?" I said to them, "Strive to enter in by the narrow door, for many, I tell you, will seek to enter in and will not be able. When I, the Master of the house, have risen up and have shut the door, and you begin to stand outside and to knock at the door, saying, 'Master, Master, open to us!' then I will answer and tell you, 'I don't know you or where you come from.' Then you will begin to say, 'We ate and drank in your presence, and you taught in our streets.' I will say, 'I tell you, I don't know where you come from. Depart from me, all you workers of iniquity.'

There will be weeping and gnashing of teeth when you see Avraham, Yitzchak, Yaakov, and all the prophets in God's kingdom, and yourselves being thrown outside. They will come from the east, west, north, and south, and will sit down in God's kingdom. Hinei! There are some who are last who will be first, and there are some who are first who will be last."

Yerushalaim (13:31-35)

On that same day, some Prushim came, saying to me, "Get out of here and go away, for Herod wants to kill you." I said to them, "Go and tell that fox, 'Hinei! I cast out shedim and perform cures today and tomorrow, and the third day I complete my mission.' Nevertheless I must go on my way today and tomorrow and the next day, for it can't be that a prophet would perish outside of Yerushalaim.

Yerushalaim, Yerushalaim, who kills the prophets and stones those who are sent to her! How often I wanted to gather your children together, like a hen gathers her own brood under her wings, and you refused. Hinei! Your house is left to you desolate.

I tell you, you will not see me until you say, 'Blessed is he who comes in the name of Hashem!'"

Dropsy (14:1-6)

When I went into the house of one of the leaders of the Prushim on a Shabbat to eat bread, they were watching me. Hinei! A certain man who had dropsy was in front of me. Answering, I spoke to the Torah experts and Prushim, saying, "Is it lawful to heal on Shabbat?" But they were silent. I took him, and healed him, and let him go. I answered them, "Which of you, if your son or an ox fell into a well, wouldn't immediately pull him out on Shabbat?"

They couldn't answer me regarding these things.

Feasts (14:7-14)

I spoke a mashal to those who were invited, when I noticed how they chose the best seats, and said to them, "When you are invited by anyone to a chatunah, don't sit in the best seat, since perhaps someone more honourable than you might be invited by him, and he who invited both of you would come and tell you, 'Make room for this person.' Then you would begin, with shame, to take the lowest place. But when you are invited, go and sit in the lowest place, so that when he who invited you comes, he may tell you, 'Friend, move up higher.' Then you will be honoured in the presence of all who sit at the table with you. For everyone who exalts himself will be humbled, and whoever humbles himself will be exalted."

I also said to the one who had invited me, "When you make a luncheon or a dinner, don't call your friends, nor your brothers, nor your mishpacha, nor rich neighbours, or perhaps they might also return the favour, and pay you back. But when you make a feast, ask the poor, the maimed, the lame, or the blind; and you will be blessed, because they don't have the resources to repay you. For you will be repaid in the resurrection of the tzaddikim."

Mashal: Banquet (14:15-24)

When one of those who sat at the table with me heard these things, he said to me, "Ashrei is he who will feast in God's kingdom!" But I said to him, "A certain man made a great banquet, and he invited many people. He sent out his servant at banquet time to tell those who were invited, 'Come, for everything is ready now.' They all as one began to make excuses. The first said to him, 'I have bought a field, and I must go and see it. Please have me excused.' "Another said, 'I have bought five yoke of oxen, and I must go try them out. Please have me excused.' Another said, 'I have married a wife, and therefore I can't come.' That servant came, and told his master these things. Then the master of the house, being angry, said to his servant, 'Go out quickly into the streets and lanes of the city, and bring in the poor, maimed, blind, and lame.' The servant said, 'Master, it is done as you commanded, and there is still room.' The master said to the servant, 'Go out into the highways and hedges, and compel them to come in, that my house may be filled. For I tell you that none of those men who were invited will taste of my banquet.'"

My Talmid (14:25-35)

Now great crowds were going with me. I turned and said to them, "If anyone comes to me, and doesn't disregard his own abba, eema, wife, children, brothers, and sisters, yes, and his own life also, he can't be my talmid. Whoever doesn't bear his own cross and come after me, can't be my talmid.

For which of you, desiring to build a tower, doesn't first sit down and count the cost, to see if he has enough to complete it? Or perhaps, when he has laid a foundation and isn't able to finish, everyone who sees begins to mock him, saying, 'This man began to build and wasn't able to finish.' Or what king, as he goes to encounter another king in war, will not sit down first and consider whether he is able with ten thousand to meet him who comes against him with twenty thousand? Or else, while the other is yet a great way off, he sends an envoy and asks for conditions of peace. So therefore, whoever of you who doesn't renounce all that he has, he can't be my talmid.

Salt is good, but if the salt becomes flat and tasteless, with what do you season it? It is fit neither for the soil nor for the manure pile. It is thrown out. He who has ears to shema, let him shema!"

Mashal: Sheep (15:1-7)

Now all the tax collectors and sinners were coming close to me to hear me. The Prushim and the scholars murmured, saying, "This man welcomes sinners, and eats with them." I told them this mashal: "Which of you men, if you had one hundred sheep and lost one of them, wouldn't leave the ninety-nine in the wilderness and go after the one that was lost, until he found it? When he has found it, he carries it on his shoulders, rejoicing. When he comes home, he calls together his friends and his neighbours, saying to them, 'Rejoice with me, for I have found my sheep which was lost!' I tell you that even so there will be more joy in heaven over one sinner who returns in teshuva, than over ninety-nine tzaddikim who don't need to return.

Mashal: Coin (15:8-10)

"Or what woman, if she had ten silver coins, if she lost one silver coin, wouldn't light a menorah, sweep the house, and seek diligently until she found it? When she has found it, she calls together her friends and neighbours, saying, 'Rejoice with me, for I have found the silver coin which I had lost!' Even so, I tell you, there is joy in the presence of the messengers of God over one sinner returning in teshuva."

Mashal: Abba (15:11-32)

I said, "A certain man had two sons. The younger of them said to his abba, 'Abba, give me my share of your property.' So he divided his livelihood between them. Not many days after, the younger son gathered all of this together and travelled into a far country. There he wasted his property with riotous living. When he had spent all of it, there arose a severe famine in that country, and he began to be in need. He went and joined himself to one of the citizens of that country, and he sent him into his fields to feed pigs. He wanted to fill his belly with the pods that the pigs ate, but no one gave him any.

But when he came to himself, he said, 'How many hired servants of my abba's have bread enough to spare, and I'm dying with hunger! I will get up and go to my abba, and will tell him, "Abba, I have sinned against heaven and in your sight. I am no more worthy to be called your son. Make me as one of your hired servants."'

He arose and came to his abba. But while he was still far off, his abba saw him and was moved with compassion, and ran, fell on his neck, and kissed him. The son said to him, 'Abba, I have sinned against heaven and in your sight. I am no longer worthy to be called your son.' But the abba said to his servants, 'Bring out the best robe and put it on him. Put a ring on his hand and sandals on his feet. Bring the fattened calf, kill it, and let's eat and celebrate; for this, my son, was dead and is alive again. He was lost and is found.' Then they began to celebrate.

Now his elder son was in the field. As he came near to the house, he heard music and dancing. He called one of the servants to him and asked what was going on. He said to him, 'Your brother has come, and your abba has killed the fattened calf, because he has received him back safe and healthy.' But he was angry and would not go in. Therefore his abba came out and begged him. But he answered his abba, 'Hinei! These many years I have served you, and I never disobeyed a commandment of yours, but you never gave me a goat, that I might celebrate with my friends. But when this your son came, who has devoured your living with prostitutes, you killed the fattened calf for him.' He said to him, 'Son, you are always with me, and all that is mine is yours. But it was appropriate to celebrate and be glad, for this, your brother, was dead, and is alive again! He was lost, and is found.'"

Mashal: Manager (16:1-8)

I also said to my talmidim, "There was a certain rich man who had a manager. An accusation was made to him that this man was wasting his possessions. He called him, and said to him, 'What is this that I hear about you? Give an accounting of your management, for you can no longer be manager.' The manager said within himself, 'What will I do, seeing that my master is taking away the management position from me? I don't have strength to dig. I am ashamed to beg. I know what I will do, so that when I am removed from management, they may receive me into their houses.' Calling each one of his master's debtors to him, he said to the first, 'How much do you owe to my master?' He said, 'A hundred measures of oil.' He said to him, 'Take your bill, and sit down quickly and write fifty.' Then he said to another, 'How much do you owe?' He said, 'A hundred measures of wheat.' He said to him, 'Take your bill, and write eighty.' His master commended the dishonest manager because he had done wisely, for the children of this world are, in their own generation, wiser than the children of the light.

Money (16:9-18)

"I tell you, make for yourselves friends by means of unrighteous wealth, so that when it fails, they may receive you into the everlasting sukkot. He who is faithful in a very little thing is faithful also in much. He who is dishonest in a very little thing is also dishonest in much. If therefore you have not been faithful in the unrighteous wealth, who will commit to your trust the true riches? If you have not been faithful in that which is another's, who will give you that which is your own? No servant can serve two masters, for either he will hate the one and love the other; or else he will hold to one and despise the other. You aren't able to serve God and wealth."

The Prushim, who were lovers of money, also heard all these things, and they scoffed at me. I said to them, "You are those who justify yourselves in the sight of men, but God knows your hearts. For that which is exalted among men is an abomination in the sight of God.

The Torah and the Prophets were until Yochanan. From that time the besorah of God's kingdom is preached, and everyone is forcing his way into it. But it is easier for heaven and earth to pass away than for one tag in the Torah to become void.

Everyone who divorces his wife and marries another commits adultery. He who marries someone who is divorced from a husband commits adultery.

Elazar (16:19-31)

"Now there was a certain rich man, and he was clothed in purple and fine linen, living in luxury every day. A certain beggar, named Elazar, was taken to his gate, full of sores, and desiring to be fed with the crumbs that fell from the rich man's table. Yes, even the dogs came and licked his sores! The beggar died, and he was carried away by the messengers to Avraham's bosom. The rich man also died and was buried.

In Sheol, he lifted up his eyes, being in torment, and saw Avraham far off, and Elazar at his bosom. He cried and said, 'Father Avraham, have mercy on me, and send Elazar, that he may dip the tip of his finger in water and cool my tongue! For I am in anguish in this flame.' But Avraham said, 'Son, remember that you, in your lifetime, received your good things, and Elazar, in the same way, bad things. But here he is now comforted and you are in anguish. Besides all this, between us and you there is a great gulf fixed, that those who want to pass from here to you are not able, and that no one may cross over from there to us.'

He said, 'I ask you therefore, father, that you would send him to my abba's house— for I have five brothers—that he may testify to them, so they won't also come into this place of torment.' But Avraham said to him, 'They have Moshe and the Prophets. Let them shema to them.' He said, 'No, father Avraham, but if someone goes to them from the dead, they will return in teshuva.' He said to him, 'If they don't shema to Moshe and the Prophets, neither will they be persuaded if someone rises from the dead.'"

Stumbling (17:1-4)

I said to the talmidim, "It is impossible that no occasions of stumbling should come, but oy to him through whom they come! It would be better for him if a millstone were hung around his neck, and he were thrown into the sea, rather than that he should cause one of these little ones to stumble.

Be careful. If your brother sins against you, be mochiach with him. If he returns in teshuva, forgive him. If he sins against you seven times in the day, and seven times returns, saying, 'I'm sorry,' you shall forgive him."

Faith (17:5-10)

The shaliachs said to me, "Increase our faith." I said, "If you had faith like a grain of mustard seed, you would tell this sycamore tree, 'Be uprooted and be planted in the sea,' and it would shema to you.

But who is there among you, having a servant ploughing or keeping sheep, that will say when he comes in from the field, 'Come immediately and sit down at the table'? Wouldn't he rather tell him, 'Prepare my dinner, clothe yourself properly, and serve me while I eat and drink. Afterward you shall eat and drink'? Does he thank that servant because he did the things that were commanded? I think not. Even so you also, when you have done all the things that are commanded you, say, 'We are unworthy servants. We have done our duty.'"

Ten Lepers (17:11-19)

As I was on my way to Yerushalaim, I was passing along the borders of Shomron and the Galil. As I entered into a certain village, ten men who were lepers met me, who stood at a distance. They lifted up their voices, saying, "Yeshua, Master, have mercy on us!" When I saw them, I said to them, "Go and show yourselves to the kohanim." As they went, they were cleansed.

One of them, when he saw that he was healed, turned back, praising God with a loud voice. He fell on his face at my feet, giving me thanks; and he was a Shomroni. I answered, "Weren't the ten cleansed? But where are the nine? Were there none found who returned to give glory to God, except this foreigner?" Then I said to him, "Get up, and go your way. Your faith has healed you."

Where (17:20-37)

Being asked by the Prushim when God's kingdom would come, I answered them, "God's kingdom doesn't come with observation; neither will they say, 'Hinei, here!' or, 'Hinei, there!' for hinei! God's kingdom is within you."

I said to the talmidim, "The days will come when you will desire to see one of the days of the Ben-Adam, and you will not see it. They will tell you, 'Hinei, here!' or 'Hinei, there!' Don't go away or follow after them, for as the lightning, when it flashes out of one part under the sky, shines to another part under the sky so will I, the Ben-Adam, be in my day. But first, I must suffer many things and be rejected by this generation.

As it was in the days of Noach, even so it will also be in the days of the Ben-Adam. They ate, they drank, they married, and they were given in marriage until the day that Noach entered into the ship, and the flood came and destroyed them all. Likewise, even as it was in the days of Lot: they ate, they drank, they bought, they sold, they planted, they built; but in the day that Lot went out from Sodom, it rained fire and sulphur from the sky and destroyed them all. It will be the same way in the day that I, the Ben-Adam, am revealed.

In that day, he who will be on the housetop and his goods in the house, let him not go down to take them away. Let him who is in the field likewise not turn back. Remember Lot's wife! Whoever seeks to save his life loses it, but whoever loses his life preserves it. I tell you, in that night there will be two people in one bed. One will be taken and the other will be left. There will be two grinding grain together. One will be taken and the other will be left." They, answering, asked me, "Where, Master?" I said to them, "Where the body is, there the vultures will also be gathered together."

Mashal: Judge (18:1-8)

I also spoke a mashal to them that they must always daven and not give up, saying, "There was a judge in a certain city who didn't fear God and didn't respect man. A widow was in that city, and she often came to him, saying, 'Defend me from my adversary!' He wouldn't for a while; but afterward he said to himself, 'Though I neither fear God nor respect man, yet because this widow bothers me, I will defend her, or else she will wear me out by her continual coming.'"

I said, "Listen to what the unrighteous judge says. Won't God avenge his chosen who are crying out to him day and night, and yet he exercises patience with them? I tell you that he will avenge them quickly. Nevertheless, when I, the Ben-Adam, come, will I find faith on the earth?"

Mashal: Tax Collector (18:9-14)

I also spoke this mashal to certain people who were convinced of their own righteousness, and who despised all others: "Two men went up into the Beit HaMikdash to daven; one was a Parush, and the other was a tax collector. The Parush stood and davened by himself like this: 'God, modeh ani that I am not like the rest of men: extortionists, unrighteous, adulterers, or even like this tax collector. I fast twice a week. I give tithes of all that I get.'

But the tax collector, standing far away, wouldn't even lift up his eyes to heaven, but beat his chest, saying, 'God, be merciful to me, a sinner!' I tell you, this man went down to his house justified rather than the other; for everyone who exalts himself will be humbled, but he who humbles himself will be exalted."

Babies (18:15-17)

They were also bringing their babies to me, that I might touch them. But when the talmidim saw it, they rebuked them. I summoned them, saying, "Allow the little children to come to me, and don't hinder them, for my kingdom belongs to such as these. Most certainly, I tell you, whoever doesn't receive my kingdom like a little child, he will in no way enter into it."

Rich Man (18:18-30)

A certain ruler asked me, saying, "Good Rabbi, what shall I do to live forever?" I asked him, "Why do you call me good? No one is good, except one: God. You know the mitzvot: 'Don't commit adultery,' 'Don't murder,' 'Don't steal,' 'Don't give false testimony,' 'Honour your father and your mother.'" He said, "I have observed all these things from my youth up." When I heard these things, I said to him, "You still lack one thing. Sell all that you have and distribute it to the poor. Then you will have treasure in heaven; then come, follow me."

But when he heard these things, he became very sad, for he was very rich. Seeing that he became very sad, I said, "How hard it is for those who have riches to enter into my kingdom! For it is easier for a camel to enter in through a needle's eye than for a rich man to enter into my kingdom." Those who heard it said, "Then who can be saved?" But I said, "The things which are impossible with men are possible with God."

Peter said, "Hinei! We have left everything and followed you." I said to them, "Most certainly I tell you, there is no one who has left house, or wife, or brothers, or parents, or children, for my kingdom's sake, who will not receive many times more in this olam, and in the olam to come, will live forever."

Aside (18:31-34)

I took the Twelve aside and said to them, "Hinei! We are going up to Yerushalaim, and all the things that are written through the prophets concerning me, the Ben-Adam, will be completed. For I will be handed over to the goyim, will be mocked, treated shamefully, and spit on. They will scourge and kill me. On the third day, I will rise again."

They understood none of these things. This saying was hidden from them, and they didn't understand the things that were said.

Blind Man (18:35-43)

As I came near Jericho, a certain blind man sat by the road, begging. Hearing a crowd going by, he asked what this meant. They told him that I was passing by. He cried out, "Yeshua, Ben-David, have mercy on me!" Those who led the way rebuked him, that he should be quiet; but he cried out all the more, "Ben-David, have mercy on me!"

Standing still, I commanded him to be brought to me. When he had come near, I asked him, "What do you want me to do?" He said, "Master, that I may see again." I said to him, "Receive your sight. Your faith has healed you." Immediately he received his sight and followed me, praising God.

All the people, when they saw it, praised God.

Zakkai (19:1-10)

I entered and was passing through Jericho. There was a man named Zakkai. He was a chief tax collector, and he was rich. He was trying to see who I was, and couldn't because of the crowd, because he was short. He ran on ahead and climbed up into a sycamore tree to see me, for I was going to pass that way. When I came to the place, I looked up and saw him, and said to him, "Zakkai, hurry and come down, for today I must stay at your house!" He hurried, came down, and received me joyfully.

When they saw it, they all murmured, saying, "He has gone in to lodge with a man who is a sinner." Zakkai stood and said to me, "Hinei! Master, half of my goods I give to the poor. If I have wrongfully exacted anything of anyone, I restore four times as much!" I said to him, "Today, yeshua has come to this house, because he also is a Ben-Avraham! For I, the Ben-Adam, came to seek and to save that which was lost."

Mashal: Ten Servants (19:11-27)

As they heard these things, I went on and told a mashal, because I was near Yerushalaim, and they supposed that God's kingdom would be revealed immediately.

I said therefore, "A certain nobleman went into a far country to receive for himself a kingdom and to return. He called ten servants of his and gave them ten pounds of silver, and told them, 'Conduct business until I come.' But his citizens hated him, and sent an envoy after him, saying, 'We don't want this man to reign over us.'

When he had come back again, having received the kingdom, he commanded these servants, to whom he had given the money, to be called to him, that he might know what they had gained by conducting business. The first came before him, saying, 'Master, your pound of silver has made ten more pounds.' He said to him, 'Well done, you good servant! Because you were found faithful with very little, you shall have authority over ten cities.' The second came, saying, 'Your pound of silver, Master, has made five pounds.' So he said to him, 'And you are to be over five cities.'

Another came, saying, 'Master, hinei! Your pound of silver, which I kept laid away in a handkerchief, for I feared you, because you are an exacting man. You take up that which you didn't lay down, and reap that which you didn't sow.' He said to him, 'Out of your own mouth I will judge you, you wicked servant! You knew that I am an exacting man, taking up that which I didn't lay down and reaping that which I didn't sow. Then why didn't you deposit my money in the bank, and at my coming, I might have earned interest on it?' He said to those who stood by, 'Take the pound away from him and give it to him who has the ten pounds.' They said to him, 'Master, he has ten pounds!' 'For I tell you that to everyone who has, will more be given; but from him who doesn't have, even that which he has will be taken away from him. But bring those enemies of mine who didn't want me to reign over them here, and kill them before me.'"

Yerushalaim (19:28-44)

Having said these things, I went on ahead, going up to Yerushalaim. When I came near to Beit-Pagei and Beit-Hini, at the hill that is called Olives, I sent two of my talmidim, saying, "Go your way into the village on the other side, in which, as you enter, you will find a colt tied, which no man has ever sat upon. Untie it and bring it. If anyone asks you, 'Why are you untying it?' say to him: 'The Master needs it.'" Those who were sent went away and found things just as I had told them. As they were untying the colt, its owners said to them, "Why are you untying the colt?" They said, "The Master needs it." Then they brought it to me.

They threw their cloaks on the colt and sat me on them. As I went, they spread their cloaks on the road. As I was now getting near, at the descent of the Hill of Olives, the whole crowd of the talmidim began to rejoice and praise God with a loud voice for all the miracles which they had seen, saying, "Blessed is the King who comes in the name of Hashem! Shalom in heaven, and glory in the highest!"

Some of the Prushim from the crowd said to me, "Rabbi, rebuke your talmidim!" I answered them, "I tell you that if these were silent, the stones would cry out."

When I came near, I saw the city and wept over it, saying, "If you, even you, had known today the things which would make for your shalom! But now, they are hidden from your eyes. For the days will come on you when your enemies will throw up a barricade against you, surround you, hem you in on every side, and will dash you and your children within you to the ground. They will not leave in you one stone on another, because you didn't know the moed of your visitation."

Beit HaMikdash (19:45-48)

I entered into the Beit HaMikdash and began to drive out those who bought and sold in it, saying to them, "It is written, 'My house is a house of tefillah,' but you have made it a 'den of robbers'!"

I was teaching daily in the Beit HaMikdash, but the chief kohanim, the scholars, and the leading men among the people sought to destroy me. They couldn't find what they might do, for all the people hung on to every word that I said.

Smicha (20:1-8)

On one of those days, as I was teaching the people in the Beit HaMikdash and proclaiming the Besorah, the kohanim and scholars came to me with the elders. They asked me, "Tell us: by what authority do you do these things? Or who is giving you smicha?" I answered them, "I also will ask you one question. Tell me: the mikvah of Yochanan, was it from heaven, or from men?" They reasoned with themselves, saying, "If we say, 'From heaven,' he will say, 'Why didn't you believe him?' But if we say, 'From men,' all the people will stone us, for they are persuaded that Yochanan was a prophet." They answered that they didn't know where it was from. I said to them, "Neither will I tell you by what authority I do these things."

Mashal: Vineyard (20:9-19)

I began to tell the people this mashal: "A man planted a vineyard and rented it out to some farmers, and went into another country for a long time. At the proper season, he sent a servant to the farmers to collect his share of the fruit of the vineyard. But the farmers beat him and sent him away empty. He sent yet another servant, and they also beat him and treated him shamefully, and sent him away empty. He sent yet a third, and they also wounded him and threw him out.

The master of the vineyard said, 'What shall I do? I will send my beloved Son. It may be that seeing him, they will respect him.' But when the farmers saw him, they reasoned among themselves, saying, 'This is the heir. Come, let's kill him, that the inheritance may be ours.' Then they threw him out of the vineyard and killed him.

What therefore will the master of the vineyard do to them? He will come and destroy these farmers, and will give the vineyard to others." When they heard that, they said, "May that never be!" But I looked at them and said, "Then what is this that is written,

'The stone which the builders rejected was made the chief cornerstone?' Everyone who falls on that stone will be broken to pieces, but it will crush whomever it falls on to dust."

The chief kohanim and the scholars sought to lay hands on me that very hour, but they feared the people—for they knew I had spoken this mashal against them.

Spies (20:20-26)

They watched me and sent out spies, who pretended to be tzaddikim, that they might trap me in something I said, so as to deliver me up to the power and authority of the governor. They asked me, "Rabbi, we know that you say and teach what is right, and aren't partial to anyone, but truly teach the way of God. Is it lawful for us to pay taxes to Caesar, or not?" But I perceived their craftiness, and said to them, "Why do you test me? Show me a denarius coin. Whose image and inscription are on it?" They answered, "Caesar's." I said to them, "Then give to Caesar the things that are Caesar's, and to God the things that are God's."

They weren't able to trap me in my words before the people. They marvelled at my answer and were silent.

Tzadukim (20:27-38)

Some of the Tzadukim came to me, those who deny that there is a resurrection. They asked me, "Rabbi, Moshe wrote to us that if a man's brother dies having a wife, and he is childless, his brother should take the wife and raise up children for his brother. There were therefore seven brothers. The first took a wife, and died childless. The second took her as wife, and he died childless. The third took her, and likewise the seven all left no children, and died. Afterward the woman also died. Therefore in the resurrection whose wife of them will she be? For the seven had her as a wife."

I said to them, "The children of this olam marry and are given in marriage. But those who are considered worthy to attain to that olam and the resurrection from the dead neither marry nor are given in marriage. For they can't die anymore, for they are like the messengers and are Bnei-Elohim, being children of the resurrection.

But that the dead are raised, even Moshe showed at the bush, when he called Hashem 'The God of Avraham, the God of Yitzchak, and the God of Yaakov.' Now he is not the God of the dead, but of the living, for all are alive to him."

Scholars (20:39-47)

Some of the scholars answered, "Rabbi, you speak well." They didn't dare to ask me any more questions. I said to them, "Why do they say that the Mashiach is David's son? David himself says in Sefer-Tehillim, 'Hashem said to my Master, "Sit at my right hand, until I make your enemies the footstool of your feet."' David therefore calls him Master, so how is he his son?"

In the hearing of all the people, I said to my talmidim, "Beware of those scholars who like to walk in long robes, and love greetings in the shuk, the best seats at shul, and the best places at feasts; who devour widows' houses, and for a pretence make long tefillot. These will receive greater condemnation."

Widow (21:1-4)

I looked up and saw the rich people who were putting their gifts into the treasury. I saw a certain poor widow casting in two tiny coins. I said, "Truly I tell you, this poor widow put in more than all of them, for all these put in gifts for God from their abundance, but she, out of her poverty, put in all that she had to live on!"

The End (21:5-19)

As some were talking about the Beit HaMikdash and how it was decorated with beautiful stones and gifts, I said, "As for these things which you see, the days will come in which there will not be left here one stone on another that will not be thrown down." They asked me, "Rabbi, so when will these things be? What is the sign that these things are about to happen?" I said, "Watch out that you don't get led astray, for many will come in my name, saying, 'I am he,' and, 'The moed is at hand.' Therefore don't follow them. When you hear of wars and disturbances, don't be terrified, for these things must happen first, but the end won't come immediately."

Then I said to them, "Nation will rise against nation, and kingdom against kingdom. There will be great earthquakes, famines, and plagues in various places. There will be terrors and great signs from heaven. But before all these things, they will lay their hands on you and will persecute you, delivering you up to synagogues and prisons, bringing you before kings and governors for my name's sake. It will turn out as a testimony for you. Settle it therefore in your hearts not to meditate beforehand how to answer, for I will give you a mouth and wisdom which all your adversaries will not be able to withstand or to contradict.

You will be handed over even by parents, brothers, mishpacha, and friends. They will cause some of you to be put to death. You will be hated by all men for my name's sake. And not a hair of your head will perish. By your endurance you will win your lives.

Yerushalaim (21:20-24)

"But when you see Yerushalaim surrounded by armies, then know that its desolation is at hand. Then let those who are in Judea flee to the mountains. Let those who are in the middle of her depart. Let those who are in the country not enter therein.

For these are days of vengeance, that all things which are written may be fulfilled.

Oy to those who are pregnant and to those who nurse infants in those days! For there will be great distress in the land and wrath to this people. They will fall by the edge of the sword, and will be led captive into all the goyim. Yerushalaim will be trampled down by the goyim until the times of the goyim are fulfilled.

My Coming (21:25-36)

"There will be signs in the sun, moon, and stars; and on the earth anxiety among goyim, in perplexity for the roaring of the sea and the waves; men fainting for fear and for expectation of the things which are coming on the world, for the powers of the heavens will be shaken. Then they will see me, the Ben-Adam, coming in a cloud with power and great glory. But when these things begin to happen, look up and lift up your heads, because your redemption is near."

I told them a mashal. "See the fig tree and all the trees. When they are already budding, you see it and know by your own selves that the summer is already near. Even so you also, when you see these things happening, know that my kingdom is near. Most certainly I tell you, this people will not pass away until all things are accomplished. Heaven and earth will pass away, but my words will by no means pass away.

So be careful, or your hearts will be loaded down with carousing, drunkenness, and cares of this life, and that day will come on you suddenly. For it will come like a snare on all those who dwell on the surface of all the earth. Therefore be watchful all the time, praying that you may be counted worthy to escape all these things that will happen, and to stand before me, the Ben-Adam."

Yehuda (21:37-22:6)

Every day I was teaching in the Beit HaMikdash, and every night I would go out and spend the night on the hill that is called Olives. All the people came early in the morning to me in the Beit HaMikdash to hear me.

Now the Festival of Matzot, which is called Pesach, was approaching. The chief kohanim and the scholars sought how they might put me to death, for they feared the people. The antagonist entered into Yehuda, who was also called Ish-Kriyot, who was counted with the Twelve. He went away and talked with the chief kohanim and captains about how he might deliver me to them. They were glad, and agreed to give him money. He consented and sought an opportunity to deliver me to them in the absence of the crowd.

Pesach (22:7-23)

The day of Matzot came, on which the Pesach must be sacrificed. I sent Peter and Yochanan, saying, "Go and prepare the Pesach for us, that we may eat." They said to me, "Where do you want us to prepare?" I said to them, "Hinei! When you have entered into the city, a man carrying a pitcher of water will meet you. Follow him into the house which he enters. Tell the master of the house, 'The Rabbi says to you, "Where is the guest room, where I may eat the Pesach with my talmidim?"' He will show you a large, furnished upper room. Make preparations there." They went, found things as I had told them, and they prepared the Pesach.

When the hour had come, I sat down with the twelve shaliachs. I said to them, "I have earnestly desired to eat this Pesach with you before I suffer, for I tell you, I will no longer by any means eat of it until it is fulfilled in my kingdom." I received a cup, and when I had made the bracha, I said, "Take this and share it among yourselves, for I tell you, I will not drink at all again from the 'pri ha'gafen', until my kingdom comes."

I took matzah, and when I had made the bracha, I broke and gave it to them, saying, "This is my body which is given for you. Do this in memory of me." Likewise, I took the cup after dinner, saying, "This cup is the renewed brit in my blood, which is poured out for you. But hinei! The hand of him who betrays me is with me on the table. I, the Ben-Adam, indeed am going as it has been determined, but oy to that man through whom I am betrayed!" They began to question among themselves which of them it was who would do this thing.

Greatest (22:24-34)

A dispute also arose among them, which of them was considered to be greatest. I said to them, "The kings of the goyim lord it over them, and those who have authority over them are called 'benefactors.' But not so with you. Rather, the one who is greater among you, let him become as the younger, and one who is governing, as one who serves. For who is greater, the one who sits at the table, or the one who serves? Isn't it he who sits at the table? But I am among you as the one who serves.

But you are those who have continued with me in my trials. I confer on you a kingdom, even as my Abba conferred on me, that you may eat and drink at my table in my kingdom. You will sit on thrones, judging the twelve tribes of Israel."

I said, "Shimon, Shimon, hinei! The antagonist asked to have each of you, that he might sift you as wheat, but I prayed for you, that your faith wouldn't fail. You, when once you have returned, strengthen your brothers." He said to me, "Master, I am ready to go with you both to prison and to death!" I said, "I tell you, Peter, the rooster will by no means crow today until you deny that you know me three times."

Olives (22:35-46)

I said to them, "When I sent you out without purse, bag, and sandals, did you lack anything?" They said, "Nothing." Then I said to them, "But now, whoever has a purse, let him take it, and likewise a bag. Whoever has none, let him sell his cloak, and buy a sword. For I tell you that this which is written must still be fulfilled in me: 'He was counted with transgressors.' For that which concerns me is being fulfilled." They said, "Master, hinei! Here are two swords." I said to them, "That is enough."

I came out and went, as my custom was, to the Hill of Olives. My talmidim also followed me. When I was at the place, I said to them, "Pray that you don't enter into temptation." I was withdrawn from them about a stone's throw, and I knelt down and prayed, saying, "Abba, if you are willing, remove this cup from me. Nevertheless, not my will, but yours, be done."

A messenger from heaven appeared to me, strengthening me. Being in agony, I prayed more earnestly. My sweat became like great drops of blood falling down on the ground. When I rose up from my tefillah, I came to the talmidim and found them sleeping because of grief, and said to them, "Why do you sleep? Rise and pray that you may not enter into temptation."

Betrayal (22:47-53)

While I was still speaking, a crowd appeared. He who was called Yehuda, one of the Twelve, was leading them. He came near to me to kiss me. But I said to him, "Yehuda, do you betray me, the Ben-Adam, with a kiss?"

When those who were around me saw what was about to happen, they said to me, "Master, shall we strike with the sword?" A certain one of them struck the servant of the Kohen Gadol, and cut off his right ear. But I answered, "Let me at least do this"—and I touched his ear and healed him.

I said to the chief kohanim, captains of the Beit HaMikdash, and elders, who had come against me, "Have you come out as against a robber, with swords and clubs? When I was with you in the Beit HaMikdash daily, you didn't stretch out your hands against me. But this is your hour, and the power of darkness."

Peter's Denial (22:54-62)

They seized me and led me away, and brought me into the Kohen Gadol's house. But Peter followed from a distance. When they had kindled a fire in the middle of the courtyard and had sat down together, Peter sat among them.

A certain servant girl saw him as he sat in the light, and looking intently at him, said, "This man also was with him." He denied me, saying, "Woman, I don't know him." After a little while someone else saw him and said, "You also are one of them!" But Peter answered, "Man, I am not!" After about one hour passed, another confidently affirmed, saying, "Truly this man also was with him, for he is a Galilean!" But Peter said, "Man, I don't know what you are talking about!" Immediately, while he was still speaking, a rooster crowed.

I turned and looked at Peter. Then Peter remembered my word, how I said to him, "Before the rooster crows you will deny me three times." He went out, and wept bitterly.

Sanhedrin (22:63-71)

The men who held me mocked me and beat me. Having blindfolded me, they struck me on the face and asked me, "Prophesy! Who is the one who struck you?" They spoke many other things against me, insulting me.

As soon as it was day, the assembly of the elders of the people were gathered together, both chief kohanim and scholars, and they led me away into their Sanhedrin, saying, "If you are the Mashiach, tell us." But I said to them, "If I tell you, you won't believe, and if I ask, you will in no way answer me or let me go. From now on I, the Ben-Adam, will be seated at the right hand of the power of God." They all said, "Are you then the Ben-Elohim?" I said to them, "You say it, because I am." They said, "Why do we need any more witness? For we ourselves have heard from his own mouth!"

Pilate & Herod (23:1-12)

The whole company of them rose up and brought me before Pilate. They began to accuse me, saying, "We found this man perverting the nation, forbidding paying taxes to Caesar, and saying that he himself is Mashiach, a king." Pilate asked me, "Are you the King of the Jewish people?" I answered him, "So you say."

Pilate said to the chief kohanim and the crowds, "I find no basis for a charge against this man." But they insisted, saying, "He stirs up the people, teaching throughout all Judea, beginning from the Galil even to this place." But when Pilate heard the Galil mentioned, he asked if the man was a Galilean. When he found out that I was in Herod's jurisdiction, he sent me to Herod, who was also in Yerushalaim during those days.

Now when Herod saw me, he was exceedingly glad, for he had wanted to see me for a long time, because he had heard many things about me. He hoped to see some miracle done by me. He questioned me with many words, but I gave no answers. The chief kohanim and the scholars stood, vehemently accusing me. Herod with his soldiers humiliated me and mocked me. Dressing me in luxurious clothing, they sent me back to Pilate. Herod and Pilate became friends with each other that very day, for before that they were enemies with each other.

Bar-Abba (23:13-25)

Pilate called together the chief kohanim, the leaders, and the people, and said to them, "You brought this man to me as someone that perverts the people, and look! Having examined him before you, I found no basis for a charge against this man concerning those things of which you accuse him. Neither has Herod, for I sent you to him, and see, nothing worthy of death has been done by him. I will therefore chastise him and release him."

Now he had to release one prisoner to them at the Festival. But they all cried out together, saying, "Away with this man! Release to us Bar-Abba!"— one who was thrown into prison for a certain revolt in the city, and for murder. Then Pilate spoke to them again, wanting to release me, but they shouted, saying, "Crucify! Crucify him!" He said to them the third time, "Why? What evil has this man done? I have found no capital crime in him. I will therefore chastise him and release him." But they were urgent with loud voices, asking that he might be crucified.

Their voices and the voices of the chief kohanim prevailed. Pilate decreed that what they asked for should be done. He released him who had been thrown into prison for insurrection and murder, for whom they asked, but he handed me over to their will.

Crucifixion (23:26-43)

When they led me away, they grabbed a certain Shimon of Cyrene, coming from the country, and laid the cross on him to carry it after me.

A great crowd of the people followed me, including women who also mourned and lamented me. But, turning to them, I said, "Daughters of Yerushalaim, don't weep for me, but weep for yourselves and for your children. For hinei! The days are coming in which they will say, 'Ashrei are the barren, the wombs that never bore, and the breasts that never nursed.' Then they will begin to tell the mountains, 'Fall on us!' and tell the hills, 'Cover us.' For if they do these things in the green tree, what will be done in the dry?"

There were also others, two criminals, led with me to be put to death. When we came to the place that is called "The Skull", they crucified me there with the criminals, one on the right and the other on the left. I said, "Abba, forgive them, for they don't know what they are doing!" Dividing my garments among them, they cast lots.

The people stood watching. The leaders with them also scoffed at me, saying, "He saved others. Let him save himself, if this is God's Mashiach, his chosen one!" The soldiers also mocked me, coming to me and offering me vinegar, and saying, "If you are the King of the Jewish people, save yourself!"

An inscription was also written over me in letters of Greek, Latin, and Hebrew: "THIS IS THE KING OF THE JEWISH PEOPLE." One of the criminals who was hanged insulted me, saying, "If you are the Mashiach, save yourself and us!" But the other answered, and rebuking him said, "Don't you even fear God, seeing you are under the same condemnation? And we indeed justly, for we receive the due reward for our deeds, but this man has done nothing wrong." He said to me, "Master, remember me when you come into your kingdom." I said to him, "Assuredly I tell you, today you will be with me in the Pardes."

Death (23:44-49)

It was now about the sixth hour, and darkness came over the whole land until the ninth hour. The sun was darkened, and the veil of the Mikdash was torn in two. Crying with a loud voice, I said, "Abba, into your hands I commit my ruach!" Having said this, I breathed my last.

When the centurion saw what was done, he praised God, saying, "Certainly this was a righteous man." All the crowds that came together to see this, when they saw the things that were done, returned home beating their breasts. All my acquaintances and the women who followed with me from the Galil stood at a distance, watching these things.

Burial (23:50-56)

Hinei! There was a man named Yosef, who was a member of the Sanhedrin, a good man and a tzaddik (he had not consented to their counsel and deed), from Ramatayim, a city of the Judeans, who was also waiting for God's kingdom. This man went to Pilate, and asked for my body. He took it down and wrapped it in a linen cloth, and laid me in a tomb that was cut in stone, where no one had ever been laid.

It was the day of the Preparation, and Shabbat was drawing near. The women who had come with me out of the Galil followed after, and saw the tomb and how my body was laid. They returned and prepared spices and ointments. On Shabbat they rested according to the mitzvah.

Dawn (24:1-12)

But on the first day of the week, at early dawn, they and some others came to the tomb, bringing the spices which they had prepared. They found the stone rolled away from the tomb. They entered in, and didn't find my body. While they were greatly perplexed about this, hinei! Two men stood by them in dazzling clothing. Becoming terrified, they bowed their faces down to the earth. The men said to them, "Why do you seek the living among the dead? He isn't here, but is risen. Remember what he told you when he was still in the Galil, saying that the Ben-Adam must be handed over into the hands of sinful men and be crucified, and the third day rise again?"

They remembered my words, returned from the tomb, and told all these things to the Eleven and to all the rest. Now they were Miriam from Magdala, Yochana, and Miriam the eema of Yaakov. The other women with them told these things to the shaliachs. These words seemed to them to be nonsense, and they didn't believe them. But Peter got up and ran to the tomb. Stooping and looking in, he saw the strips of linen lying by themselves, and he departed to his home, wondering what had happened.

Emmaus (24:13-35)

Hinei! Two of them were going that very day to a village named Emmaus, which was seven miles from Yerushalaim. They talked with each other about all of these things which had happened. While they talked and questioned together, I myself came near, and went with them. But their eyes were kept from recognizing me.

I said to them, "What are you talking about as you walk, and are sad?" One of them, named Chalfai, answered me, "Are you the only stranger in Yerushalaim who doesn't know the things which have happened there in these days?" I said to them, "What things?" They said to me, "The things concerning Yeshua of Natzeret, who was a prophet mighty in deed and word before God and all the people; and how the chief kohanim and our leaders handed him over to be condemned to death, and crucified him. But we were hoping that it was he who would redeem Israel. Yes, and besides all this, it is now the third day since these things happened. Also, certain women of our company amazed us, having arrived early at the tomb; and when they didn't find his body, they came saying that they had also seen a vision of messengers, who said that he was alive. Some of us went to the tomb and found it just like the women had said, but they didn't see him."

I said to them, "Foolish people, and slow of heart to believe in all that the prophets have spoken! Didn't the Mashiach have to suffer these things and to enter into his glory?" Beginning from Moshe and from all the prophets, I explained to them in all the Tanach the things concerning myself.

We came near to the village where they were going, and I acted like I would go further. They urged me, saying, "Stay with us, for it is almost evening, and the day is almost over." I went in to stay with them. When I had sat down at the table with them, I took the matzah and made the bracha. Breaking it, I gave it to them. Their eyes were opened and they recognized me; then I vanished out of their sight.

They said to one another, "Weren't our hearts burning within us while he spoke to us along the way, and while he opened the Tanach to us?" They rose up that very hour, returned to Yerushalaim, and found the Eleven gathered together, and those who were with them, saying, "The Master is risen indeed, and has appeared to Shimon!" They related the things that happened along the way, and how I was recognized by them in the breaking of the matzah.

Myself (24:36-45)

As they said these things, I myself stood among them, and said to them, "Shalom aleichem!" But they were terrified and filled with fear, and supposed that they had seen a spirit. I said to them, "Why are you troubled? Why do doubts arise in your hearts? See my hands and my feet, that it is truly me. Touch me and see, for a spirit doesn't have flesh and bones, as you see that I have." When I had said this, I showed them my hands and my feet. While they still didn't believe for joy, and wondered, I said to them, "Do you have anything here to eat?" They gave me a piece of a broiled fish and some honeycomb. I took them, and ate in front of them.

I said to them, "This is what I told you while I was still with you, that all things which are written in the Torah of Moshe, the Prophets, and Tehillim concerning me must be fulfilled." Then I opened their minds, that they might understand the Tanach.

Heaven (24:46-53)

I said to them, "Thus it is written, and thus it was necessary for me, the Mashiach, to suffer and to rise from the dead the third day, and that returning in teshuva and forgiveness of sins should be preached in my name to all the goyim, beginning at Yerushalaim. You are witnesses of these things. Hinei! I send out the promise of my Abba on you. But wait in the city of Yerushalaim until you are clothed with power from on high."

I led them out as far as Beit-Hini, and I lifted up my hands and blessed them. While I blessed them, I withdrew from them and was carried up into heaven. They bowed down to me and returned to Yerushalaim with great joy, and were continually in the Beit HaMikdash, praising and blessing God.

AS TOLD TO YOCHANAN

The Word (1:1-18)

In the beginning was me, the Word; and I was with God, and I was God. I was in the beginning with God. All things were made through me. Without me, nothing was made that has been made. In me was life, and the life was the light of men. The light shines in the darkness, and the darkness hasn't overcome it.

There came a man sent from God, whose name was Yochanan. He came as a witness, that he might testify about the light, that all might believe through him. He was not the light, but was sent that he might testify about the light. The true light that enlightens everyone was coming into the world.

I was in the world, and the world was made through me, and the world didn't recognize me. I came to my own, and those who were my own didn't receive me. But as many as received me, to them I gave the right to become Bnei-Elohim, to those who believe in my name: who were born, not of blood, nor of the will of the flesh, nor of the will of man, but of God.

I, the Word, became flesh and lived among them. They saw my glory, such glory as of the unique Son of the Father, full of grace and truth. Yochanan testified about me. He cried out, saying, "This was he of whom I said, 'He who comes after me has surpassed me, for he was before me.'"

From my fullness they all received grace upon grace. For the Torah was given through Moshe. Grace and truth were realized through me, the Mashiach. No one has seen God at any time. I, the unique Son, who am in the bosom of my Abba, have declared him.

Yochanan (1:19-28)

This is Yochanan's testimony, when the Judeans sent kohanim and Levites from Yerushalaim to ask him, "Who are you?" He declared, and didn't deny, but he declared, "I am not the Mashiach." They asked him, "What then? Are you Eliyahu?" He said, "I am not." "Are you the Prophet?" He answered, "No." They said therefore to him, "Who are you? Give us an answer to take back to those who sent us. What do you say about yourself?" He said, "I am the voice of someone crying in the wilderness, 'Make straight the way of Hashem,' as Yeshaya the prophet said."

Those who had been sent were from the Prushim. They asked him, "Why then do you immerse if you are not the Mashiach, nor Eliyahu, nor the Prophet?" Yochanan answered them, "I immerse in water, but among you stands someone whom you don't know. He is the one who comes after me, who is preferred before me, whose sandal strap I'm not worthy to loosen."

These things were done in Beit-Anya beyond the Yarden, where Yochanan was immersing.

This Is He (1:29-34)

The next day, he saw me coming to him, and said, "Hinei! The Lamb of God, who takes away the sin of the world! This is he of whom I said, 'After me comes a man who is preferred before me, for he was before me.' I didn't know him, but for this reason I came immersing in water, that he would be revealed to Israel."

Yochanan testified, saying, "I have seen the Ruach descending like a dove out of heaven, and it stayed on him. I didn't recognize him, but he who sent me to immerse in water said to me, 'He on whom you will see the Ruach descending and staying, this is he who immerses in Ruach HaKodesh.' I have seen and have testified that this is the Ben-Elohim."

Andrew & Shimon (1:35-42)

Again, the next day, Yochanan was standing with two of his talmidim, and he looked at me as I walked, and said, "Hinei, the Lamb of God!" The two talmidim heard him speak, and they followed me. I turned and saw them following, and said to them, "What are you looking for?" They said to me, "Rabbi" (which is to say, being translated, Teacher), "where are you staying?" I said to them, "Come and see." They came and saw where I was staying, and they stayed with me that day. It was about the tenth hour.

One of the two who heard Yochanan and followed me was Andrew, Shimon Peter's brother. He first found his own brother, Shimon, and said to him, "We have found the Mashiach!" (which is, being translated, Anointed One). He brought him to me. I looked at him and said, "You are Shimon Ben-Yonah. You shall be called Kefa" (which is by translation, Rock).

Philip & Netanel (1:43-51)

On the next day, I was determined to go out into the Galil, and I found Philip. I said to him, "Follow me." Now Philip was from Beit-Tzaida, the city of Andrew and Peter. Philip found Netanel, and said to him, "We have found him of whom Moshe in the Torah and also the prophets, wrote: Yeshua Ben-Yosef, from Natzeret!" Netanel said to him, "Can any good thing come out of Natzeret?" Philip said to him, "Come and see."

I saw Netanel coming to me, and said about him, "Hinei! An Israelite indeed, in whom is no deceit!" Netanel said to me, "How do you know me?" I answered him, "Before Philip called you, when you were under the fig tree, I saw you." Netanel answered me, "Rabbi, you are the Ben-Elohim! You are the Melech-

Yisrael!" I answered him, "Because I told you, 'I saw you underneath the fig tree,' do you believe? You will see greater things than these!" I said to him, "Most certainly, I tell you all, hereafter you will see heaven opened, and the messengers of God ascending and descending on me, the Ben-Adam."

Wedding in Kana (2:1-12)

The third day, there was a wedding in Kana in the Galil. My eema was there. I also was invited, with my talmidim, to the wedding. When the wine ran out, my eema said to me, "They have no wine." I said to her, "Woman, what does that have to do with you and me? My hour has not yet come." My eema said to the servants, "Whatever he says to you, do it."

Now there were six water pots of stone set there after the Jewish people's way of purifying, containing twenty to thirty gallons apiece. I said to them, "Fill the water pots with water." So they filled them up to the brim. I said to them, "Now draw some out, and take it to the master of ceremonies." So they took it.

When the master of ceremonies tasted the water now become wine, and didn't know where it came from (but the servants who had drawn the water knew), the master of ceremonies called the chattan and said to him, "Everyone serves the good wine first, and when the guests have drunk freely, then that which is worse. You have kept the good wine until now!"

This beginning of my signs I did in Kana in the Galil, and revealed my glory; and my talmidim believed in me. After this, I went down to Kfar-Nachum—I, and my eema, my brothers, and my talmidim; and we stayed there a few days.

Beit HaMikdash (2:13-25)

Pesach in Judea was at hand, and I went up to Yerushalaim. I found in the Beit HaMikdash those who sold oxen, sheep, and doves, and the changers of money sitting. I made a whip of cords and drove all out of the Beit HaMikdash, both the sheep and the oxen; and I poured out the changers' money and overthrew their tables. To those who sold the doves, I said, "Take these things out of here! Don't make my Abba's house a shuk!" My talmidim remembered that it was written, "Zeal for your house will eat me up."

The Judeans therefore answered me, "What sign do you show us, seeing that you do these things?" I answered them, "Destroy this mikdash, and in three days I will raise it up." The Judeans therefore said, "It took forty-six years to build this Mikdash! Will you raise it up in three days?" But I spoke of the mikdash of my body. When therefore I was raised from the dead, my talmidim remembered that I said this, and they believed the Tanach and the word which I had said.

Now when I was in Yerushalaim at Pesach, during the Festival, many believed in my name, observing my signs which I did. But I didn't entrust myself to them, because I knew everyone, and because I didn't need for anyone to testify concerning man; for I myself knew what was in man.

Nakdimon (3:1-21)

Now there was a man of the Prushim named Nakdimon, a leader of the Judeans. He came to me by night and said to me, "Rabbi, we know that you are a teacher come from God, for no one can do these signs that you do, unless God is with him."

I answered him, "Most certainly I tell you, unless someone is born anew, he can't see my kingdom." Nakdimon said to me, "How can a man be born when he is old? Can he enter a second time into his mother's womb and be born?" I answered, "Most certainly I tell you, unless someone is born of water and ruach, he can't enter into my kingdom. That which is born of the flesh is flesh. That which is born of the Ruach is ruach. Don't marvel that I said to you, 'You must be born anew.' The wind blows where it wants to, and you hear its sound, but don't know where it comes from and where it is going. So is everyone who is born of the Ruach."

Nakdimon answered me, "How can these things be?" I answered him, "Are you the teacher of Israel, and don't understand these things? Most certainly I tell you, we speak that which we know and testify of that which we have seen, and you people don't receive our witness. If I told you earthly things and you don't believe, how will you believe if I tell you heavenly things? No one has ascended into heaven but me, who descended out of heaven—I, the Ben-Adam, who am in heaven. As Moshe lifted up the serpent in the wilderness, even so must I, the Ben-Adam, be lifted up in hagbah, that whoever believes in me should not perish, but live forever. For God so loved the world, that he gave me, his unique Son, that whoever believes in me should not perish, but live forever.

For God didn't send me into the world to judge the world, but that the world should be saved through me. He who believes in me is not judged. He who doesn't believe has been judged already, because he has not believed in my name—the unique Ben-Elohim. This is the judgement, that the light has come into the world, and men loved the darkness rather than the light, for their actions were evil. For everyone who does evil hates the light and doesn't come to the light, lest his actions would be exposed. But he who does the truth comes to the light, that his actions may be revealed, that they have been done in God."

Yochanan (3:22-36)

After these things, I came with my talmidim into the land of Judea. I was staying there with them and immersing. Yochanan also was immersing in Einon near Shalem, because there was much water there. They were coming and were being immersed; for Yochanan was not yet thrown into prison.

Therefore a dispute arose on the part of Yochanan's talmidim with some Judeans about purification. They came to Yochanan and said to him, "Rabbi, he who was with you beyond the Yarden, to whom you have testified, hinei! He immerses, and everyone is coming to him." Yochanan answered, "A man can receive nothing unless it has been given him from heaven. You yourselves testify that I said, 'I am not the Mashiach,' but, 'I have been sent before him.' He who has the kallah is the chattan; but the shoshvin of the chattan, who stands and hears him, rejoices greatly because of the chattan's voice. Therefore my joy is made full. He must increase, but I must decrease."

I, who come from above, am above all. He who is from the earth belongs to the earth and speaks of the earth. I, who came from heaven, am above all. What I have seen and heard, of that I testify; and no one receives my witness. He who receives my witness sets his seal to this, that God is true. For I, whom God has sent, speak the words of God; for God gives the Ruach without measure. My Abba loves me, his Son, and has given all things into my hand. Anyone who believes in me, his Son, lives forever, but anyone who disobeys me won't see life, but the wrath of God remains on him.

Shomron (4:1-29)

Therefore when I knew that the Prushim had heard that I was making and immersing more talmidim than Yochanan (although I myself didn't immerse, but my talmidim), I left Judea and departed into the Galil. I needed to pass through Shomron. So I came to a city of Shomron called Shechem, near the parcel of ground that Yaakov gave to his son Yosef. Yaakov's well was there. I therefore, being tired from my journey, sat down by the well. It was about the sixth hour.

A woman of Shomron came to draw water. I said to her, "Give me a drink." For my talmidim had gone away into the city to buy food. The Shomroni woman therefore said to me, "How is it that you, being a Jewish person, ask for a drink from me, a Shomroni woman?" (For Jewish people have no dealings with Shomronim.) I answered her, "If you knew the gift of God, and who I am who says to you, 'Give me a drink,' you would have asked me, and I would have given you living water."

The woman said to me, "Sir, you have nothing to draw with, and the well is deep. So where do you get that living water? Are you greater than our father Yaakov, who gave us the well and drank from it himself, as did his children and his livestock?" I answered her, "Everyone who drinks of this water will thirst again, but whoever drinks of the water that I will give him will never thirst again; but the water that I will give him will become in him a well of water springing up to life forever."

The woman said to me, "Sir, give me this water, so that I don't get thirsty, neither come all the way here to draw." I said to her, "Go, call your husband, and come here." The woman answered, "I have no husband." I said to her, "You said well, 'I have no husband,' for you have had five husbands; and he whom you now have is not your husband. This you have said truly."

The woman said to me, "Sir, I perceive that you are a prophet. Our fathers worshipped in this mountain, and you Jewish people say that in Yerushalaim is the place where people ought to worship." I said to her, "Woman, believe me, the hour is coming when neither in this mountain nor in Yerushalaim will you worship my Abba. You worship that which you don't know. We worship that which we know; for yeshua is from the Jewish people. But the hour comes, and now is, when the true worshippers will worship my Abba in ruach and truth, for my Abba seeks such to be his worshippers. God is ruach, and those who worship him must worship in ruach and truth."

The woman said to me, "I know that the Mashiach is coming, he who is called the Anointed One. When he has come, he will declare to us all things." I said to her, "I am he, the one speaking to you!" Just then, my talmidim came. They marvelled that I was speaking with a woman; yet no one said, "What are you looking for?" or, "Why do you speak with her?" So the woman left her water pot, went away into the city, and said to the people, "Come, see a man who told me everything that I have done. Could this be the Mashiach?"

Shomronim (4:30-42)

They went out of the city, and were coming to me. In the meanwhile, the talmidim urged me, saying, "Rabbi, eat." But I said to them, "I have food to eat that you don't know about." The talmidim therefore said to one another, "Has anyone brought him something to eat?"

I said to them, "My food is to do the will of him who sent me and to accomplish his work. Don't you say, 'There are yet four months until the harvest?' Hinei! I tell you, lift up your eyes and look at the fields, that they are white for harvest already. He who reaps receives wages and gathers fruit to life forever, that both he who sows and he who reaps may rejoice together. For in this the saying is true, 'One sows, and another reaps.' I sent you to reap that for which you haven't laboured. Others have laboured, and you have entered into their labour."

From that city many of the Shomronim believed in me because of the word of the woman, who testified, "He told me everything that I have done." So when the Shomronim came to me, they begged me to stay with them. I stayed there two days. Many more believed because of my word. They said to the woman, "Now we believe, not because of your speaking; for we have heard for ourselves, and know that this is indeed the Mashiach, the Saviour of the world."

Nobleman's Son (4:43-54)

After the two days I went out from there and went into the Galil. For I myself testified that a prophet has no honour in his own country. So when I came into the Galil, the Galileans received me, having seen all the things that I did in Yerushalaim at the Festival, for they also went to the Festival. I came therefore again to Kana in the Galil, where I made the water into wine.

There was a certain nobleman whose son was sick at Kfar-Nachum. When he heard that I had come out of Judea into the Galil, he went to me and begged me that I would come down and heal his son, for he was at the point of death. I therefore said to him, "Unless you people see signs and wonders, you will in no way believe." The nobleman said to him, "Sir, come down before my child dies." I said to him, "Go your way. Your son lives." The man believed the word that I spoke to him, and he went his way. As he was going down, his servants met him and reported, saying "Your child lives!" So he enquired of them the hour when he began to get better. They said therefore to him, "Yesterday at the seventh hour, the fever left him." So the abba knew that it was at that hour in which I said to him, "Your son lives." He believed, as did his whole house.

This is again the second sign that I did, having come out of Judea into the Galil.

Beit-Chisda (5:1-16)

After these things, there was a Jewish festival, and I went up to Yerushalaim. Now in Yerushalaim by the sheep gate, there is a pool, which is called in Hebrew, "Beit-Chisda", having five porches. In these lay a great crowd of those who were sick, blind, lame, or paralyzed, waiting for the moving of the water; for a messenger went down at certain times into the pool and stirred up the water. Whoever stepped in first after the stirring of the water was healed of whatever disease he had.

A certain man was there who had been sick for thirty-eight years. When I saw him lying there, and knew that he had been sick for a long time, I asked him, "Do you want to be made well?" The sick man answered me, "Sir, I have no one to put me into the pool when the water is stirred up, but while I'm coming, another steps down before me." I said to him, "Arise, take up your mat, and walk." Immediately, the man was made well, and took up his mat and walked.

Now that day was Shabbat. So the Judeans said to him who was cured, "It is Shabbat. It is not lawful for you to carry the mat." He answered them, "He who made me well said to me, 'Take up your mat and walk.'" Then they asked him, "Who is the man who said to you, 'Take up your mat and walk'?" But he who was healed didn't know who it was, for I had withdrawn, a crowd being in the place.

Afterward I found him in the Beit HaMikdash and said to him, "Hinei! You are made well. Sin no more, so that nothing worse happens to you." The man went away, and told the Judeans that it was I who had made him well. For this cause the Judeans persecuted me and sought to kill me, because I did these things on Shabbat.

Son (5:17-30)

But I answered them, "My Abba is still working, so I am working, too." For this cause therefore the Judeans sought all the more to kill me, because I not only broke Shabbat, but also called God my own Abba, making myself equal with God. I therefore answered them, "Most certainly, I tell you: I the Son, can do nothing of myself, but what I see my Abba doing. For whatever things he does, these I also do likewise. For my Abba has affection for me, his Son, and shows me all things that he himself does. He will show me greater accomplishments than these, that you may marvel.

For as my Abba raises the dead and gives them life, even so I, his Son, also give life to whom I desire. For my Abba judges no one, but he has given all judgement to me, his Son, that all may honour me, even as they honour my Abba. He who doesn't honour me, his Son, doesn't honour my Abba who sent me. Most certainly I tell you, he who hears my word and believes him who sent me lives forever, and doesn't come into judgement, but has passed out of death into life. Most certainly I tell you, the hour comes, and now is, when the dead will shema to the Ben-Elohim's voice; and those who shema will live. For as my Abba has life in himself, even so he gave to me, his Son, also to have life in myself. He also gave me authority to execute judgement, because I am a Ben-Adam. Don't marvel at this, for the hour is coming in which all who are in the tombs will hear my voice and will come out; those who have done good, to the resurrection of life; and those who have done evil, to the resurrection of judgement.

I can of myself do nothing. As I hear, I judge; and my judgement is righteous, because I don't seek my own will, but the will of my Abba who sent me.

Testimony (5:31-47)

"If I testify about myself, my witness is not valid. It is another who testifies about me. I know that the testimony which he testifies about me is true. You have sent to Yochanan, and he has testified to the truth. But the testimony which I receive is not from man. However, I say these things that you may be saved. He was the burning and shining menorah, and you were willing to rejoice for a while in his light.

But the testimony which I have is greater than that of Yochanan; for the work which my Abba gave me to accomplish, the very work that I do, testifies about me, that my Abba has sent me. My Abba himself, who sent me, has testified about me. You have neither heard his voice at any time, nor seen his form. You don't have his word living in you, because you don't believe me whom he sent. You search the Tanach, because you think that in it you will live forever; and it is this which testifies about me. Yet you will not come to me, that you may have life!

I don't receive glory from men. But I know you, that you don't have God's love in yourselves. I have come in my Abba's name, and you don't receive me. If another comes in his own name, you will receive him. How can you believe, who receive glory from one another, and you don't seek the glory that comes from the only God?

Don't think that I will accuse you to my Abba. There is someone who accuses you, even Moshe, on whom you have set your hope. For if you believed Moshe, you would believe me; for he wrote about me. But if you don't believe his writings, how will you believe my words?"

Five Loaves (6:1-15)

After these things, I went away to the other side of the Kinneret, which is also called the Sea of Tiverya. A great crowd followed me, because they saw my signs which I did on those who were sick. I went up onto the mountain, and I sat there with my talmidim. Now Pesach, the Jewish festival, was at hand.

Therefore, lifting up my eyes and seeing that a great crowd was coming to me, I said to Philip, "Where are we to buy bread, that these may eat?" I said this to test him, for I myself knew what I would do. Philip answered me, "Two hundred days' wages worth of bread is not sufficient for them, that every one of them may receive a little." One of my talmidim, Andrew, Shimon Peter's brother, said to me, "There is a boy here who has five barley loaves and two fish, but what are these among so many?" I said, "Have the people sit down." Now there was much grass in that place. So the men sat down, in number about five thousand. I took the loaves, and having made the bracha, I distributed to the talmidim, and the talmidim to those who were sitting down, likewise also of the fish as much as they desired.

When they were filled, I said to my talmidim, "Gather up the broken pieces which are left over, that nothing be lost." So they gathered them up, and filled twelve baskets with broken pieces from the five barley loaves, which were left over by those who had eaten.

When therefore the people saw the sign which I did, they said, "This is truly the Prophet who comes into the world!" Therefore, perceiving that they were about to come and take me by force to make me king, I withdrew again to the mountain by myself.

Sea (6:16-21)

When evening came, my talmidim went down to the sea. They entered into the boat, and were going over the sea to Kfar-Nachum. It was now dark, and I had not come to them. The sea was tossed by a great wind blowing. When therefore they had rowed about three or four miles, they saw me walking on the sea and drawing near to the boat; and they were afraid. But I said to them, "It's me! Don't be afraid." They were willing therefore to receive me into the boat. Immediately the boat was at the land where we were going.

Kfar-Nachum (6:22-51)

On the next day, the crowd that stood on the other side of the sea saw that there was no other boat there, except the one in which my talmidim had embarked, and that I hadn't entered with my talmidim into the boat, but my talmidim had gone away alone. However, boats from Tiverya came near to the place where they ate the bread after I had made the bracha. When the crowd therefore saw that I wasn't there, nor my talmidim, they themselves got into the boats and came to Kfar-Nachum, seeking me.

When they found me on the other side of the sea, they asked me, "Rabbi, when did you come here?" I answered them, "Most certainly I tell you, you seek me, not because you saw signs, but because you ate of the loaves and were filled. Don't work for the food which perishes, but for the food which lasts to life forever which I, the Ben-Adam, will give to you. For God my Abba has sealed me."

They said therefore to me, "What must we do, that we may do the work of God?" I answered them, "This is the work of God, that you believe in me whom he has sent." They said therefore to me, "What then do you do for a sign, that we may see and believe you? What work do you do? Our fathers ate the manna in the wilderness. As it is written, 'He gave them bread out of heaven to eat.'" I therefore said to them, "Most certainly, I tell you, it wasn't Moshe who gave you the bread out of heaven, but my Abba gives you the true bread out of heaven. For the bread of God is that which comes down out of heaven and gives life to the world."

They said therefore to me, "Master, always give us this bread." I said to them, "I am the bread of life. Whoever comes to me will not be hungry, and whoever believes in me will never be thirsty. But I told you that you have seen me, and yet you don't believe. All those whom my Abba gives me will come to me. He who comes to me I will in no way throw out. For I have come down from heaven, not to do my own will, but the will of him who sent me. This is the will of my Abba who sent me, that of all he has given to me I should lose nothing, but should raise him up at the last day. This is the will of the one who sent me, that everyone who sees me, his Son, and believes in me should live forever; and I will raise him up at the last day."

Judeans (6:52-59)

The Judeans therefore murmured concerning me, because I said, "I am the bread which came down out of heaven." They said, "Isn't this Yeshua Ben-Yosef, whose abba and eema we know? How then does he say, 'I have come down out of heaven?'"

Therefore I answered them, "Don't murmur among yourselves. No one can come to me unless my Abba who sent me draws him; and I will raise him up in the last day. It is written in the Prophets, 'They will all be taught by God.' Therefore everyone who hears and has learned from my Abba, comes to me. Not that anyone has seen my Abba, except me—I who am from God. I have seen my Abba. Most certainly, I tell you, he who believes in me lives forever. I am the bread of life. Your fathers ate the manna in the wilderness and they died. This is the bread which comes down out of heaven, that anyone may eat of it and not die. I am the living bread which came down out of heaven. If anyone eats of this bread, he will live forever. Yes, the bread which I will give for the life of the world is my flesh."

The Judeans therefore contended with one another, saying, "How can this man give us his flesh to eat?" I therefore said to them, "Most certainly I tell you, unless you eat the flesh of the Ben-Adam and drink his blood, you don't have life in yourselves. He who eats my flesh and drinks my blood lives forever, and I will raise him up at the last day. For my flesh is food indeed, and my blood is drink indeed. He who eats my flesh and drinks my blood lives in me, and I in him. As my living Abba sent me, and I live because of my Abba, so he who partakes of me will also live because of me. This is the bread which came down out of heaven—not as our fathers ate the manna and died. He who eats this bread will live forever."

I said these things in the shul, as I taught in Kfar-Nachum.

Hard Saying (6:60-71)

Therefore many of my talmidim, when they heard this, said, "This is a hard saying! Who can listen to it?" But, knowing in myself that my talmidim murmured at this, I said to them, "Does this cause you to stumble? Then what if you would see me, the Ben-Adam, ascending to where I was before? It is the Ruach who gives life. The flesh profits nothing. The words that I speak to you are ruach, and are life. But there are some of you who don't believe." For I knew from the beginning who they were who didn't believe, and who it was who would betray me. I said, "For this cause I have said to you that no one can come to me, unless it is given to him by my Abba."

At this, many of my talmidim went back and walked no more with me. I said therefore to the Twelve, "You don't also want to go away, do you?" Shimon Peter answered me, "Master, to whom would we go? You have the words of life forever. We have come to believe and know that you are the Mashiach, the Son of the living God." I answered them, "Didn't I choose you, the Twelve, and one of you is an accuser?" Now I spoke of Yehuda Ben-Shimon from Kriyot, for it was he who would betray me, being one of the Twelve.

Sukkot (7:1-13)

After these things, I was walking in the Galil, for I wouldn't walk in Judea, because the Judeans sought to kill me. Now the Jewish festival of Sukkot was at hand. My brothers therefore said to me, "Depart from here and go into Judea, that your talmidim also may see the things which you do. For no one does anything in secret while he seeks to be known openly. If you do these things, reveal yourself to the world." For even my brothers didn't believe in me.

I therefore said to them, "My moed has not yet come, but your time is always ready. The world can't hate you, but it hates me, because I testify about it, that its actions are evil. You go up to the Festival. I am not yet going up to this Festival, because my moed is not yet fulfilled." Having said these things to them, I stayed in the Galil. But when my brothers had gone up to the Festival, then I also went up, not publicly, but as it were in secret.

The Judeans therefore sought me at the Festival, and said, "Where is he?" There was much murmuring among the crowds concerning me. Some said, "He is a good man." Others said, "Not so, but he leads the crowd astray." Yet no one spoke openly of me for fear of the Judeans.

Chol HaMoed (7:14-24)

But when it was now the middle of the Festival, I went up into the Beit HaMikdash and taught. The Judeans therefore marvelled, saying, "How is this man so literate without having studied?" I therefore answered them, "My torah is not mine, but his who sent me. If anyone desires to do his will, he will know about the torah, whether it is from God or if I am speaking from myself. He who speaks from himself seeks his own glory, but I who seek the glory of him who sent me am true, and no unrighteousness is in me.

Didn't Moshe give you the Torah, and yet none of you keeps the Torah? Why do you seek to kill me?" The crowd answered, "You have a shed! Who seeks to kill you?" I answered them, "I did one work and you all marvel because of it. Moshe has given you circumcision (not that it is of Moshe, but of the fathers), and on Shabbat you circumcise a boy. If a boy receives circumcision on Shabbat, that the Torah of Moshe may not be broken, are you angry with me because I made a man completely healthy on Shabbat? Don't judge according to appearance, but judge righteous judgement."

Murmurings (7:25-36)

Therefore some of the people of Yerushalaim said, "Isn't this he whom they seek to kill? Hinei! He speaks openly, and they say nothing to him. Can it be that the leaders indeed know that this is truly the Mashiach? However, we know where this man comes from, but when the Mashiach comes, no one will know where he comes from."

I therefore cried out in the Beit HaMikdash, teaching and saying, "You both know me, and know where I am from. I have not come of myself, but he who sent me is true, whom you don't know. I know him, because I am from him, and he sent me." They sought therefore to take me; but no one laid a hand on me, because my hour had not yet come. But of the crowd, many believed in me. They said, "When the Mashiach comes, he won't do more signs than those which this man has done, will he?"

The Prushim heard the crowd murmuring these things concerning me, and the chief kohanim and the Prushim sent officers to arrest me. Then I said, "I will be with you a little while longer, then I go to him who sent me. You will seek me and won't find me. You can't come where I am." The Judeans therefore said among themselves, "Where will this man go that we won't find him? Will he go to the Diaspora among the Hellenistic Jews and teach them? What is this word that he said, 'You will seek me, and won't find me;' and 'Where I am, you can't come'?"

Hoshana Rabbah (7:37-8:1)

Now on the last and greatest day of the Festival, I stood and cried out, "If anyone is thirsty, let him come to me and drink! He who believes in me, as the Tanach has said, from within him will flow rivers of living water." But I said this about the Ruach, which those believing in me were to receive. For Ruach HaKodesh was not yet given, because I wasn't yet glorified.

Many of the crowd therefore, when they heard these words, said, "This is truly the Prophet." Others said, "This is the Mashiach!" But some said, "What, does the Mashiach come out of the Galil? Hasn't the Tanach said that the Mashiach comes of the offspring of David, and from Beit-Lechem, the village where David was?" So a division arose in the crowd because of me. Some of them would have arrested me, but no one laid hands on me.

The officers therefore came to the chief kohanim and Prushim; and they said to them, "Why didn't you bring him?" The officers answered, "No man ever spoke like this man!" The Prushim therefore answered them, "You aren't also led astray, are you? Have any of the leaders or any of the Prushim believed in him? But this crowd that doesn't know the Torah is cursed." Nakdimon (he who came to me by night, being one of them) said to them, "Does our Law judge a man unless it first hears from him personally and knows what he does?" They answered him, "Are you also from the Galil? Search and see that no prophet has arisen out of the Galil."

Everyone went to his own house. But I went to the Hill of Olives.

Adulteress (8:2-11)

Now very early in the morning, I came again into the Beit HaMikdash, and all the people came to me. I sat down and taught them. The scholars and the Prushim brought a woman taken in adultery. Having set her in the middle, they told me, "Rabbi, we found this woman in adultery, in the very act. Now in our Torah, Moshe commanded us to stone such women. What then do you say about her?" They said this testing me, that they might have something to accuse me of. But I stooped down and wrote on the ground with my finger.

But when they continued asking me, I looked up and said to them, "He who is without sin among you, let him throw the first stone at her." Again I stooped down and wrote on the ground with my finger. They, when they heard it, being convicted by their conscience, went out one by one, beginning from the oldest, even to the last. I was left alone with the woman where she was, in the middle.

Standing up, I saw her and said, "Woman, where are your accusers? Did no one condemn you?" She said, "No one, sir." I said, "Neither do I condemn you. Go your way. From now on, sin no more."

Treasury (8:12-20)

Again, therefore, I spoke to them, saying, "I am the light of the world. He who follows me will not walk in the darkness, but will have the light of life."

The Prushim therefore said to me, "You testify about yourself. Your testimony is not valid." I answered them, "Even if I testify about myself, my testimony is true, for I know where I came from, and where I am going; but you don't know where I came from, or where I am going. You judge according to the flesh. I judge no one. Even if I do judge, my judgement is true, for I am not alone, but I am with my Abba who sent me. It's also written in your Torah that the testimony of two people is valid. I am someone who testifies about myself, and my Abba who sent me testifies about me." They said therefore to me, "Where is your Abba?" I answered, "You know neither me nor my Abba. If you knew me, you would know my Abba also."

I spoke these words in the Treasury, as I taught in the Beit HaMikdash. Yet no one arrested me, because my hour had not yet come.

Truth (8:21-32)

I said therefore again to them, "I am going away, and you will seek me, and you will die in your sins. Where I go, you can't come." The Judeans therefore said, "Will he kill himself, because he says, 'Where I am going, you can't come'?" I said to them, "You are from below. I am from above. You are of this world. I am not of this world. I said therefore to you that you will die in your sins; for unless you believe that I am he, you will die in your sins." They said therefore to me, "Who are you?" I said to them, "Just what I have been saying to you from the beginning. I have many things to speak and to judge concerning you. However, he who sent me is true; and the things which I heard from him, these I say to the world."

They didn't understand that I spoke to them about my Abba. I therefore said to them, "When you have lifted up the Ben-Adam in hagbah, then you will know that I am he, and I do nothing of myself, but as my Abba taught me, I say these things. He who sent me is with me. My Abba hasn't left me alone, for I always do the things that are pleasing to him."

As I spoke these things, many believed in me. I therefore said to those Judeans who had believed me, "If you stay in my word, then you are truly my talmidim. You will know the truth, and the truth will make you free."

Your Father (8:33-47)

They answered me, "We are Avraham's offspring, and have never been in bondage to anyone. How do you say, 'You will be made free'?" I answered them, "Most certainly I tell you, everyone who commits sin is the bondservant of sin. A bondservant doesn't live in the house forever. A son stays forever. If therefore I, the Son, make you free, you will be free indeed. I know that you are Avraham's offspring, yet you seek to kill me, because my word finds no place in you. I say the things which I have seen with my Abba; and you also do the things which you have seen with your father."

They answered me, "Our father is Avraham." I said to them, "If you were Bnei-Avraham, you would do the deeds of Avraham. But now you seek to kill me, a man who has told you the truth which I heard from God. Avraham didn't do this. You do the deeds of your father."

They said to me, "We were not born of sexual immorality. We have one father, God." Therefore I said to them, "If God were your father, you would love me, for I came out and have come from God. For I haven't come of myself, but he sent me. Why don't you understand my speech? Because you can't hear my word. You are of your father the accuser, and you want to do the desires of your father. He was a murderer from the beginning, and doesn't stand in the truth, because there is no truth in him. When he speaks a lie, he speaks on his own; for he is a liar, and the father of lies. But because I tell the truth, you don't believe me. Which of you convicts me of sin? If I tell the truth, why do you not believe me? He who is of God hears the words of God. For this cause you don't hear, because you are not of God."

My Abba (8:48-59)

Then the Judeans answered me, "Don't we say well that you are a Shomroni, and have a shed?" I answered, "I don't have a shed, but I honour my Abba and you dishonour me. But I don't seek my own glory. There is someone who seeks and judges. Most certainly, I tell you, if a person keeps my word, he will never see death."

Then the Judeans said to me, "Now we know that you have a shed. Avraham died, as did the prophets; and you say, 'If a man keeps my word, he will never taste of death.' Are you greater than our father Avraham, who died? The prophets died. Who do you make yourself out to be?" I answered, "If I glorify myself, my glory is nothing. It is my Abba who glorifies me, of whom you say that 'he is our God!' You have not known him, but I know him. If I said, 'I don't know him,' I would be like you, a liar. But I know him and keep his word. Your father Avraham rejoiced to see my day. He saw it and was glad."

The Judeans therefore said to me, "You are not yet fifty years old! Have you seen Avraham?" I said to them, "Most certainly, I tell you, before Avraham came into existence, I AM." Therefore they took up stones to throw at me, but I hid myself and went out of the Beit HaMikdash, having gone through the middle of them, and so passed by.

Blind Man (9:1-12)

As I passed by, I saw a man blind from birth. My talmidim asked me, "Rabbi, who sinned, this man or his parents, that he was born blind?" I answered, "This man didn't sin, nor did his parents, but that the work of God might be revealed in him. I must do the work of him who sent me while it is day. The night is coming, when no one can work. While I am in the world, I am the light of the world." When I had said this, I spat on the ground, made mud with the saliva, anointed the blind man's eyes with the mud, and said to him, "Go, wash in the pool of Shiloach" (which means "Sent"). So he went away, washed, and came back seeing.

Therefore the neighbours and those who saw that he was blind before said, "Isn't this he who sat and begged?" Others were saying, "It is he." Still others were saying, "He looks like him." He said, "I am he!" They therefore were asking him, "How were your eyes opened?" He answered, "A man called Yeshua made mud, anointed my eyes, and said to me, 'Go to the pool of Shiloach and wash.' So I went away and washed, and I received sight." Then they asked him, "Where is he?" He said, "I don't know."

Judean Authorities (9:13-23)

They brought him who had been blind to the Prushim. It was Shabbat when I made the mud and opened his eyes. Again therefore the Prushim also asked him how he received his sight. He said to them, "He put mud on my eyes, I washed, and I see." Some therefore of the Prushim said, "This man is not from God, because he doesn't keep Shabbat." Others said, "How can a man who is a sinner do such signs?" So there was division among them. Therefore they asked the blind man again, "What do you say about him, because he opened your eyes?" He said, "He is a prophet."

The Judeans therefore didn't believe concerning him, that he had been blind and had received his sight, until they called the parents of him who had received his sight, and asked them, "Is this your son, whom you say was born blind? How then does he now see?" His parents answered them, "We know that this is our son, and that he was born blind; but how he now sees, we don't know; or who opened his eyes, we don't know. He is of age. Ask him. He will speak for himself." His parents said these things because they feared the Judeans; for the Judeans had already agreed that if any man would confess me as Mashiach, he would be put out of the shul. Therefore his parents said, "He is of age. Ask him."

Thrown Out (9:24-41)

So they called the man who was blind a second time, and said to him, "Give glory to God. We know that this man is a sinner." He therefore answered, "I don't know if he is a sinner. One thing I do know: that though I was blind, now I see."

They said to him again, "What did he do to you? How did he open your eyes?" He answered them, "I told you already, and you didn't listen. Why do you want to hear it again? You don't also want to become his talmidim, do you?" They insulted him and said, "You are his talmid, but we are talmidim of Moshe. We know that God has spoken to Moshe. But as for this man, we don't know where he comes from." The man answered them, "How amazing! You don't know where he comes from, yet he opened my eyes. We know that God doesn't listen to sinners, but if anyone is a worshipper of God and does his will, he listens to him. Since the world began it has never been heard of that anyone opened the eyes of someone born blind. If this man were not from God, he could do nothing." They answered him, "You were altogether born in sins, and do you teach us?" Then they threw him out.

I heard that they had thrown him out, and finding him, I said, "Do you believe in the Ben-Adam?" He answered, "Who is he, sir, that I may believe in him?" I said to him, "You have both seen him, and it is he who speaks with you." He said, "Master, I believe!" and he bowed down to me. I said, "I came into this world for judgement, that those who don't see may see; and that those who see may become blind." Those of the Prushim who were with me heard these things, and said to me, "Are we also blind?" I said to them, "If you were blind, you would have no sin; but now you say, 'We see.' Therefore your sin remains.

Mashal: Door (10:1-10)

"Most certainly, I tell you, anyone who doesn't enter by the door into the sheep fold, but climbs up some other way, is a thief and a robber. But the one who enters in by the door is the shepherd of the sheep. The gatekeeper opens the gate for him, and the sheep listen to his voice. He calls his own sheep by name and leads them out. Whenever he brings out his own sheep, he goes before them; and the sheep follow him, for they know his voice. They will by no means follow a stranger, but will flee from him; for they don't know the voice of strangers."

I spoke this mashal to them, but they didn't understand what I was telling them. I therefore said to them again, "Most certainly, I tell you, I am the sheep's door. All who came before me are thieves and robbers, but the sheep didn't listen to them. I am the door. If anyone enters in by me, he will be saved, and will go in and go out and will find pasture. The thief only comes to steal, kill, and destroy. I came that they may have life, and may have it abundantly.

Mashal: Shepherd (10:11-21)

"I am the good shepherd. The good shepherd lays down his life for the sheep. He who is a hired hand, and not a shepherd, who doesn't own the sheep, sees the wolf coming, leaves the sheep, and flees. The wolf snatches the sheep and scatters them. The hired hand flees because he is a hired hand and doesn't care for the sheep.

I am the good shepherd. I know my own, and my own know me; even as my Abba knows me, and I know my Abba. I lay down my life for the sheep. I have other sheep which are not of this fold. I must bring them also, and they will shema to my voice. They will become one flock with one shepherd. Therefore my Abba loves me, because I lay down my life, that I may take it up again. No one takes it away from me, but I lay it down by myself. I have power to lay it down, and I have power to take it up again. I received this mitzvah from my Abba."

Therefore a division arose again among the Judeans because of these words. Many of them said, "He has a shed and is insane! Why do you listen to him?" Others said, "These are not the sayings of someone possessed by a shed. It isn't possible for a shed to open the eyes of the blind, is it?"

Chanukah (10:22-42)

It was the Festival of Chanukah at Yerushalaim. It was winter, and I was walking in the Beit HaMikdash, in Shlomo's porch. The Judeans therefore came around me and said to me, "How long will you hold us in suspense? If you are the Mashiach, tell us plainly." I answered them, "I told you, and you don't believe. The things that I do in my Abba's name, these testify about me. But you don't believe, because you are not of my sheep, as I told you. My sheep shema to my voice, and I know them, and they follow me. I give life forever to them. They will never perish, and no one will snatch them out of my hand. My Abba who has given them to me is greater than all. No one is able to snatch them out of my Abba's hand. I and my Abba are echad."

Therefore the Judeans took up stones again to stone me. I answered them, "I have shown you many good deeds from my

Abba. For which of those do you stone me?" The Judeans answered me, "We don't stone you for a good deed, but for blasphemy, because you, being a man, make yourself out to be God." I answered them, "Isn't it written in your Torah, 'I said, you are elohim'? If he called them elohim, to whom the word of God came (and the Tanach can't be broken), do you say of me whom my Abba sanctified and sent into the world, 'You blaspheme,' because I said, 'I am a son of Elohim'? If I don't do the work of my Abba, don't believe me. But if I do it, though you don't believe me, believe the work, that you may know and believe that my Abba is in me, and I in my Abba."

They sought again to seize me, and I went out of their hand. I went away again beyond the Yarden into the place where Yochanan was immersing at first, and I stayed there. Many came to me. They said, "Yochanan indeed did no sign, but everything that Yochanan said about this man is true." Many believed in me there.

Elazar (11:1-17)

Now a certain man was sick, Elazar from Beit-Hini, of the village of Miriam and her sister, Marta. It was that Miriam who had anointed me with perfume and wiped my feet with her hair, whose brother Elazar was sick. The sisters therefore sent to me, saying, "Master, hinei! He for whom you have great affection is sick." But when I heard it, I said, "This sickness is not to death, but for the glory of God, that I, the Ben-Elohim, may be glorified by it."

Now I loved Marta, and her sister, and Elazar. When therefore I heard that he was sick, I stayed two days in the place where I was. Then after this I said to the talmidim, "Let's go into Judea again." The talmidim asked me, "Rabbi, the Judeans were just trying to stone you. Are you going there again?" I answered, "Aren't there twelve hours of daylight? If a man walks in the day, he doesn't stumble, because he sees the light of this world. But if a man walks in the night, he stumbles, because the light isn't in him."

I said these things, and after that, I said to them, "Our friend Elazar has fallen asleep, but I am going so that I may awaken him out of sleep." The talmidim therefore said, "Master, if he has fallen asleep, he will recover." Now I had spoken of his death, but they thought that I spoke of taking rest in sleep. So I said to them plainly then, "Elazar is dead. I am glad for your sakes that I was not there, so that you may believe. Nevertheless, let's go to him." Toma therefore, who is called the Twin, said to his fellow talmidim, "Let's also go, that we may die with him."

So when I came, I found that he had been in the tomb four days already.

Marta & Miriam (11:18-32)

Now Beit-Hini was near Yerushalaim, about two miles away. Many of the Judeans had joined the women around Marta and Miriam, to console them concerning their brother.

Then when Marta heard that I was coming, she went and met me, but Miriam stayed in the house. Therefore Marta said to me, "Master, if you would have been here, my brother wouldn't have died. Even now I know that whatever you ask of God, God will give you." I said to her, "Your brother will rise again." Marta said to me, "I know that he will rise again in the resurrection at the last day." I said to her, "I am the resurrection and the life. He who believes in me will still live, even if he dies. Whoever lives and believes in me will never die. Do you believe this?" She said to me, "Yes, Master. I have come to believe that you are the Mashiach, the Ben-Elohim, he who comes into the world."

When she had said this, she went away and called Miriam, her sister, secretly, saying, "The Rabbi is here and is calling you." When she heard this, she arose quickly and went to me. Now I had not yet come into the village, but was in the place where

Marta met me. Then the Judeans who were with her in the house and were consoling her, when they saw Miriam, that she rose up quickly and went out, followed her, saying, "She is going to the tomb to weep there." Therefore when Miriam came to where I was and saw me, she fell down at my feet, saying to me, "Master, if you would have been here, my brother wouldn't have died!"

Tomb (11:33-44)

When I therefore saw her weeping, and the Judeans weeping who came with her, I groaned in the Ruach and was troubled, and said, "Where have you laid him?" They told me, "Master, come and see." I wept. The Judeans therefore said, "See how much affection he had for him!" Some of them said, "Couldn't this man, who opened the eyes of him who was blind, have also kept this man from dying?"

I therefore, again groaning in myself, came to the tomb. Now it was a cave, and a stone lay against it. I said, "Take away the stone." Marta, the sister of him who was dead, said to me, "Master, by this time there is a stench, for he has been dead four days." I said to her, "Didn't I tell you that if you believed, you would see God's glory?" So they took away the stone from the place where the dead man was lying.

I lifted up my eyes and said, "Abba, modeh ani that you listened to me. I know that you always listen to me, but because of the crowd standing around I said this, that they may believe that you sent me." When I had said this, I cried with a loud voice, "Elazar, come out!" He who was dead came out, bound hand and foot with wrappings, and his face was wrapped around with a cloth. I said to them, "Free him, and let him go."

Sanhedrin (11:45-57)

Therefore many of the Judeans who came to Miriam and saw what I did believed in me. But some of them went away to the Prushim and told them the things which I had done. The chief kohanim therefore and the Prushim gathered a sanhedrin, and said, "What are we doing? For this man does many signs. If we leave him alone like this, everyone will believe in him, and the Romans will come and take away both our place and our nation."

But a certain one of them, Kayafa, being Kohen Gadol that year, said to them, "You know nothing at all, nor do you consider that it is advantageous for us that one man should die for the people, and that the whole nation not perish." Now he didn't say this of himself, but being Kohen Gadol that year, he prophesied that I would die for the nation, and not for the nation only, but that I might also gather together as echad the Bnei-Elohim who are scattered abroad.

So from that day forward they took counsel that they might put me to death. I therefore walked no more openly among the Judeans, but departed from there into the country near the wilderness, to a city called Ephraim. I stayed there with my talmidim.

Now Pesach in Judea was at hand. Many went up from the country to Yerushalaim before Pesach, to purify themselves. Then they sought for me and spoke with one another as they stood in the Beit HaMikdash, "What do you think—that he isn't coming to the Festival at all?" Now the chief kohanim and the Prushim had commanded that if anyone knew where I was, he should report it, that they might seize me.

Anointing (12:1-8)

Then, six days before Pesach, I came to Beit-Hini, where Elazar was, who had been dead, whom I raised from the dead. So they made me a dinner there. Marta served, but Elazar was one of those who sat at the table with me.

Therefore Miriam took a pound of perfume of pure nard, very precious, and anointed my feet and wiped my feet with her hair. The house was filled with the fragrance of the perfume.

Then Yehuda from Kriyot, Shimon's son, one of my talmidim, who would betray me, said, "Why wasn't this perfume sold for three hundred days' wages and given to the poor?" Now he said this, not because he cared for the poor, but because he was a thief, and having the money box, used to steal what was put into it. But I said, "Leave her alone. She has kept this for the day of my burial. For you always have the poor with you, but you don't always have me."

Yerushalaim (12:9-19)

A large crowd therefore of the Judeans learned that I was there; and they came, not for my sake only, but that they might see Elazar also, whom I had raised from the dead. But the chief kohanim conspired to put Elazar to death also, because on account of him many of the Judeans went away and believed in me.

On the next day a great crowd had come to the Festival. When they heard that I was coming to Yerushalaim, they took the branches of the palm trees and went out to meet me, and cried out, "Hoshia-na! Blessed is he who comes in the name of Hashem, the Melech-Yisrael!" Having found a young donkey, I sat on it. As it is written, "Don't be afraid, Bat-Tzion. Hinei! Your King comes, sitting on a donkey's colt." My talmidim didn't understand these things at first, but when I was glorified, then they remembered that these things were written about me, and that they had done these things to me.

The crowd therefore that was with me when I called Elazar out of the tomb and raised him from the dead was testifying about it. For this cause also the crowd went and met me, because they heard that I had done this sign. The Prushim therefore said among themselves, "See how you accomplish nothing. Hinei! The world has gone after him."

Hellenistic Jews (12:20-36)

Now there were certain Hellenistic Jews among those who went up to worship at the Festival. Therefore, these came to Philip, who was from Beit-Tzaida in the Galil, and asked him, saying, "Sir, we want to see Yeshua." Philip came and told Andrew, and in turn, Andrew came with Philip, and they told me. I answered them, "The time has come for me, the Ben-Adam, to be glorified. Most certainly I tell you, unless a grain of wheat falls into the earth and dies, it remains by itself alone. But if it dies, it bears much fruit. He who loves his life will lose it. He who hates his life in this olam will keep it to life forever. If anyone serves me, let him follow me. Where I am, there my servant will also be. If anyone serves me, my Abba will honour him.

Now my soul is troubled. What shall I say? 'Abba, save me from this time?' But I came to this time for this cause. Abba, glorify your name!" Then a Bat-Kol came out of the sky, saying, "I have both glorified it and will glorify it again." Therefore the crowd who stood by and heard it said that it had thundered. Others said, "A messenger has spoken to him!" I answered, "This Bat-Kol hasn't come for my sake, but for your sakes. Now is the judgement of this world. Now the prince of this world will be cast out. And I, if I am lifted up in hagbah from the earth, will draw all people to myself." But I said this, signifying by what kind of death I should die.

The crowd answered me, "We have heard out of the Torah that the Mashiach lasts forever. How do you say, 'The Ben-Adam must be lifted up in hagbah?' Who is this Ben-Adam?" I therefore said to them, "Yet a little while the light is with you. Walk while you have the light, that darkness doesn't overtake you. He who walks in the darkness doesn't know where he is going. While you have the light, believe in the light, that you may become children of light."

Departed (12:36-50)

I said these things, and I departed and hid myself from them. But though I had done so many signs before them, yet they didn't believe in me, that the word of Yeshaya the prophet might be fulfilled, which he spoke: "Hashem, who has believed our report? To whom has the arm of Hashem been revealed?" For this cause they couldn't believe, for Yeshaya said again: "He has blinded their eyes and he hardened their heart, lest they should see with their eyes, and perceive with their heart, and would turn, and I would heal them." Yeshaya said these things when he saw my glory, and spoke of me.

Nevertheless, even many of the leaders believed in me, but because of the Prushim they didn't confess it, so that they wouldn't be put out of the shul, for they loved men's praise more than God's praise.

I cried out and said, "Whoever believes in me, believes not in me, but in him who sent me. He who sees me sees him who sent me. I have come as a light into the world, that whoever believes in me may not stay in the darkness. If anyone listens to my sayings and doesn't believe, I don't judge him. For I came not to judge the world, but to save the world. He who rejects me, and doesn't receive my sayings, has someone who judges him. The word that I spoke will judge him in the last day. For I spoke not from myself, but my Abba who sent me gave me a mitzvah, what I should say and what I should speak. I know that his mitzvah is life forever. The things therefore which I speak, even as my Abba has said to me, so I speak."

Seder (13:1-17)

Now before the Festival of Pesach, knowing that my time had come that I would depart from this olam to my Abba, having loved my own who were in the world, I loved them to the end. During the Seder, the accuser having already put into the heart of Yehuda from Kriyot, Shimon's son, to betray me, knowing that my Abba had given all things into my hands, and that I came from God and was going to God, I arose from dinner, and laid aside my outer garments. I took a towel and wrapped a towel around my waist. Then I poured water into the basin, and began to wash the talmidim's feet and to wipe them with the towel that was wrapped around me.

Then I came to Shimon Peter. He said to me, "Master, do you wash my feet?" I answered him, "You don't know what I am doing now, but you will understand later." Peter said to me, "You will never wash my feet!" I answered him, "If I don't wash you, you have no part with me." Shimon Peter said to me, "Master, not my feet only, but also my hands and my head!" I said to him, "Someone who has bathed only needs to have his feet washed, but is completely clean. You are clean, but not all of you." For I knew him who would betray me; therefore I said, "You are not all clean."

So when I had washed their feet, put my outer garment back on, and sat down again, I said to them, "Do you know what I have done to you? You call me, 'Rabbi' and 'Master.' You say so correctly, for so I am. If I then, the Master and the Rabbi, have washed your feet, you also ought to wash one another's feet. For I have given you an example, that you should also do as I have done to you. Most certainly I tell you, a servant is not greater than his master, neither is someone who is sent greater than he who sent him.

If you know these things, ashrei are you if you do them.

Yehuda from Kriyot (13:18-32)

"I don't speak concerning all of you. I know whom I have chosen; but that the Scripture may be fulfilled, 'He who eats bread with me has lifted up his heel against me.' From now on, I tell you before it happens, that when it happens, you may believe that I am he. Most certainly I tell you, he who receives whomever I send, receives me; and he who receives me, receives him who sent me."

When I had said this, I was troubled in my ruach, and testified, "Most certainly I tell you that one of you will betray me." The talmidim looked at one another, perplexed about whom I spoke. One of my talmidim, whom I loved, was at the table, leaning against my chest. Shimon Peter therefore beckoned to him, and said to him, "Tell us who it is of whom he speaks." He, leaning back, as he was, on my chest, asked me, "Master, who is it?" I therefore answered, "It is he to whom I will give this piece of matzah when I have dipped it."

So when I had dipped the piece of matzah, I gave it to Yehuda Ben-Shimon from Kriyot. After the piece of matzah, then the antagonist entered into him. Then I said to him, "What you do, do quickly." Now nobody at the table knew why I said this to him. For some thought, because Yehuda had the money box, that I said to him, "Buy what things we need for the Festival," or that he should give something to the poor. Therefore having received that morsel, he went out immediately. It was night.

When he had gone out, I said, "Now I, the Ben-Adam, have been glorified, and God has been glorified in me. If God has been glorified in me, God will also glorify me in himself, and he will glorify me immediately.

Shimon Peter (13:33-14:1)

"My sons, I will be with you a little while longer. You will seek me, and as I said to the Judeans, 'Where I am going, you can't come,' so now I tell you. A new mitzvah I give to you, that you love one another. Just as I have loved you, you also love one another. By this everyone will know that you are my talmidim, if you have love for one another."

Shimon Peter said to me, "Master, where are you going?" I answered, "Where I am going, you can't follow now, but you will follow afterwards." Peter said to me, "Master, why can't I follow you now? I will lay down my life for you." I answered him, "Will you lay down your life for me? Most certainly I tell you, the rooster won't crow until you have denied me three times.

Don't let your heart be troubled! Believe in God. Believe also in me.

Toma (14:2-7)

"In my Abba's house are many homes. If it weren't so, I would have told you. I am going to prepare a place for you. If I go and prepare a place for you, I will come again and will receive you to myself; that where I am, you may be there also. You know where I go, and you know the way."

Toma said to me, "Master, we don't know where you are going. How can we know the way?" I said to him, "I am the way, the truth, and the life. No one comes to my Abba, except through me. If you had known me, you would have known my Abba also. From now on, you know him and have seen him."

Philip (14:8-20)

Philip said to me, "Master, show us your Abba, and that will be enough for us." I said to him, "Have I been with you such a long time, and do you not know me, Philip? He who has seen me has seen my Abba. How do you say, 'Show us your Abba?' Don't you believe that I am in my Abba, and my Abba in me? The words that I tell you, I speak not from myself; but my Abba who lives in me does his work. Believe me that I am in my Abba, and my Abba in me; or else believe me for the very work's sake.

Most certainly I tell you, he who believes in me, the things that I do, he will do also; and he will do greater things than these, because I am going to my Abba. Whatever you will ask in my name, I will do it, that my Abba may be glorified in me, his Son. If you will ask anything in my name, I will do it.

If you love me, keep my mitzvot.

I will pray to my Abba, and he will give you another Helper, that he may be with you forever: the Ruach-Emet, whom the world can't receive, for it doesn't see him and doesn't know him. You know him, for he lives with you and will be in you. I will not leave you orphans. I will come to you. Yet a little while, and the world will see me no more; but you will see me. Because I live, you will live also. In that day you will know that I am in my Abba, and you in me, and I in you.

Yehuda (14:21-30)

"Anyone who has my mitzvot and keeps them, that person is the one who loves me. Anyone who loves me will be loved by my Abba, and I will love him, and will reveal myself to him."

Yehuda (not from Kriyot) said to me, "Master, what has happened that you are about to reveal yourself to us, and not to the world?" I answered him, "If a man loves me, he will keep my word. My Abba will love him, and we will come to him and make our home with him. He who doesn't love me doesn't keep my words. The word which you hear isn't mine, but my Abba's who sent me. I have said these things to you while still living with you. But the Helper, Ruach HaKodesh, whom my Abba will send in my name, will teach you all things, and will remind you of all that I said to you.

Shalom I leave with you. My shalom I give to you! Not as the world gives, I give to you. Don't let your heart be troubled, neither let it be fearful. You heard how I told you, 'I am going away, and I will come back to you.' If you loved me, you would have rejoiced because I said 'I am going to my Abba;' for my Abba is greater than I! Now I have told you before it happens so that when it happens, you may believe. I will no more speak much with you, for the prince of the world comes, and he has nothing in me. But that the world may know that I love my Abba, and as my Abba commanded me, even so I do.

Arise, let's go from here.

Vine (15:1-8)

"I am the true vine, and my Abba is the farmer. Every branch in me that doesn't bear fruit, he takes away. Every branch that bears fruit, he prunes, that it may bear more fruit. You are already pruned clean because of the word which I have spoken to you.

Stay in me, and I in you. As the branch can't bear fruit by itself unless it stays in the vine, so neither can you, unless you stay in me. I am the vine. You are the branches. He who stays in me and I in him bears much fruit, for apart from me you can do nothing. If a man doesn't stay in me, he is thrown out as a branch and is withered; and they gather them, throw them into the fire, and they are burned.

If you stay in me, and my words stay in you, you will ask whatever you desire, and it will be done for you. In this my Abba is glorified, that you bear much fruit; and so you will be my talmidim.

Love (15:9-25)

"Even as my Abba has loved me, I also have loved you. Stay in my love. If you keep my mitzvot, you will stay in my love, even as I have kept my Abba's mitzvot and stay in his love. I have spoken these things to you, that my joy may stay in you, and that your joy may be made full.

This is my mitzvah, that you love one another, even as I have loved you. Greater love has no one than this, that someone lay down his life for his friends. You are my friends if you do whatever I command you. No longer do I call you servants, for the servant doesn't know what his master does. But I have called you friends, for everything that I heard from my Abba, I have made known to you. You didn't choose me, but I chose you and appointed you, that you should go and bear fruit, and that your fruit should last; that whatever you will ask of my Abba in my name, he may give it to you.

I command these things to you, that you may love one another. If the world hates you, you know that it has hated me before it hated you. If you were of the world, the world would love its own. But because you are not of the world, since I chose you out of the world, therefore the world hates you. Remember the word that I said to you: 'A servant is not greater than his master.' If they persecuted me, they will also persecute you. If they kept my word, they will also keep yours. But they will do all these things to you for my name's sake, because they don't know him who sent me.

If I had not come and spoken to them, they would not have had sin; but now they have no excuse for their sin. He who hates me, hates my Abba also. If I hadn't done among them the things which no one else did, they wouldn't have had sin. But now they have seen and also hated both me and my Abba. But this happened so that the word may be fulfilled which was written in their Torah, 'They hated me without a cause.'

Helper (15:26-16:15)

"When the Helper has come, whom I will send to you from my Abba, the Ruach-Emet, who proceeds from my Abba, he will testify about me. You will also testify, because you have been with me from the beginning.

I have said these things to you so that you wouldn't be caused to stumble. They will put you out of the shuls. Yes, the time is coming that whoever kills you will think that he offers service to God. They will do these things because they have not known my Abba nor me. But I have told you these things so that when the time comes, you may remember that I told you about them. I didn't tell you these things from the beginning, because I was with you.

But now I am going to him who sent me, and none of you asks me, 'Where are you going?' But because I have told you these things, sorrow has filled your heart. Nevertheless I tell you the truth: It is to your advantage that I go away; for if I don't go away, the Helper won't come to you. But if I go, I will send him to you. When he has come, he will be mochiach with the world about sin, about righteousness, and about judgement; about sin, because they don't believe in me; about righteousness, because I am going to my Abba, and you won't see me anymore; about judgement, because the prince of this world has been judged.

I still have many things to tell you, but you can't bear them now. However, when he, the Ruach-Emet, has come, he will guide you into all truth, for he will not speak from himself; but whatever he hears, he will speak. He will declare to you things that are coming. He will glorify me, for he will take from what is mine and will declare it to you. All things that my Abba has are mine; therefore I said that he takes of mine and will declare it to you.

Talmidim (16:16-33)

"A little while, and you will not see me. Again a little while, and you will see me." Some of my talmidim therefore said to one another, "What is this that he says to us, 'A little while, and you won't see me, and again a little while, and you will see me;' and, 'Because I go to my Abba'?" They said therefore, "What is this that he says, 'A little while'? We don't know what he is saying."

Therefore I perceived that they wanted to ask me, and I said to them, "Do you enquire among yourselves concerning this, that I said, 'A little while, and you won't see me, and again a little while, and you will see me?' Most certainly I tell you that you will weep and lament, but the world will rejoice. You will be sorrowful, but your sorrow will be turned into joy. A woman, when she gives birth, has sorrow because her time has come. But when she has delivered the child, she doesn't remember the anguish anymore, for the joy that a human being is born into the world. Therefore you now have sorrow, but I will see you again, and your heart will rejoice, and no one will take your joy away from you. In that day you will ask me no questions. Most certainly I tell you, whatever you may ask of my Abba in my name, he will give it to you. Until now, you have asked nothing in my name. Ask, and you will receive, that your joy may be made full.

I have spoken these things to you in figures of speech. But the time is coming when I will no more speak to you in figures of speech, but will tell you plainly about my Abba. In that day you will ask in my name; and I don't say to you that I will pray to my Abba for you, for my Abba himself loves you, because you have loved me, and have believed that I came from God. I came from my Abba and have come into the world. Again, I leave the world and go to my Abba."

My talmidim said to me, "Hinei! Now you are speaking plainly, and using no figures of speech! Now we know that you know all things, and don't need for anyone to question you. By this we believe that you came from God." I answered them, "Do you now believe? Hinei! The time is coming, yes, and has now come, that you will be scattered, everyone to his own place, and you will leave me alone. Yet I am not alone, because my Abba is with me. I have told you these things, that in me you may have shalom. In the world you have trouble; but cheer up! I have overcome the world."

Tefillah (17:1-8)

I said these things; then, lifting up my eyes to heaven, I said, "Abba, the time has come. Glorify me, your Son, that I may also glorify you; even as you gave me authority over all flesh, that I might give life forever to all whom you have given me. This is life forever, that they should know you, the only true God, and me, the Mashiach whom you sent.

I glorified you on the earth. I have accomplished the work which you have given me to do. Now, Abba, glorify me with your own self with the glory which I had with you before this olam existed. I revealed your name to the people whom you have given me out of the world. They were yours, and you have given them to me. They have kept your word. Now they have known that all things whatever you have given me are from you, for the words which you have given me I have given to them; and they received them, and knew for sure that I came from you. They have believed that you sent me.

For Them (17:9-19)

"I pray for them. I don't pray for the world, but for those whom you have given me, for they are yours. All things that are mine are yours, and yours are mine, and I am glorified in them. I am no more in this olam, but these are in the world, and I am coming to you. Holy Abba, keep them through your name which you have given me, that they may be echad, even as we are. While I was with them in the world, I kept them in your name. I have kept those whom you have given me. None of them is lost except the son of destruction, that the Scripture might be fulfilled.

But now I come to you, and I say these things in the world, that they may have my joy made full in themselves. I have given them your word. The world hated them because they are not of the world, even as I am not of the world. I pray not that you would take them from the world, but that you would keep them from the evil one. They are not of the world, even as I am not of the world. Sanctify them in your truth. Your word is truth. As you sent me into the world, even so I have sent them into the world. For their sakes I sanctify myself, that they themselves also may be sanctified in truth.

For You (17:20-26)

"Not for these only do I pray, but for those also who will believe in me through their word, that they may all be echad; even as you, Abba, are in me, and I in you, that they also may be echad in us; that the world may believe that you sent me. The glory which you have given me, I have given to them, that they may be echad, even as we are echad: I in them, and you in me, that they may be perfectly echad, that the world may know that you sent me and loved them, even as you loved me.

Abba, I desire that they also whom you have given me be with me where I am, that they may see my glory which you have given me, for you loved me before the foundation of the world. Righteous Abba, the world hasn't known you, but I knew you; and these knew that you sent me. I made known to them your name, and will make it known; that the love with which you loved me may be in them, and I in them."

Betrayal (18:1-11)

When I had spoken these words, I went out with my talmidim over the brook Kidron, where there was a garden, into which I and my talmidim entered. Now Yehuda, who betrayed me, also knew the place, for I often met there with my talmidim. Yehuda then, having taken a detachment of soldiers and officers from the chief kohanim and the Prushim, came there with lanterns, torches, and weapons.

I therefore, knowing all the things that were happening to me, went out and said to them, "Who are you looking for?" They answered me, "Yeshua of Natzeret." I said to them, "I am he."

Yehuda also, who betrayed me, was standing with them. When therefore I said to them, "I am he," they went backward and fell to the ground. Again therefore I asked them, "Who are you looking for?" They said, "Yeshua of Natzeret." I answered, "I told you that I am he. If therefore you seek me, let these go their way," that the word might be fulfilled which I spoke, "Of those whom you have given me, I have lost none."

Shimon Peter therefore, having a sword, drew it, struck the Kohen Gadol's servant, and cut off his right ear. The servant's name was Malchus. I therefore said to Peter, "Put the sword into its sheath. The cup which my Abba has given me, shall I not surely drink it?"

Peter's Denial (18:12-27)

So the detachment, the commanding officer, and the officers of the Judeans seized me and bound me, and led me to Chanan first, for he was father-in-law to Kayafa, who was Kohen Gadol that year. Now it was Kayafa who advised the Judeans that it was expedient that one man should perish for the people.

Shimon Peter followed me, as did another talmid. Now that talmid was known to the Kohen Gadol, and entered in with me into the court of the Kohen Gadol; but Peter was standing at the door outside. So the other talmid, who was known to the Kohen Gadol, went out and spoke to her who kept the door, and brought in Peter. Then the maid who kept the door said to Peter, "Are you also one of this man's talmidim?" He said, "I am not." Now the servants and the officers were standing there, having made a fire of coals, for it was cold. They were warming themselves. Peter was with them, standing and warming himself.

The Kohen Gadol therefore asked me about my talmidim and about my torah. I answered him, "I spoke openly to the world. I always taught at shuls and in the Beit HaMikdash, where the Judeans always meet. I said nothing in secret. Why do you ask me? Ask those who have heard me what I said to them. Hinei! They know the things which I said." When he had said this, one of the officers standing by slapped me with his hand, saying, "Do you answer the Kohen Gadol like that?" I answered him, "If I have spoken evil, testify of the evil; but if well, why do you beat me?" Chanan sent me bound to Kayafa, the Kohen Gadol.

Now Shimon Peter was standing and warming himself. They said therefore to him, "You aren't also one of his talmidim, are you?" He denied it and said, "I am not." One of the servants of the Kohen Gadol, being a relative of him whose ear Peter had cut off, said, "Didn't I see you in the garden with him?" Peter therefore denied it again, and immediately the rooster crowed.

Praetorium (18:28-38)

They led me therefore from Kayafa into the Praetorium. It was early, and they themselves didn't enter into the Praetorium, that they might not be defiled, but might eat the Pesach. Pilate therefore went out to them and said, "What accusation do you bring against this man?" They answered him, "If this man weren't an evildoer, we wouldn't have handed him over to you." Pilate therefore said to them, "Take him yourselves, and judge him according to your law." Therefore the Judeans said to him, "It is illegal for us to put anyone to death," that my word might be fulfilled, which I spoke, signifying by what kind of death I should die.

Pilate therefore entered again into the Praetorium, called me, and said to me, "Are you the King of the Jewish people?" I answered him, "Do you say this by yourself, or did others tell you about me?" Pilate answered, "I'm not a Jewish person, am I? Your own nation and the chief kohanim handed you over to me. What have you done?" I answered, "My kingdom is not of this world. If my kingdom were of this world, then my servants would fight, that I wouldn't be handed over to the Judeans. But now my kingdom is not from here." Pilate therefore said to me, "Are you a king then?" I answered, "You say that I am a king. For this reason I have been born, and for this reason I have come into the world, that I should testify to the truth. Everyone who is of the truth listens to my voice." Pilate said to me, "What is truth?"

Gavta (18:38-19:16)

When he had said this, he went out again to the Judeans, and said to them, "I find no basis for a charge against him. But you have a custom that I should release someone to you at Pesach. Therefore, do you want me to release to you the King of the Jewish people?" Then they all shouted again, saying, "Not this man, but Bar-Abba!" Now Bar-Abba was a robber.

So Pilate then took me and flogged me. The soldiers twisted thorns into a crown and put it on my head, and dressed me in a purple garment. They kept saying, "Hail, King of the Jewish people!" and they kept slapping me. Then Pilate went out again, and said to them, "Look! I bring him out to you, that you may know that I find no basis for a charge against him." I therefore came out, wearing the crown of thorns and the purple garment. Pilate said to them, "Behold, the man!" When therefore the chief kohanim and the officers saw me, they shouted, saying, "Crucify! Crucify!" Pilate said to them, "Take him yourselves and crucify him, for I find no basis for a charge against him." The Judeans answered him, "We have a law, and by our law he ought to die, because he made himself out to be a son of God."

When therefore Pilate heard this saying, he was more afraid. He entered into the Praetorium again, and said to me, "Where are you from?" But I gave him no answer. Pilate therefore said to me, "Aren't you speaking to me? Don't you know that I have power to release you and have power to crucify you?" I answered, "You would have no power at all against me, unless it were given to you from above. Therefore he who handed me over to you has greater sin."

At this, Pilate was seeking to release me, but the Judeans cried out, saying, "If you release this man, you aren't Caesar's friend! Everyone who makes himself a king speaks against Caesar!" When Pilate therefore heard these words, he brought me out and sat down on the judgement seat at a place called "The Pavement", but in Hebrew, "Gavta." Now it was the Preparation Day of Pesach, at about the sixth hour. He said to the Judeans, "Behold, your King!" They cried out, "Away with him! Away with him! Crucify him!" Pilate said to them, "Shall I crucify your King?" The chief kohanim answered, "We have no king but Caesar." So then he handed me over to them to be crucified.

Crucifixion (19:17-27)

So they took me and led me away. I went out, bearing my cross, to the place called "The Place of a Skull", which is called in Hebrew, "Golgolta", where they crucified me, and with me two others, on either side one, and me in the middle.

Pilate wrote a title also, and put it on the cross. There was written, "YESHUA OF NAZARETH, THE KING OF THE JEWISH PEOPLE." Therefore many of the Judeans read this title, for the place where I was crucified was near the city; and it was written in Hebrew, in Latin, and in Greek. The chief kohanim of the Judeans therefore said to Pilate, "Don't write, 'The King of the Jewish people,' but, 'he said, "I am King of the Jewish people."'" Pilate answered, "What I have written, I have written."

Then the soldiers, when they had crucified me, took my garments and made four parts, to every soldier a part; and also the tunic. Now the tunic was without seam, woven from the top throughout. Then they said to one another, "Let's not tear it, but cast lots for it to decide whose it will be," that the Scripture might be fulfilled, which says, "They parted my garments among them. They cast lots for my clothing." Therefore the soldiers did these things.

But standing by my cross were my eema, my eema's sister, Miriam the wife of Chalfai, and Miriam from Magdala. Therefore when I saw my eema, and the talmid whom I loved standing there, I said to my eema, "Woman, hinei! Your son!" Then I said to the talmid, "Hinei! Your eema!" From that hour, the talmid took her to his own home.

Death (19:28-37)

After this, seeing that all things were now finished, that the Scripture might be fulfilled, I said, "I am thirsty!" Now a vessel full of vinegar was set there; so they put a sponge full of the vinegar on hyssop, and held it at my mouth. When I therefore had received the vinegar, I said, "It is finished!" Then I bowed my head and gave up my ruach.

Therefore the Judeans, because it was the Preparation Day, so that the bodies wouldn't remain on the cross on Shabbat (for that Shabbat was a Yom Tov), asked of Pilate that their legs might be broken and that they might be taken away. Therefore the soldiers came and broke the legs of the first and of the other who was crucified with me; but when they came to me and saw that I was already dead, they didn't break my legs. However, one of the soldiers pierced my side with a spear, and immediately blood and water came out.

He who has seen has testified, and his testimony is true. He knows that he tells the truth, that you may believe. For these things happened that the Scripture might be fulfilled, "A bone of him will not be broken." Again another Scripture says, "They will look on him whom they pierced."

Burial (19:38-42)

After these things, Yosef of Ramatayim, being a talmid of mine, but secretly for fear of the Judeans, asked of Pilate that he might take away my body. Pilate gave him permission. He came therefore and took away my body. Nakdimon, who at first came to me by night, also came bringing a mixture of myrrh and aloes, about a hundred Roman pounds. So they took my body, and bound it in linen cloths with the spices, as the custom of the Judeans is to bury.

Now in the place where I was crucified there was a garden. In the garden was a new tomb in which no man had ever yet been laid. Then, because of the Judeans' Preparation Day (for the tomb was near at hand), they laid me there.

Dawn (20:1-10)

Now on the first day of the week, Miriam from Magdala went early, while it was still dark, to the tomb, and saw that the stone had been taken away from the tomb. Therefore she ran and came to Shimon Peter and to the other talmid whom I loved, and said to them, "They have taken away the Master out of the tomb, and we don't know where they have laid him!"

Therefore Peter and the other talmid went out, and they went towards the tomb. They both ran together. The other talmid outran Peter and came to the tomb first. Stooping and looking in, he saw the linen cloths lying there; yet he didn't enter in. Then Shimon Peter came, following him, and entered into the tomb. He saw the linen cloths lying, and the cloth that had been on my head, not lying with the linen cloths, but rolled up in a place by itself. So then the other talmid who came first to the tomb also entered in, and he saw and believed. For as yet they didn't know the Scripture, that I must rise from the dead.

So the talmidim went away again to their own homes.

Miriam (20:11-18)

But Miriam was standing outside at the tomb weeping. So as she wept, she stooped and looked into the tomb, and she saw two messengers in white sitting, one at the head and one at the feet, where my body had lain. They asked her, "Woman, why are you weeping?" She said to them, "Because they have taken away my Master, and I don't know where they have laid him."

When she had said this, she turned around and saw me standing, and didn't know that it was me. I said to her, "Woman, why are you weeping? Who are you looking for?" Supposing me to be the gardener, she said to me, "Sir, if you have carried him away, tell me where you have laid him, and I will take him away." I said to her, "Miriam." She turned and said to me, "Ribboni!" which is to say, "Rabbi!" I said to her, "Don't hold me, for I haven't yet ascended to my Abba; but go to my brothers and tell them, 'I am ascending to my Abba and your Abba, to my God and your God.'"

Miriam from Magdala came and told the talmidim that she had seen me, and that I had said these things to her.

Talmidim (20:19-23)

When therefore it was evening on that day, the first day of the week, and when the doors were locked where the talmidim were assembled, for fear of the Judeans, I came and stood in the middle and said to them, "Shalom aleichem!" When I had said this, I showed them my hands and my side. The talmidim therefore were glad when they saw me.

I therefore said to them again, "Shalom be to you. As my Abba has sent me, even so I send you." When I had said this, I breathed on them, and said to them, "Receive Ruach HaKodesh! If you forgive anyone's sins, they have been forgiven them. If you retain anyone's sins, they have been retained."

Toma (20:24-31)

But Toma, one of the Twelve, called the Twin, wasn't with them when I came. The other talmidim therefore said to him, "We have seen the Master!" But he said to them, "Unless I see in his hands the print of the nails, put my finger into the print of the nails, and put my hand into his side, I will not believe."

After eight days, again my talmidim were inside and Toma was with them. I came, the doors being locked, and stood in the middle, and said, "Shalom aleichem!" Then I said to Toma, "Reach here your finger, and see my hands. Reach here your hand, and put it into my side. Don't be unbelieving, but believing." Toma answered me, "My Master and my God!" I said to him, "Because you have seen me, you have believed. Ashrei are those who have not seen and have believed."

Therefore I did many other signs in the presence of my talmidim, which are not written in this sefer; but these are written that you may believe that I am the Mashiach, the Ben-Elohim, and that believing you may have life in my name.

Tiverya (21:1-14)

After these things, I revealed myself again to the talmidim at the sea of Tiverya. I revealed myself this way: Shimon Peter, Toma called the Twin, Netanel of Kana in the Galil, and the sons of Zavdai, and two others of my talmidim were together. Shimon Peter said to them, "I'm going fishing." They told him, "We are also coming with you." They immediately went out and entered into the boat. That night, they caught nothing.

But when day had already come, I stood on the beach; yet the talmidim didn't know that it was me. I therefore said to them, "My sons, have you anything to eat?" They answered me, "No." I said to them, "Cast the net on the right side of the boat, and you will find some." They cast it therefore, and now they weren't able to draw it in for the crowd of fish. That talmid therefore whom I loved said to Peter, "It's the Master!" So when Shimon Peter heard that it was me, he wrapped his coat around himself (for he was naked), and threw himself into the sea. But the other talmidim came in the little boat (for they were not far from the land, but about two hundred cubits away), dragging the net full of fish.

So when they got out on the land, they saw a fire of coals there, with fish and bread laid on it. I said to them, "Bring some of the fish which you have just caught." Shimon Peter went up, and drew the net to land, full of one hundred and fifty-three great fish. Even though there were so many, the net wasn't torn. I said to them, "Come and eat breakfast!" None of the talmidim dared enquire of me, "Who are you?" knowing that it was me. Then I came and took the bread, gave it to them, and the fish likewise.

This is now the third time that I was revealed to my talmidim after I had risen from the dead.

Shimon Peter (21:15-25)

So when they had eaten their breakfast, I said to Shimon Peter, "Shimon Ben-Yonah, do you love me more than these?" He said to me, "Yes, Master; you know that I have affection for you." I said to him, "Feed my lambs." I said to him again a second time, "Shimon Ben-Yonah, do you love me?" He said to me, "Yes, Master; you know that I have affection for you." I said to him, "Tend my sheep." I said to him the third time, "Shimon Ben-Yonah, do you have affection for me?" Peter was grieved because I asked him the third time, "Do you have affection for me?" He said to me, "Master, you know everything. You know that I have affection for you." I said to him, "Feed my sheep. Most certainly I tell you, when you were young, you dressed yourself and walked where you wanted to. But when you are old, you will stretch out your hands, and another will dress you and carry you where you don't want to go." Now I said this, signifying by what kind of death he would glorify God. When I had said this, I said to him, "Follow me."

Then Peter, turning around, saw a talmid following. This was the talmid whom I loved, the one who had also leaned on my chest at the dinner and asked, "Master, who is going to betray you?" Peter, seeing him, said to me, "Master, what about this man?" I said to him, "If I desire that he stay until I come, what is that to you? You follow me."

This saying therefore went out among the brothers that this talmid wouldn't die. Yet I didn't say to him that he wouldn't die, but, "If I desire that he stay until I come, what is that to you?" This is the talmid who testifies about these things, and wrote these things. We know that his witness is true. There are also many other things which I did, which if they would all be written, he supposes that even the world itself wouldn't have room for the books that would be written.

EPILOGUE

Forty Days (Acts 1:1-11)

The first book Luke wrote to Theophilus concerned all that I began both to do and to teach, until the day in which I was received up, after I had given mitzvah through Ruach HaKodesh to the shaliachs whom I had chosen. To these I also showed myself alive after I suffered, by many proofs, appearing to them over a period of forty days and speaking about my kingdom. Being assembled together with them, I commanded them, "Don't depart from Yerushalaim, but wait for the promise of my Abba, which you heard from me. For Yochanan indeed immersed in water, but you will be immersed in Ruach HaKodesh not many days from now."

Therefore, when we had come together, they asked me, "Master, are you now restoring the kingdom to Israel?" I said to them, "It isn't for you to know moadim or seasons which my Abba has set within his own authority. But you will receive power when Ruach HaKodesh has come upon you. You will be witnesses to me in Yerushalaim, in all Judea and Shomron, and to the uttermost parts of the earth."

When I had said these things, as they were looking, I was taken up, and a cloud received me out of their sight. While they were staring into the sky as I went, hinei! Two men stood by them in white clothing, who also said, "You men of the Galil, why do you stand looking into the sky? This Yeshua, who was received up from you into the sky, will come back in the same way as you saw him going into the sky."

I hope this experience was everything you hoped for, and more.

If you didn't already, <u>would you share your experience of Yeshua First-Person in a review, or even just give five stars</u>? I will personally read your testimony, and it really will help spread the word. Just scan the heart code below with your phone's camera to leave a review.

What's next after that? Visit yeshuafirstperson.com to join our annual reading movement, read testimonies, learn Hebrew with me, and more. Just scan the book code above with the camera app on your phone.

Izzy Avraham

Director, Holy Language Institute

P.S. Don't forget to get copies of Yeshua First-Person for the Jewish people in your life!

Made in the USA
Columbia, SC
26 August 2024